THE WICKED TENANTS AND GETHSEMANE

University of South Florida
INTERNATIONAL STUDIES IN FORMATIVE
CHRISTIANITY AND JUDAISM

VOLUME 4
THE WICKED TENANTS AND GETHSEMANE
Isaiah in the Wicked Tenants' Vineyard, and Moses and the High Priest in Gethsemane:
Judaic Traditions in Mark 12:1–9 and 14:32–42
Roger David Aus

THE WICKED TENANTS AND GETHSEMANE

Isaiah in the Wicked Tenants' Vineyard, and Moses and the High Priest in Gethsemane: Judaic Traditions in Mark 12:1–9 and 14:32–42

ROGER DAVID AUS

Scholars Press
Atlanta, Georgia

THE WICKED TENANTS AND GETHSEMANE

Isaiah in the Wicked Tenants' Vineyard, and Moses and the High Priest in Gethsemane: Judaic Traditions in Mark 12:1–9 and 14:32–42

by

Roger David Aus

Published by Scholars Press
for the University of South Florida

© 1996
University of South Florida

Library of Congress Cataloging in Publication Data
Aus, Roger, 1940–
    The wicked tenants and Gethsemane : Isaiah in the wicked tenants'
vineyard, and Moses and the high priest in Gethsemane : Judaic
traditions in Mark 12:1–9 and 14:32–42 / by Roger David Aus.
        p.   cm. — (University of South Florida international studies
in formative Christianity and Judaism ; v. 4)
    Includes bibliographical references and index.
    ISBN 0-7885-0261-1 (cloth : alk. paper)
    1. Bible. N.T. Mark XII, 1–9—Criticism, interpretation, etc.
2. Bible. N.T. Mark XIV, 32–42—Criticism, interpretation, etc.
3. Bible. N.T. Mark—Relation to the Old Testament. 4. Bible.
O.T.—Relation to Mark. 5. Bible. N.T. Mark—Relation to Isaiah.
6. Bible. O.T. Isaiah—Relation to Mark. 7. Wicked husbandmen
(Parable) 8. Jesus Christ—Prayer in Gethsemane. 9. Rabbinical
literature—Relation to the New Testament. I. Title. II. Series.
BS2585.2.A87   1996
226.3'06—dc20   96-13044

Printed in the United States of America
on acid-free paper

Dedication

To

Hans Conzelmann

Nils Alstrup Dahl

Joseph Fitzmyer, S.J.

Judah Goldin

Rowan Greer III

Helmut Koester

Abraham Malherbe

Wayne Meeks

Paul Minear

John Schütz

Krister Stendahl

and G. Ernest Wright

In deep gratitude to my teachers at Harvard and Yale who helped me to lay a foundation in Biblical Studies in the 1960's.

"The fear of the LORD is the beginning of knowledge."

(Prov 1:7)

"Reverence for your teacher is like reverence for Heaven."

(*Exod. Rab.* Shemoth 3/17 on Exod 4:16)

TABLE OF CONTENTS

CHAPTER TWO

Jesus in Gethsemane (Mark 14:32-42 par.): Psalm 116, Moses' Struggle with Death at the Very End of His Life, and The High Priest and the Day of Atonement

APPENDIX ONE

Paul's Calling and Re-commissioning in 2 Cor 12:1-10
and
Moses' Calling and Death Scene

APPENDIX TWO

The Contrast of God's Taking Away Moses' Soul Through a Kiss,
and
Judas' Handing Jesus Over to Certain Death Through a Kiss

Preface

For almost all those scholars who consider the narrative genuine, Jesus meant himself to be the "beloved son" whom the owner (God) finally sent to his vineyard in the parable of the Wicked Tenants (Mark 12:1-9, par.), which I analyze in Chapter One. This is because the "son" of the owner was killed last. On the basis of Judaic sources with the expression "My (God's) son," I propose instead that Jesus meant the extremely popular prophet Isaiah, although he *may* also have considered himself as following in the latter's footsteps. According to Palestinian Judaic tradition, Isaiah too was martyred in Jerusalem, where Jesus told the parable in the Temple, often characterized as a "vineyard." Allusions to the Song of the Vineyard in Isaiah 5 also point to who are meant by the wicked tenants who abuse and kill the servant-prophets sent to them. Members of the Temple hierarchy, especially the wealthy, land-owning high priestly families, are severely reproached by Jesus as "usurping occupants" for actively preventing God's message of the necessity of repentance from reaching the people. Next to Jesus' prophetic "cleansing of the Temple," this narrative did more than anything else to infuriate the Temple hierarchy and to cause Jesus' death. Told just before the Passover pilgrimage festival, the parable also reflects expressions and imagery from Exod 15:1-18, part of the Torah lesson for the last day of Passover.

Chapter Two deals with Jesus in Gethsemane (Mark 14:32-42, par.). The Palestinian Jewish Christian author of this very moving narrative in a masterful way employed motifs and expressions from Psalm 116, one of the Hallel psalms which had just been recited / sung by Jesus and his disciples at the Passover Seder meal; elements from Moses' struggle with death at the very end of his life; and motifs and expressions used for the high priest on the Day of Atonement, including the preceding night. To buttress the latter, I point out a large number of other usages of such high priest language for Jesus in the Passion Narratives of the gospels. Several side effects from this study are new proposals for the Semitic background of the terms "Golgotha" and "Gethsemane," the puzzling expression ἀπέχει ("It is enough") in Mark 14:41, and Peter's "spreading" (ἐπιβάλλω – his garment over himself in shame) and weeping in Mark 14:72. While a Palestinian Jewish Christian composed the Gethsemane narrative, he may have incorporated some historical elements. Basically, however, the account is not historical. Nevertheless, it does convey very important *religious* truths, which I describe.

Two appendices are added, the first more extensively dealing with Paul's calling and re-commissioning in 2 Cor 12:1-10 and Moses' calling and death scene in Judaic tradition. My main concern here, however, is to point out how Paul's beseeching the Lord three times to remove the thorn in his flesh, and the Lord's answer that "My grace is sufficient for you" in vv 8-9, derive from the same Judaic complex as Jesus' threefold prayer in Gethsemane: the scene of Moses' impending death, based on early interpretation of Deut 3:23-26.

Appendix Two points out a contrast between God's taking away Moses' soul with a kiss, and Judas' handing Jesus over to certain death through a kiss.

The large number of Judaic sources which I employ are enumerated in the bibliography at the end of this volume. In the text only the standard abbreviations are given. While an index of the biblical and post-biblical passages cited would be simply too voluminous, an index of modern authors has been included. It helps to indicate where my own conclusions agree with, or more often differ from those of contemporary scholarship. Wherever possible, I have tried to dialogue with the most important secondary literature, without, however, overburdening the footnotes.

The dating of rabbinic sources, which I extensively quote, will always remain problematical. While many materials are patently late, others, especially those from the Tannaitic period, should not be rejected out of hand simply because they do not precede 70 C.E. Many NT scholars unfortunately employ the dating problem as a cheap pretext for not even considering rabbinic traditions, which they find hard to locate and read in the original Hebrew or Aramaic. Each individual case, however, must be judged on its own merits, which I try to do. The problem of dating remains, yet so does the relevance of particular rabbinic sources.

Non-familiarity with Palestinian Judaic sources, customs and the nature of halakha and haggadah has long hindered a better understanding of the parable of the Wicked Tenants and the Gethsemane narrative. I would hope that the two chapters in this volume may lead to a better appreciation by non-Jewish Christians, and by interested Jews, of these two accounts. Jesus' own narrative and theological artistry, as well as that of the Palestinian Jewish Christian author of the Gethsemane narrative, should also be admired for what they are.

My sincere thanks go to Professor Étan Levine of Haifa and to Professor Klyne Snodgrass of Chicago for reading a first draft of Chapter One, to Dr. Niko Oswald of Berlin for doing the same with Chapter Two, and to Professor Christian Wolff of Berlin for commenting on Appendix One. Professor Lieselotte Kötzsche of Berlin graciously provided me with a photocopy of the illustration, before Chapter One, of Isaiah being sawed in two. The Rev. Paul Hoffman, kindly helped me in proofreading. Finally, I would like to greatly thank Professor Jacob Neusner for accepting this volume in the series *International Studies in Formative Christianity and Judaism*. His methodological studies and numerous translations of early Judaic sources have greatly aided many others to navigate in the "sea" of the Talmud and in other rabbinic writings. In the above study on Gethsemane, his renderings of the tractate *Yoma* in the Tosefta and Jerusalem Talmud were especially helpful.

As a parish pastor, I have had to sacrifice much of my vacation in recent years in order to write the first drafts of the studies in this volume. If I have succeeded at least in provoking a discussion of new solutions, leading to a better understanding of the parable of the Wicked Tenants and Gethsemane, or in whetting others' appetites to deal more extensively with Judaic, especially rabbinic sources, then that sacrifice will have been well worthwhile.

Roger David Aus
June 1995
Berlin, Germany

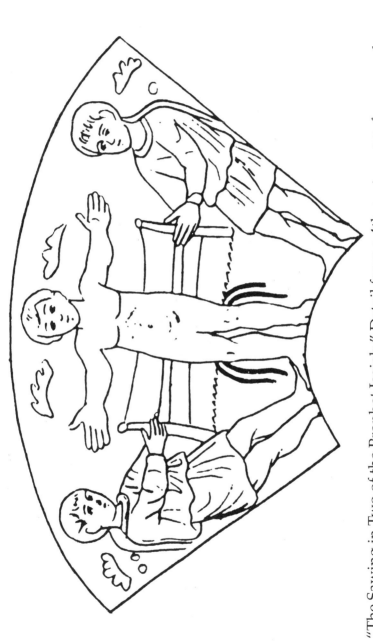

"The Sawing in Two of the Prophet Isaiah." Detail from a 4th century C.E. funerary glass, Rome. Reproduction from A. Kisa, *Das Glas im Altertume* (Leipzig, 1908; reprint Rome: L'Erma di Bretschneider, 1968) 3.881.

Chapter One

The Parable of the Wicked Tenants (Mark 12:1-9), The Song of the Vineyard (Isa 5:1-7), The Song at the Sea (Exod 15:1-18), and the Martyrdom of Isaiah

Introduction

C.H. Dodd remarked that the narrative of the Wicked Tenants is "The most difficult of the parables referring directly to the existing situation...."[1] J. Ernst spoke of it as "derart komplex...,"[2] and E. Haenchen of "ihrem geheimnisvollen Helldunkel...."[3] In the most recent monograph on the pericope, K. Snodgrass wrote in 1983: "Despite its importance...the Parable of the Wicked Tenants has been an enigma to modern interpreters."[4]

---

[1] *The Parables of the Kingdom* (London: Collins, 1963) 93. He is followed here by M. Hengel in "Das Gleichnis von den Weingärtnern Mc 12, 1-12 im Lichte der Zenonpapyri und der rabbinischen Gleichnisse" in *ZNW* 59 (1968) 9. My reasons for considering only Mark 12:1-9 as belonging to the original parable will be given below.

[2] *Das Evangelium nach Markus* (RNT; Regensburg: Pustet, 1981) 343.

[3] *Der Weg Jesu* (Berlin: de Gruyter, 1968[2]) 401.

[4] *The Parable of the Wicked Tenants* (WUNT 27; Tübingen: Mohr, 1983) 1. For bibliography on the Markan form of the parable, which I consider the oldest version and to which I deliberately limit myself, see his pp. 119-126; M. Hubaut, *La parabole des vignerons homicides* (CahRB 16; Paris: Gabalda, 1976) 147-148; J. Gnilka, *Das Evangelium nach Markus (Mk 8, 27 – 16, 20)* (EKK 11/2; Zurich:

1

Part of the problem lies in the fact that the narrative clearly alludes several times to another text, the Song of the Vineyard in Isaiah 5, which itself is an allegory. Who or what is then meant by the vineyard in Jesus' parable? Another major difficulty is the identity of the owner's "son," whom the tenants kill. Almost all the interpreters who consider the parable historical believe Jesus rather openly alluded to himself here.[5] Others say he never would have spoken in such a manner, thus the narrative was definitely composed later in an early Christian community.

The following study aims to address and clarify these and similar problems in the Markan version of the parable. Section I. deals with the Temple setting of Mark 12:1-9; section II. with the Song of the Vineyard (Isa 5:1-7) and the Temple; section III. with the Song at the Sea (Exod 15:1-18) and the Temple; section IV. with the Martyrdom of Isaiah and Isa 66:1; section V. with the "beloved son" and Isa 5:1; section VI. with the extent of the narrative; section VII. with the original language; section VIII. with the question of historicity; and section IX. with Mark's understanding of the parable. These are followed by section X., several concluding remarks.

Throughout this study I quote Judaic sources extensively, often with my own version of the Semitic original. This should be of aid especially to those interpreters whose expertise lies elsewhere. In addition, a number of the rabbinic sources are not easily accessible.

Finally, A. Jülicher maintained that in the parable "alle dichterische Frische fehlt."[6] In contrast to him and others, I point out how the author, whom I consider to be Jesus, very artistically combined motifs and even vocabulary, primarily from Judaic traditions on the Song of the Vineyard and the Song at the Sea, into a narrative which even today remains not only challenging and forceful,[7] but also of great importance in regard to

---

Benziger; Neukirchen-Vluyn: Neukirchener, 1989[3]) 141; and *The Gospel of Mark. A Cumulative Bibliography 1950-1990*, ed. F. Neirynck et al. (BETL 102; Leuven: University Press, 1992) 602-603. See also R. Gundry, *Mark. A Commentary on His Apology for the Cross* (Grand Rapids: Eerdmans, 1993) 659-664 and 682-691.

[5] Cf. for example J. Jeremias, *The Parables of Jesus* (New York: Scribners, 1963) 72-73: "There can be no doubt that in the sending of the son Jesus himself had his own sending in mind...."

[6] Cf. *Die Gleichnisreden Jesu* (Tübingen: Mohr, 1910) 2.406. A. Loisy in *Les Evangiles Synoptiques* (Ceffonds, 1908) 2.319 remarked that the parable is distinguished neither by originality nor by invention.

[7] Cf. the statement by Snodgrass, *The Parable* 111-112: "The artistry and force of the parable make it one of the most important and effective of all of Jesus' parables," as well as Hengel, "Das Gleichnis" 34: "its inner tension and short, balanced form" make it superior to all the similar rabbinic parables.

how Jesus viewed himself, the Jerusalem Temple authorities, and the Temple itself at the very end of his life.

I. The Temple Setting of Mark 12:1-9.

In its Markan context, Jesus relates the parable of the Wicked Tenants while he is within the Jerusalem Temple. After his first short view of the Temple precincts late in the day, 11:11 notes that Jesus retired with the disciples to Bethany. The next day he again entered the Temple and performed the so-called "cleansing,"[8] with the result that the chief priests and the scribes sought a way to eliminate him (11:15-19). On the third day, while walking in the Temple, Jesus was confronted by the chief priests, scribes and elders with the question of the source of the authority for his deeds (11:27-33). Then the prophet from Nazareth told his parable of the Wicked Tenants, which led to "their" trying to arrest him (12:12), which refers back to the chief priests, scribes and elders of 11:27. Following the questions of paying taxes to Caesar, the resurrection and the great commandment, Jesus is again portrayed as teaching in the Temple (12:35, 38; cf. 14:49), including an incident opposite the treasury (12:41). Only after this does he leave the Temple, predicting in regard to Herod's wonderful buildings: "There will not be left here one stone upon another, that will not be thrown down" (13:2).

The parable of the Wicked Tenants is thus set squarely in the middle of Jesus' Temple activity, both of deed and word. There is no reason to believe Jesus did not relate it there. (On the question of its historicity, see section VIII. below.) The Evangelist Mark knew of its setting within the Temple context and correctly retained this setting when he composed our first gospel.[9] This Temple context for Jesus' parable is corroborated by very early Judaic interpretation of Isa 5:1-7, to which Jesus alludes at the outset and within his parable, and by the golden vine decorations of the Herodian Temple. To these I now turn.

II. The Song of the Vineyard (Isa 5:1-7) and the Temple.

Before discussing early Judaic interpretation of Isa 5:1-7 as referring to the Temple, Jesus' allusions to the Song of the Vineyard should be

---

[8] On recent secondary literature concerning this, cf. D. Seeley, "Jesus' Temple Act" in *CBQ* 55 (1993) 263-283, especially 263, n. 1.

[9] Cf. Snodgrass, *The Parable* 46, referring to Hengel and others; and R. Pesch, *Das Markusevangelium, II. Teil* (HTKNT 2; Freiburg: Herder, 1984[3]) 213-214.

pointed out, for some important modern critics have considered them to be "secondary editorial activity," based on the Septuagint.[10]

A. *Jesus' Allusions to Isaiah 5.*

In Mark 12:1 and 9 Jesus relates his parable of the Wicked Tenants of the Vineyard to Isaiah's Song of the Vineyard by clearly alluding to it five times.

1) Most of the phrase ἀμπελῶνα ἄνθρωπος ἐφύτευσεν, "a man planted a vineyard," in Mark 12:1 derives from Isa 5:2. After referring to a vineyard (כֶּרֶם) in v 1, the MT in v 2 states that "he planted it with choice vines" (וַיִּטָּעֵהוּ שֹׂרֵק). The LXX simply transliterates the Hebrew for "choice vines," but inserts "vineyard" and changes the phrase into the first person singular: καὶ ἐφύτευσα ἄμπελον σωρηχ, "and I planted a vineyard of sorech."

Here Jesus appears to have combined the "vineyard" from Isa 5:1 with "he planted" from v 2, and to have introduced as its subject "a man," necessary for his narrative. He was definitely not influenced by the first person singular of the LXX.

2) The phrase περιέθηκεν θραγμόν,[11] "and he set a hedge around it," in Mark 12:1 now resembles LXX Isa 5:2, καὶ φραγμὸν περιέθηκα: "and I set a hedge around it." Again, the LXX turns the third person into the first person singular. It here attempts to interpret the rare Hebrew וַיְעַזְּקֵהוּ, "and he dug it about," a *hapax legomenon* meaning he dug a ditch around the entire vineyard.[12] The typically stony Palestinian soil thus provided him with building material for a wall when he "cleared it (the vineyard) of stones." Since the verb עזק in later Hebrew means "to break clods and level the ground; to break ground; to till,"[13] the LXX felt it necessary to paraphrase it.

---

[10] Cf. for example Jeremias, *The Parables* 70-71. Hubaut in *La parabole* 131 unconvincingly proposes that the allusions to Isa 5:1-7 in 12:1 and 9 were later added to a primitive version of the parable. The same is maintained by H. Weder, *Die Gleichnisse Jesu als Metaphern* (FRLANT 120; Göttingen: Vandenhoeck & Ruprecht, 1990⁴) 147-148, 150. E. Klostermann in *Das Markusevangelium* (HNT 3; Tübingen: Mohr, 1950⁴) 121 considers the details from Isa 5:1-2 in Mark 12:1 to be only a poetic description; in their new context they are actually "meaningless."

[11] The noun means fence, paling, hedge (LSJ 1952).

[12] BDB 740.

[13] Jastrow, *A Dictionary* 1062.

I suggest that Jesus borrowed the noun גָּדֵר, "wall, fence,"[14] from Isa 5:5, which already in the MT had an equivalent verbal form, גָּדֵר, "wall up or off, build a wall."[15] It is found both in later Hebrew and Aramaic as "to surround with a גָּדֵר, fence in."[16] Jesus then paraphrased Isa 5:2's "he dug it and cleared it of stones" with the one verbal form, גָּדֵר. A vineyard wall was usually made from the stones cleared from the field and surrounding ditch, and a hedge of thorn and briar was frequently erected on top of this.[17]

When a Hellenistic Jewish Christian translated Jesus' term נדר, he logically employed the phrase φραγμὸν περιέθηκα from LXX Isa 5:2, for he easily recognized the very well-known Song of the Vineyard as the background of the setting of Jesus' parable.

3) The phrase καὶ ὤρυξεν ὑπολήνιον,[18] "and he dug a pit / vat beneath the wine press," in Mark 12:1 recalls LXX Isa 5:2's καὶ προλήνιον ὤρυξα, "and I dug a pit / vat in front of the wine press."[19] Again, the LXX verb is in the first person singular. The Hebrew noun יֶקֶב,[20] which was not "dug out" but "hewed out" in the MT, is translated by ὑπολήνιον in LXX Isa 16:10; Joel 3:13; Hag 2:17; and Zech 14:10. The fact that ὑπο – and not προλήνιον is employed in Mark 12:1 shows the Hellenistic Jewish Christian translator's independence of the LXX here.

4) The phrase καὶ ᾠκοδόμησεν πύργον, "and he built a tower," in Mark 12:1 recalls LXX Isa 5:2's καὶ ᾠκοδόμησα πύργον, "and I built a tower," yet here again it is in the first person singular. A different Greek translation of the Hebrew וַיִּבֶן מִגְדָּל was hardly possible.

5) The question τί (οὖν) ποιήσει ὁ κύριος τοῦ ἀμπελῶνος; "What (therefore) will the owner of the vineyard do?" in Mark 12:9 also recalls Isa 5:5. The MT has "what I am doing to My vineyard," meant, however,

---

[14] BDB 154-155. It also occurs in Ps 80:13 (Eng. 12) in a context of God's bringing a vine (Israel) out of Egypt, important in section III. below, also because of God's "son" in v 16 (Eng. 15).

[15] *Ibid.*, 154.

[16] Jastrow 214-215.

[17] Cf. Krauss, *Talmudische Archäologie* 184, including Mishnaic references to a ditch (חריץ) as always forming the border of a vineyard.

[18] This noun only occurs here in the NT.

[19] The only passage cited for προλήνιον in LSJ 1488 is here.

[20] BDB 428: wine-vat, sometimes wine-press. Cf. Krauss, *Talmudische Archäologie* 233, for the upper vat as גַּת, or פּוּרָה (BDB 807), יֶקֶב as the lower. See also the art. "Wine" by J. Ross in *IDB* 4.850-851.

as future. One action is that it (the vineyard) "will be destroyed" (לְבָעֵר).[21] This verb, בער in the piel, may be behind the following answer in Mark 12:9, "He will come and 'destroy' (ἀπολέσει) the tenants...."[22] The Targum of Isa 5:5 makes the future explicit: "what I am about (עתיד) to do to My people."[23] The LXX has τί ποιήσω τῷ ἀμπελῶνί μου, "what I will do to My vineyard," again in the first person singular.[24]

The question "What will he (e.g. the owner) do?" occurs a number of times in rabbinic comment on a vineyard after a preliminary negative reaction on the part of others.[25] For this reason there is no dependence on the LXX here, with its "I," but on a common phrase adapted by Jesus from the content of Isa 5:5.

(For my proposal that the term "beloved" – ἀγαπητός – for the son in Mark 12:6 ultimately derives from the "beloved" of Isa 5:1, see section V. below.)

*   *   *

Jesus thus very probably alludes in Mark 12:1 and 9 five times to Isaiah 5, the Song of the Vineyard. The four introductory phrases in his parable follow neither the order now found in the MT nor in the LXX. He creatively reworked the material from Isaiah. The LXX form of narration, "I" instead of "he," definitely did not influence him. The use of ὑπο – and not προλήνιον also shows independence of the LXX. As remarked above, the Hellenistic Jewish Christian who translated Jesus' narrative into Greek easily recognized the five allusions to Isaiah 5 and very appropriately chose expressions from there for his own rendering. The

---

[21] The piel of this verb means here "be for destruction, be destroyed" (BDB 129, end of 3.).

[22] Cf. 2 Sam 4:11, where David threatens to "destroy" wicked men who have slain a man.

[23] Cf. Stenning, *The Targum of Isaiah* 16-17. Stenning believes the Isaiah Targum acquired a fixed form much earlier than the fifth century C.E. (vii; the third century C.E.? – ix). Yet it incorporated much earlier material, and each case must be interpreted individually. See also Chilton, *The Isaiah Targum* xxiii, for two phases of development, one Tannaitic and one Amoraic.

[24] The question in Isa 5:4, "What else should I do (lit. to do) for My vineyard, and I have not done it to it?" may also have influenced Jesus' own phrase.

[25] Cf. for example "When a vineyard does not yield fruit, 'what does its owner do to it?' He uproots it!" in *Gen. Rab.* Noah 38/9 on Gen 11:6 (Soncino English 1.308); "What will I do to them?", with destruction, in *Exod. Rab.* Mishpatim 30/1 on Exod 21:1 (Soncino 3.346); and "What will He (God at the Judgment) say to them? 'It is you who have devoured the vineyard' (Isa 3:14)," in *Exod. Rab.* Shemoth 5/12 on Exod 4:29 (Soncino 3.92).

five allusions, four of them very close together in Mark 12:1, all go back to Jesus' own creative use of Isaiah 5,[26] and are not later "secondary editorial activity."

B. *Isaiah 5:1-7 and the Temple*

In the Jerusalem Temple wine accompanied numerous offerings. The daily burnt offering in the morning and in the evening included a fourth of a hin of wine as a libation (Exod 29:40; Num 28:7). The same amount applied to the offering of first fruits (Lev 23:13), and to others.[27] Already in the first fourth of the second century B.C.E., Sir 50:15 describes the high priest in Jerusalem so: "he poured a libation of the blood of the grape; he poured it out at the foot of the altar."[28] Josephus, a native of Jerusalem who wrote at the end of the first century C.E., speaks of the priests as "pouring the wine as a libation around the altar."[29]

This libation wine was then collected in a pit (שׁית)[30] at the side of the altar. Such were the quantities of wine which flowed into it that the pit had to be periodically cleaned.[31]

---

[26] Cf. the statement of A. Milavec regarding Jesus' use of Isaiah 5 in Mark 12:1 in "A Fresh Analysis of the Parable of the Wicked Husbandmen in the Light of Jewish-Catholic Dialogue" in *Parables and Story in Judaism and Christianity*, ed. C. Thoma and M. Wyschogrod (New York: Paulist, 1989) 91-92: "By borrowing and noticeably modifying the familiar opening, an artful storyteller evokes the mood and theme of a familiar story at the same time that he signals a *new* version of this old parable is about to be presented." Jesus also employed vineyard imagery in a creative way in two other parables: Matt 20:1-15 and 21:28-32. See also Luke 13:6-9. U. Mell in *Die "anderen" Winzer: eine exegetische Studie zur Vollmacht Jesu Christi nach Markus 11, 27-12, 34* (WUNT 77; Tübingen: Mohr-Siebeck, 1994) deals with Mark 12:1b-11 on pp. 74-172. He finds literary and structural connections to LXX Isa 5:1-9a (pp. 78-88), yet concludes from this that the author of this pre-Markan judgment allegory should be sought in early Hellenistic Judaism. For him there are no Semitisms in the pericope, therefore Jesus cannot be the narrator (114, with n. 228).

[27] Cf. Num 15:5, 7 (1/3), 10 (1/2); 28:14 (1/2, 1/3, 1/4).

[28] Cf. G. Nickelsburg, *Jewish Literature Between the Bible and the Mishnah* 64-65, for the dating and the work as originally having been written in Hebrew, in Jerusalem (55).

[29] *Ant.* 3.234 in regard to Num 15:4-10. See *Vita* 7 for Jerusalem, and *Ant.* 20.267 for Josephus's completing the *Antiquities* in 93-94 C.E. For these and other references, see Ross, "Wine" 851, as well as the art. "Sacrifices" by T. Gaster in *IDB* 4.156.

[30] Jastrow 1570. A noun with the same consonants, meaning "thorn-bushes" (BDB 1011), is found in Isa 5:6.

[31] Cf. *m. Midd.* 3:3 (English in Danby, *The Mishnah* 594), and *t. Sukk.* 3:15 (English in Neusner, *The Tosefta* 2.221-222), which mentions once every seventy years; as

Each projection at the four corners of the altar was called a "horn," קֶרֶן.[32] The same Hebrew term is employed only once in the MT in the sense of "hill," and that is in Isa 5:1, "My Beloved (God) had a vineyard on a very fertile 'hill.'" In Judaic tradition this is the Temple Mount in Jerusalem. For Targum Jonathan, the "lofty mountain" of Isa 5:1 is the place regarding which God says: "I established them like the plant of a chosen vine; and I built My sanctuary among them; yea, I gave them My altar to make atonement for their sins" (5:2).[33]

This information aids in understanding the following Tannaitic tradition found, for example, in *t. Sukk.* 3:15. It begins by mentioning the "pit" and quotes Num 28:7 regarding pouring out a drink offering of "strong drink" (שֵׁכָר) to the Lord in the holy place, that is, at the altar in the Temple. "Strong drink" in the MT is usually parallel to "wine," meant here as undiluted.[34]

"R. Yose (b. Ḥalafta, a third generation Tanna)[35] says, 'The cavity of the pit[36] descended to the abyss.'" He quotes Isa 5:1-2 as his proof text. Then he interprets v 2 as follows:

> "'And He built a tower in the midst of it' – this is the sanctuary.
> 'He hewed out a vat therein' – this is the altar.
> And also 'He hewed out a vat therein' – this is the pit."[37]

---

well as *m. Meʿil.* 3:3 (Danby 577). In *m. Sukk.* 4:9 (Danby 179) a bowl containing wine upon the eastern side of the altar is mentioned.

[32] Cf. Exod 27:2; Lev 4:7, 18; and other references in BDB 902.

[33] Cf. Stenning, *The Targum of Isaiah* 16-17. See also *Sifre* Deut. 'Eqeb § 37 on Deut 11:9 (Hebrew in Finkelstein, *Sifre on Deuteronomy* 73, and English in Hammer, *Sifre* 73) with Isa 5:1, *qeren* and the Temple.

[34] Cf. BDB 1016, especially Isa 5:11 and 22.

[35] Cf. Strack and Stemberger, *Introduction* 84. In *y. Ḥag.* 3:1, 78d (English in Neusner, *The Talmud of the Land of Israel* 20.84) R. Yose is one of seven elders who ostensibly interpreted Isa 5:1 in seven different ways.

[36] Neusner in 2.221 has the plural. The singular is found in Zuckermandel and Liebermann, *Tosephta* 197. I slightly modify Neusner's translation here.

[37] This tradition is also found in *t. Meʿil.* 1:16 (Neusner 5.236; Zuckermandel / Liebermann 558); *y. Sukk.* 4:6, 54d (Neusner 17.108); and *b. Sukk.* 49a (Soncino 230), which has the school of R. Ishmael state that God created the pit (of the altar, at the time of the world's creation: Gen 1:1); here the "choice vine" of Isa 5:2 is the Temple. P. Billerbeck had called attention to these texts in Str-B 1.867. Following him, C. Evans cited several of them in "On the Vineyard Parables of Isaiah 5 and Mark 12" in *BZ* 28 (1984) 82-86.

R. Yose repeats the phrase "He hewed out a vat therein" because he was well aware of there being an upper and a lower part to the vat or wine press.[38]

In his commentary on Matthew, Origen, who probably died in Palestine ca. 251 C.E.,[39] considered the tower of Jesus' parable of the Wicked Tenants in Matt 21:22 to be the Jerusalem Temple, the hedge as evidence of God's care, and the wine press as the place of the libations.[40] He thus appears to have been acquainted with something like the Tannaitic tradition cited above.

Rabbinic comment on Isa 5:1-7, often in the form of parables, also frequently interprets the "vineyard,"[41] or the "beloved" (ידיד),[42] as the Temple. The entire narrative also appears to lie behind a parable by R.

---

[38] Cf. n. 20.

[39] Cf. Walker, *A History of the Christian Church* 74.

[40] Cf. his *Commentaria in Evangelium secundum Matthaeum* in *P.G.* 13.1488-89. Other interpretations of the parable of the Wicked Tenants by the church fathers are found in Gnilka, *Das Evangelium nach Markus* (Mk 8, 27 – 16, 20) 149-150. See also Snodgrass, *The Parable* 3, n. 1.

[41] Cf. the parable in *Exod. Rab.* Beshallaḥ 20/5 on Exod 13:17 (Soncino 3.246-247, with n. 1 on p. 247 on the tower of Isa 5:2 as the Temple); Terumah 34/3 on Exod 25:10 (Soncino 3.427-428); *Pesiq. Rav Kah.* 16/9 on Isa 40:1 (English in Braude and Kapstein, *Pesikta de-Rab Kahana* 298, dealing with the Ninth of Ab, which commemorates the destruction of the Temple; see p. 297); and *Pesiq. R.* 29/30.B, 3 (English in Braude, *Pesikta Rabbati* 586 on Isa 40:1) on Nebuchadnezzar's destroying the first Temple.

[42] Cf. *b. Menaḥ.* 53a-b (Soncino 320); *'Avot R. Nat.* B 43 (Hebrew in Schechter, *Aboth de Rabbi Nathan* 121; English in Saldarini, *The Fathers According to Rabbi Nathan [B]* 265); *Sifre* Deut. Berakah § 352 on Deut 33:12 (Finkelstein 409; Hammer 364-365); and *Midr. Ps.* 84/1 on Ps 84:1 (Hebrew in Buber, *Midrasch Tehillim* 185b or p. 370; English in Braude, *The Midrash on Psalms* 2.64). In *Som.* 2.172-173, Philo of Alexandria also comments on Isa 5:7, yet as usual he allegorizes, making the fruit of the vineyard into virtue. *Pseudo-Philo* 28:4, Eleazar the priest's words to the sons of Israel, is another early example of the haggadic interpretation of Isaiah 5, Israel as a plant taken from God's vineyard. Despite His care, it destroys its own fruit and refuses to yield it to God. See *OTP* 2.341, and 298-299 for the writing as originally in Hebrew, from Palestine, and from about the time of Jesus. In *DJD* 5, col. I (pp. 15-16; cf. Martínez 186-187) offers a pesher from Qumran on Isa 5:5-6, referring the text to "the end of days" and "the men of scoffing who are in Jerusalem." If the (high) priests, who were in charge of the Temple worship services, are meant here, as is probable, this is another argument for interpreting the tenants of Jesus' parable as the priestly hierarchy in Jerusalem (see below). Unfortunately, 4Q Benediction (4Q500; Martínez 402), which mentions a winepress and "the gate of the holy height," is too short and truncated to relate it to the Temple. See on this J. Baumgarten, "4Q500 and the Ancient Exegesis of the Lord's Vineyard" in *JJS* 40 (1989) 1-6.

Simeon b. Yehoṣadaq, a first generation Palestinian Amora,[43] regarding a
king who tells a "tenant" (אָרִיס) to convert an uncultivated field into a
vineyard.[44] This parable quotes Hos 11:1, "out of Egypt I called My son,"
of relevance to the "son" of Mark 12:6, as I shall point out below. It also
shows that Jesus was not the only Palestinian teacher to base a parable
with a tenant on Isa 5:1-7.

All of the above makes it quite probable that Jesus, who based the
setting and a later phrase in his parable of the Wicked Tenants on Isa 5:1-
7, also meant the Temple as the vineyard which will be given to "others"
(Mark 12:9). This is due to the very negative behavior of the Temple
authorities, to which I shall turn after indicating one more possible
influence on Jesus' vineyard parable.

Josephus, of priestly descent and – as noted above – a native of
Jerusalem, was well acquainted with the Herodian Temple structure. He
relates that above the Sanctuary gate, which itself was overlaid with
gold, there were golden vines. Grape clusters as tall as a human being
hung down from these.[45] The Mishnah in *Midd.* 3:8 notes that the golden
vine was trained over poles. Whoever donated a (piece of gold shaped
like a) leaf, grape or cluster, brought it, and (the priests) hung it on the
vine. R. Eleazar b. R. Ṣadoq, an older second generation Tanna,[46] remarks
that it was once necessary for 300 priests to clear it (because the
donations were so numerous).[47] This shows its great popularity.

H. Danby comments that "when the Temple treasury was in need,
the treasurer took from the vine as much (gold) as was required."[48] If this
is correct, as seems plausible, the Temple administrators, themselves
wealthy, gleaned from the golden Temple vine-vineyard what they
considered appropriate. Jesus, sitting in the Temple precincts, from
which the golden vine because of its height was visible from many
angles, related a parable about the wicked tenants of a vineyard, the

---

[43] Strack and Stemberger, *Introduction* 92.

[44] Cf. *Exod. Rab.* Ki Thissa 43/9 on Exod 32:11 (Soncino 3.504-505, and n. 1;
Hebrew in Mirqin, *Midrash Rabbah* 6.160).

[45] Cf. *Bell.* 5.210. In *Ant.* 15.395 he notes that the golden vine was "a marvel of size
and artistry to all who saw with what costliness of material it had been
constructed." Thackeray on the *Bellum* passage states that Tacitus in his *History*
V.5 also alludes to it.

[46] Strack and Stemberger, *Introduction* 78.

[47] Hebrew in Albeck, *Shisha Sidre Mishna* 5.328; English in Danby 595. Cf. also *b.*
Ḥull. 90b (Soncino 506).

[48] *The Mishnah* 595, n. 6.

administrators of the Jerusalem Temple. The setting was very appropriate.[49]

C. *Those Meant by Isa 5:1-7.*

The five allusions to Isa 5:1-7 found in Mark 12:1-9, as pointed out above, make it possible that the context of the Song of the Vineyard can help to indicate those against whom Jesus directed his parable. This is indeed the case.

Targum Jonathan of Isa 5:7b reads:

"I (God) thought (lit. said) that they (Israel and Judah)
would perform justice,
and behold, *usurpers* (אָנוֹסִין);
that they would perform favorable judgment,
and behold, they increase transgression."[50]

The MT has מִשְׂפָּח, "bloodshed,"[51] as the background of אָנוֹסין. The latter term is the plural participle of the verb אנס, to do violence, take by force, snatch, rob, oppress.[52] "Usurpers," who take others' property by violence, are meant here, as the next verse in the Targum (5:8) indicates:

"Woe to those who join house to house,
attaching field (estate, farm by) *usurpation* (אוּנְסָא)
to their fields (estates, farms), saying:
'Until we take possession of every place,'
thinking that they will dwell alone in the midst of the land."[53]

The Targum enforces this motif in v 11 by mentioning "the wine of *usurpation* inflaming them," and in v 24: "the wealth (מָמוֹן) which they have *obtained by usurpation* (shall be) like dust that flies away."[54]

---

[49] Cf. the reference to Josephus (without concrete sources) by E. Lohmeyer in "Das Gleichnis von den bösen Weingärtnern (Mark 12, 1-12)" in *ZST* 18 (1941) 247. M. Hubaut in *La parabole* 139 mentions Lohmeyer and others who believed the golden Temple vine "was the trigger" for Jesus' parable. That is certainly exaggerated, for the main background of the parable is found in the vineyard of Isa 5:1-7, interpreted of the Temple, and in the Song at the Sea and Isaiah's martyrdom in the Jerusalem Temple, to be shown below.

[50] I slightly modify the translation of Stenning 16-17.

[51] BDB 705; it only occurs here.

[52] Jastrow 86.

[53] Stenning 16-17, again modified. On חקל as estate, farm, field, cf. Jastrow 497. For אונסא, see Jastrow 29, and 488 on חסן, af. as to take possession (for oneself and heirs).

[54] My modification of Stenning 16-19.

Rabbinic interpretation of Isa 5:8 corroborates the motif of usurpation found in the Targum. R. Yoḥanan (bar Nappaḥa), a second generation Palestinian Amora,[55] interpreted "Woe unto those who join house to house" as those "who make a loan on a man's house and field to take them from him," thinking that they will "inherit" (ירש) the land alone. Yet God swears that many of these extortioners' houses will become "desolate," as v 9 is interpreted.[56]

The commentators point to the background of Isa 5:8 in the owners of far-off, large rural estates who now live in Jerusalem. They employ tenants for the real work, themselves reaping the greater profits without exerting themselves. In part, they have acquired the estates illegally, amassing great wealth, which then remains in the hands of a very few.[57]

The situation had hardly changed at the time of Jesus and in the first centuries C.E., as seen in the Targum's very similar interpretation of the Hebrew, certainly reflecting actual contemporary conditions.[58] It was

---

[55] Strack and Stemberger, *Introduction* 94-95; he died in 279 C.E.

[56] Interestingly, Yoḥanan's brother-in-law Simeon b. Laqish (*Introduction* 95) interpreted the same Isaianic verse, 5:9, to mean the "destruction" (חוּרְבָּן) of both the first and the second Temples. Cf. *Lam. Rab.*, Proem 22 (Soncino 7.27-28; Hebrew in Buber, *Midrasch Ekha Rabbati* 8b or p. 16), where the מָקוֹם, "place" of 5:8, is treated as the Temple.

[57] Cf. H. Wildenberger, *Jesaja* (BKAT X/1; Neukirchen-Vluyn: Neukirchener, 1972) 184; R. Kilian, *Jesaja 1-12* (NEB; Würzburg: Echter, 1986) 42; and G. Fohrer, *Das Buch Jesaja*, 1. Band, Kapitel 1-23 (ZBK; Zurich and Stuttgart: Zwingli, 1966²) 79. See already 1 Chron 27:27 for the vineyards of King David, 2 Chron 26:10 for King Uzziah's vinedressers, and Cant 8:11 for King Solomon's vineyard at Baalhemon, which he "let out" to keepers, i.e. tenants. The latter verse is associated with Isa 5:7 in *Cant. Rab.* 8:11 § 1 (Soncino 9.317).

[58] Cf. J. Herz, "Grossgrundbesitz in Palästina im Zeitalter Jesu" in *PJ* 24 (1928) 98-113, as well as Hengel's analysis of sources primarily from the third century B.C.E. in "Das Gleichnis" 1-39. See also *b. Sukk.* 44b (Soncino 205), where someone stated in the presence of Aibu, the father of Rab, a first generation Palestinian Amora (Strack and Stemberger, *Introduction* 93): "I possess cities, vineyards and olive trees...." In *b. B. Bat.* 14a (Soncino 67) it is also stated that R. Yannai, a first generation Palestinian Amora (Strack and Stemberger, *Introduction* 91), planted "400 vineyards...." These vineyards had to be let out to tenants or supervisors, since the wealthy owners could not care for them themselves. S. Freyne's analysis of economic conditions in Galilee before 70 C.E. shows that in that region there was no great disaffection leading to revolt. See his *Galilee, Jesus and the Gospels* (Philadelphia: Fortress, 1988) 155-167. This speaks strongly against the proposal of J. and R. Newell that the Galilean Jesus in his parable "attacks the methods of the first century Zealot movement." See their "The Parable of the Wicked Tenants" in *NovT* 14 (1972) 226-237, quotation p. 226. W. Herzog in "Peasant Revolt and the Spiral of Violence. The Parable of the Wicked Tenants (Mark 12:1-12)" in *Parables as Subversive Speech: Jesus as Pedagogue of the Oppressed* (Louisville: Westminster / John Knox Press, 1994) 98-113, considers the parable to deal with a

perhaps furthered by gifts of property, for example fields and vineyards, made to the Jerusalem Temple.[59] If so, the Temple administrators not only took care of the regular Temple "business." They also had to care for estates which had been donated to the Sanctuary. These administrators, especially the aristocratic high priests, were well-known for their own wealth, including large estates.[60]

Isa 3:12-15.

Before analyzing the behavior of a "usurper" of a vineyard or other property in Judaic sources in regard to Mark 12:1-9, I would first like to call attention to Isaiah's tirade against the Jerusalem elders and princes who have "devoured the vineyard" (Isa 3:12-15).[61]

"small rebellion." It "codifies the spiral of violence by describing a local peasant revolt on a great estate" (p. 109). In *New Documents Illustrating Early Christianity,* vol. 6, "§ 13. Self-Help and Legal Redress: The Parable of the Wicked Tenants" (Macquarie University, 1992) 86-105, S. Llewelyn deals extensively with papyrological and rabbinic sources on leases. He warns against using too early and too late materials to interpret the parable of the Wicked Tenants. In light of the papyri he concludes that "new vineyards were worked by contract labour rather than leased to tenants" (p. 105). My proposal below concerning tenants as "violent usurpers" contradicts this view.

[59] Cf. *Mek. R. Ish.* Nezikim 14 on Exod 22:4 (Lauterbach, *Mekilta de-Rabbi Ishmael* 3.109, with n. 2, and 310).

[60] Cf. *t. Menaḥ.* 13:22 (Neusner 5.162), where high priests "love money"; *Ant.* 13.298 for the Sadducees' association with the wealthy (the high priests were for the most part Sadducees); the second generation Tanna R. Eleazar b. Azaryah, described as an "aristocratic, rich priest" (Strack and Stemberger, *Introduction* 78); as well as the discussion in Jeremias, *Jerusalem in the Time of Jesus* 92-99 and 196-198. On a severe criticism of the Jerusalem priesthood as avaricious, see *Test. Moses* 7:5 (*OTP* 1.930, with similar texts from Qumran and the *Psalms of Solomon* in n. "e"). In his volume *The Social History of Palestine in the Herodian Period: The Land is Mine* (Studies in the Bible and Early Christianity, 20; Lewiston, NY: Mellen, 1991), D. Fiensy deals with the period from 37 B.C.E. to 70 C.E. He states: "Perhaps the most significant class of wealthy landowners was the class of aristocratic priests and especially the High Priestly families" (p. 51). See also p. 178: "The aristocrats – Herodians, High Priestly families, and lay aristocrats – were large estate owners who exploited the labor of the peasants." Fiensy deals with "Tenant Farmers in Palestine" on pp. 80-85; he considers early rabbinic materials, together with sources from Wadi Murabaat and Nahal Hever, as most important in understanding the situation of the Palestinian tenant farmers (p. 80).

[61] For a similar critique on the part of the prophet Jeremiah regarding the "shepherds" who have destroyed God's vineyard, cf. Jer 12:10. Chilton in *The Isaiah Targum* xxiv calls attention to "attacks on the priestly hierarchy" before 70 C.E. See Targ Isa 22:15-25 and 28:1-4 (Chilton 44-45 and 54, with his notes).

The vineyard of 5:1-7 stands for the people of Israel and Judah (v 7).[62] The Song of the Vineyard was also interpreted, however, as if it were directed against the leaders of the people, i.e. the Jerusalem aristocracy, especially the high priests. These are castigated in 3:12-15.[63] The Lord will enter into judgment with the people's elders and princes because they have devoured His "vineyard," they have exploited the poor, crushing and grinding them. Rabbinic comment on 3:14 strongly emphasizes this motif.[64]

The Targum similarly reproves the leaders / officers of the people, who reside in Jerusalem. In 3:12 they "plunder it (the people) like the gleaners of a vineyard, and like creditors do they rule over it." They cause the people to err, they have corrupted their paths. On 3:14 it states that the Lord will judge the elders and leaders / officers, who have "usurped / oppressed / done violence to" (אנס) His people. They will not be able to escape this judgment, for "the plunder of the poor is in your houses."[65]

I suggest that the Hebrew of 3:14, "the LORD (simultaneously also the Lord of the vineyard) will come (יבא) in judgment" over the elders and princes of His people, stands behind the phrase in Mark 12:9, where the lord of the vineyard "will come" (ἐλεύσεται – in judgment) and destroy the tenants.[66] As pointed out above, the vineyard will be "devoured / destroyed" in Isa 5:5, employing the same verb, בער, as here in 3:14 of the elders and princes' "devouring" the vineyard.

Jesus directs his parable of the Wicked Tenants of the Vineyard against the very same group as the prophet Isaiah did in 3:12-15, the "leaders" of God's vineyard, here the people of Israel. Instead of dealing graciously with the poor, the Jerusalem aristocracy devoured or "usurped" their property, thereby amassing even more wealth for

---

[62] In v 3 the inhabitants of Jerusalem are specifically addressed.

[63] Cf. for example *Exod. Rab.* Shemoth 5/12 on Exod 4:29 (Soncino 3.91), associating Isa 3:14 and 5:7.

[64] Cf. *b. Šabb.* 54b-55a (Soncino 252), where the religious elders do not restrain the secular princes; *Deut. Rab.* Debarim 1/10 on Deut 1:13 (Soncino 7.9-10) in parable form accuses the leaders of not attending to the people's needs and wants, thereby becoming guilty; and *Ruth Rab.* Proem 6 (Soncino 8.9), where "the great do not bear the burden of the small upon them." See also *Esth. Rab.* 3/2 on Esth 1:9 (Soncino 9.45), which interprets Isa 3:12 to mean: "they are exacting towards them (the people)," "they pluck their tiny grapes," "they bring false charges against them," and "they pounced on them like a creditor."

[65] Stenning 12-13.

[66] The Lord's "coming" to judge is a standard phrase in the MT, as in Ps 96:13, 98:9 and 143:2. Cf. Wildberger, *Jesaja* X/1, p. 132.

themselves. For this reason the Lord will judge them, and they themselves will be devoured / destroyed. One of the main aspects of Jesus' prophetic call to repentance was that the rich should treat the poor more equitably.[67] If they refused to do so, the consequences were clear – God's severe judgment of them. This was especially true of the spiritual leadership of God's people, Israel, those responsible for the Jerusalem Temple, also considered God's "vineyard."

Jesus was not the only one to threaten the wealthy Temple administrators with destruction for exploiting the common people. One example just before his time is that of Baba b. Buta, according to rabbinic tradition the same person who counseled Herod to pull down and rebuild the Jerusalem Temple.[68]

In *y. Beṣa (Yom Ṭob)* 2:4, 61c it is related that Baba b. Buta once came to the courtyard (עזרה) of the Jerusalem Temple. He found it "desolate" (שוממת, i.e. empty of sacrificial animals because the Temple officials had allowed the price to be driven up so high that the people could no longer afford the animals).[69] He then stated regarding the high priests and other Temple administrators: "May the houses of those who 'desolated' (השימו) the house of God 'be made desolate' (ישמו)!"[70]

To rectify the situation, he went and brought 3000 animals from the Kedar herd, set them up in the courtyard, and invited those required to bring whole offerings and peace offerings to serve themselves, which they did.[71]

---

[67] Cf. the articles on *ptōchos* etc. by E. Bammel in *TDNT* 6.902-908, *ploutos* etc. by F. Hauck and W. Kasch in 6.327-328, and *mamōnas* by F. Hauck in 4.389-390.

[68] Cf. *b. B. Bat.* 3b-4a (Soncino 10-12). The "rabbis" whom Herod kills here are probably the Sons of Baba, who opposed him and favored Antigonus. See Josephus, *Ant.* 15.260-266. The rebuilding of the Temple is related as of 15.380.

[69] Cf. a similar incident in *m. Ker.* 1:7 (Danby 564) with R. Simeon b. Gamaliel I, a first generation Tanna (Strack and Stemberger, *Introduction* 74).

[70] Neusner 18.64.

[71] Neusner inserts his English translation of *t. Ḥag.* 2:11 (Neusner 2.317) here, yet the Yerushalmi's version has 3000. "The whole herd" is found in Zuckermandel and Liebermann 236. On the herd of Kedar, cf. Isa 60:7, which states that "they shall come up with acceptance on My altar, and I will glorify My glorious house (the Temple)." The number 3000 is not to be taken literally; it simply signifies very many, enough for all those who wished to sacrifice. On the large numbers of sacrificial animals donated (in part by the Temple administrators) at King Josiah's renewed Passover festival, cf. 2 Chron 35:7-9 and 1 Esdr 1:7-9.

Baba b. Buta must have infuriated the high priests and other Temple administrators with this curse and with his action, yet his authority[72] prevented them from retaliating.[73] The opposite was the case with Jesus, whose prophetic and symbolic "cleansing" of the Temple and veiled allusion to the Temple administrators as the wicked tenants of God's vineyard, the Temple, infuriated them so much that they sought to arrest and kill him. This parable was also told by Jesus within the Temple precincts.

Returning to the motif of a "usurping occupant," I would like to point out that it is significant that *Targum Jonathan* employs the term אנס in Isa 3:14 for those who have devoured the vineyard in the MT. Early rabbinic employment of the noun אַנָּס greatly helps to understand the violent behavior of the tenants of the vineyard in Mark 12:1-9.[74]

An *'annas* is basically "one who acts violently, a violent man." This is clearly shown in *t. Ter.* 1:16, which speaks of "a thief, an *'annas*, and a robber."[75] If such a person forcibly appropriated another's piece of property, the best English translation for him, as in Targ Isa 5:7b-8, 11 and 24 (employing a verbal form), is "usurping occupant." This is shown in *m. Kil.* 7:6, which deals with a vineyard, as in Jesus' parable of the violent tenants, who through their killing the heir (son) seek to gain permanent possession of the owner's vineyard. It reads: "If a *usurping occupant* sowed a vineyard and it was recovered from him...."[76]

H. Danby defines such a person as "one who had seized the property of those absent or killed or taken captive in war...."[77] The first possibility

---

[72] Cf. the Sons of Baba as having "a high position and great influence with the masses"; they "were held in esteem and honor by all the people" in *Ant.* 15.261 and 264.

[73] The Tosefta ends the episode by saying: "and no one said a thing about it."

[74] A striking scriptural example of violent seizure of someone else's vineyard is found in 1 Kings 21, where Jezebel and her husband King Ahab, with the help of elders and nobles, obtain possession of / inherit Naboth's vineyard by killing him. Here too the perpetrators are to suffer a similar fate (vv 19-24). The incident is similar to the violence employed in Mark 12:7-8, followed by the perpetrators' destruction (v 9).

[75] Cf. Zuckermandel and Liebermann 25; Neusner 1.131 translates "extortioner" here. See also *t. Ma'aś. Š.* 1:7 (Zuckermandel and Liebermann 86), where Neusner translates "thug" (1.295).

[76] Albeck 1.123; Danby 36.

[77] *The Mishnah* 313, n. 6. It should not be confused with a similar term, סיקריקון (Jastrow 986, who plausibly considers it a disguised form of καισαρίκιον: the possessor of confiscated property). In *m. Giṭ.* 5:6 and *Bik.* 1:2 and 2:3 (Albeck 3.287, and 1.311 and 315; Danby 313, 93 and 95), this term most probably refers to those who usurped the property of the victims of the Hadrianic persecution of

fits the situation of Jesus' parable of the Wicked Tenants admirably, for the owner of the vineyard "went off to a distant country" (Mark 12:1).[78] The tenants then took advantage of the situation by usurping his property.

The Mishnah continues by asking: "After what time is the vineyard called by the name of the usurping occupant? After (the name of its first owner) is forgotten." The latter phrase employs the passive of שָׁקַע, to be depressed, sink, go down.[79] Maimonides interprets: "From such time as he, i.e. the original owner, has sunk, i.e. disappeared, withdrawn himself, hidden, to avoid terrorization by the *'annas*."[80]

The Jerusalem or Palestinian Talmud discusses this situation extensively by considering whether the rightful owner of the vineyard had "despaired" or "not (yet) despaired" (of recovering it). It then asks: "But can real property be stolen...?" R. La, a third generation Palestinian Amora,[81] then states: "Even though real property cannot be stolen, despair (of recovering it) does affect (the status of) real property."[82] I. Mandelbaum explains this by the following: "Although the usurper

---

132-135 C.E. See the remainder of Danby's note in 313, n. 6. The *'annasim* of *m. Sanh.* 3:3 are also irrelevant here, for they are later tax-gatherers (Albeck 4.176 and Danby 385; cf. *b. Sanh.* 26a in Soncino 150).

[78] This is a stock phrase found in early Judaic sources: הלך למדינת־הַיָם. It occurs thirty-five times in the Mishnah alone. Danby (*The Mishnah* 221, n. 1) defines it as "any place beyond the borders of the land of Israel." Elsewhere he notes the one exception as Babylon (307, n. 2). Jesus employs it elsewhere in Luke 15:13 and 19:12 (cf. Matt 25:14), both parables. Three other examples of the phrase in early rabbinic parables are *Mek. R. Ish.* Beshallaḥ 2 on Exod 14:5 (Lauterbach 1.198); Shirata 3 on Exod 15:2 (Lauterbach 2.27); and *Tanḥ.* B Beshallaḥ 7 on Exod 13:17, with a tenant (Hebrew in Buber, *Midrasch Tanchuma* 2.29a or p. 55; German in Bietenhard, *Midrasch Tanḥuma* B 1.350). Of special interest to Mark 12:1-9 are examples in *b. B. Meṣ.* 38b (Soncino 233). The issue dealt with is that of an abandoned estate, and who may take it over if the owner, who had gone to a far-off country, died or was not heard of again. Then the next of kin may do so.

[79] Jastrow 1624, who cites b. *'Arak.* 6b: "as long as the name of its owner is not merged (but is still traceable)." Soncino 31 translates: "has become forgotten." Against J. Derrett, who in *Law in the New Testament* (London: Darton, 1970; the relevant chapter revises his article which appeared in *RIDA* 10 [1963] 11-41) 303-304 believes the term יָאַשׁ (Jastrow 560) is involved here. Derrett concludes his study by proposing that in his parable Jesus referred to Adam, the keeper of the Garden of Eden, who with his wife was tempted, judged and expelled. Jesus then added several more episodes to this (310-312). There is nothing in the parable to substantiate Derrett's proposal.

[80] Quoted in Soncino, *b. Kilaim* 128.

[81] Strack and Stemberger, *Introduction* 99; Str-B 5/6.202.

[82] See *y. Kil.* 7:4(6), 31a (Neusner / Mandelbaum 4.220).

cannot gain ownership of the vineyard by stealing it, the rightful owner's despair does enable him to be considered the vineyard's owner with regard to rabbinic prohibition of sowing another kind (*kilaim*) in it."[83]

This major legal topos from early Judaic tradition, the "violent seizing of" or "usurping" a vineyard, is the main background to Jesus' parable of the Wicked Tenants. They repeatedly beat, wound, shamefully treat and kill the servants[84] of the owner, who is in a far-off country and can take no direct legal action. Finally, they even kill the owner's son, the (only) heir,[85] hoping that he will "despair" completely of ever recovering his vineyard. To avoid further terrorization by the *'annas*, the owner will then withdraw, i.e. his name will gradually be "forgotten," and the usurper can act as if he legally owns the seized property. He may then even render certain duties from the vineyard, as if he were the proper owner now fulfilling his religious obligations.

Jesus' parable is thus shown to have its background in a legal situation which occurred so often in rural Palestine that it was later codified in the Mishnah, precisely by means of the example of a vineyard. This background was not far-fetched for the original hearers of Jesus' parable. They knew of such situations from daily life.

*   *   *

The second major influence on the content of Jesus' parable, after the Song of the Vineyard, was the Song at the Sea, to which I now turn.

III. The Song at the Sea (Exod 15:1-18) and the Temple.

A. *Teaching Regarding the Passover Texts in the Temple Precincts.*

Jesus told his parable of the Wicked Tenants within the Temple precincts shortly before Passover (Mark 14:1, 12), the great pilgrimage festival commemorating God's redeeming the Israelites from bondage in Egypt by leading them through the Red (Reed) Sea (Exod 12:1 – 15:21).

---

[83] *Ibid.*

[84] On the servants as prophets sent by God to Israel, see my discussion in section IV below. Targ Isa 5:6 inserts the motif of prophets into the MT (Stenning 16-17).

[85] If the son as ἀγαπητός in Mark 12:6 derives from יָחִיד, he is the "only" son. Cf. Jastrow 574. See, for example, Gen 22:2, 12, 16; Amos 8:10; and Zech 12:10. Below, however, I argue for the derivation from חביב. There is also no indication in the parable that the father made a gift of the vineyard to his son, who then had to take possession of it; otherwise it would be forfeited and could be appropriated by others. Against E. Bammel, "Das Gleichnis von den bösen Winzern (Mark. 12, 1-12) und das jüdische Erbrecht" in *RIDA* 6 (1959) 11-17.

It was customary for the festival pilgrims also to be concerned with the study of the Torah in Jerusalem, encouraged by their viewing the Sages of the Sanhedrin and their disciples doing this.[1] A baraitha in *b. Pesaḥ.* 26a relates that R. Yoḥanan b. Zakkai, a first generation Tanna,[2] "was sitting in the shadow of the Temple and teaching all day."[3] H. Freedman explains that he "was lecturing on the laws of Festivals to the masses, this being within thirty days before a Festival."[4] In *b. Pesaḥ.* 6a another baraitha is quoted which states: "Questions are asked and lectures are given on the laws of Passover for thirty days before Passover." R. Simeon b. Gamaliel (I, a contemporary of Yoḥanan b. Zakkai)[5] maintained, however, that it was for only two weeks.[6]

These lectures also referred to the basic Passover texts in the Bible, to which the "Song at the Sea" (Exod 15:1-18) belongs. Exod 13:17 – 15:26 was the Torah lesson for the seventh or last day of the Passover feast.[7] According to the official chronology of early Judaism, *Seder 'Olam*, Israel sang the Song the morning after they passed through the Red Sea. "It

---

[1] Cf. the excellent study by S. Safrai, *Die Wallfahrt im Zeitalter des Zweiten Tempels* (Forschungen zum jüdisch-christlichen Dialog 3; Neukirchen: Neukirchener, 1981) 260. For the population of Jerusalem at Passover swelling from some 25-30,000 to possibly 180,000, see Jeremias, *Jerusalem* 77-84; Jeremias later considered the latter figure "a little too high" (p. 84). Safrai (97) speaks of "10,000's"; one cannot be more exact. A. Edersheim in *The Life and Times of Jesus the Messiah* (Grand Rapids, Michigan: Eerdmans, 1942) 1.243 estimates that the Temple alone held ca. 210,000 persons.

[2] Strack and Stemberger, *Introduction* 74-75.

[3] Soncino 117.

[4] *Ibid.*, n. 1.

[5] Strack and Stemberger, *Introduction* 74.

[6] Soncino 23-24, including 6b. Cf. also *t. Meg.* 3:5 (Zuckermandel / Liebermann 225; Neusner 2.289), quoted in *y. Pesaḥ.* 1:1, 27b (Neusner / Bokser 13.10-11), and *b. Meg.* 32a (Soncino 195). On Hillel's explanation of an important Passover regulation (before the festival), see the sources cited by Edersheim in *The Life* 1.248.

[7] Cf. *b. Meg.* 31a (Soncino 187, where n. 17 should read Exod 13:17, to be translated in the text as "he [Pharaoh] sent"), as well as Braude and Kapstein, *Pesikta deRab Kahana* 201, n. 1, and Braude's table in *Pesikta Rabbati* 909, and 392. According to J. Mann in *The Bible As Read and Preached in the Old Synagogue* (Cincinnati, 1940) 1.430, in the Palestinian triennial cycle of readings, the haftarah or prophetic reading for Exod 14:15 ff. (including the "Song" of 15:1-18) was Isa 65:24 – 66:10. If this particular reading already prevailed in the first century C.E., it helps to explain how Jesus associated motifs and terms from the Song with the martyrdom of Isaiah, connected to Isa 66:1 (see below).

was the seventh day; it was the last festival day of Passover."[8] When Jesus in his parable of the Wicked Tenants employs expressions and motifs from this passage and from Judaic comment on it, his Passover hearers may possibly have recognized the source of these background materials. They were part of God's holy word discussed in Jerusalem precisely at that time, just before the Passover feast. The term "Song," which Moses and the people sang, may also have helped to connect this passage to the "Song" of the Vineyard in Isa 5:1-7, alluded to five times within Jesus' parable of the Wicked Tenants.[9]

Some time shortly before Jesus related his parable in the Temple, the chief priests, scribes and elders confronted him there with the question of his authority (Mark 11:27-33). The authoritative, master copy of the Torah was kept in the Temple Courtyard, and at the pilgrimage festivals, including Passover, other copies could be compared to it.[10]

More importantly, as noted above, the Sages of the Sanhedrin, Israel's highest court, taught the people on these occasions within the Temple precincts. The pilgrims and the local residents considered their teaching to be authoritative. If a popular prophet from Galilee also taught in the Temple on the same occasion, within "hearing distance" of these "authorized" teachers, and if he made veiled allusions to the leaders' and Temple administrators' exploiting the vineyard – Temple of God, they would have immediately considered their own (and God's) authority as seriously put in question. Rightly, they would have held Jesus to be intentionally on a collision course with them. Mark 12:12 states they perceived that Jesus had told the parable of the Wicked Tenants against them. Therefore they tried to arrest him. The Evangelist Mark certainly has retained this statement from the tradition of the Passion available to him. In light of the proposal made above, there is no reason to doubt its plausibility.

---

[8] Cf. Milikowsky, "Seder Olam: A Rabbinic Chronography," chapter 5 on Exod 15:1 (Hebrew 244-245, English 463). In *Exod. Rab.* Beshallah 22/3 on Exod 14:31 (Soncino 3.276-277) a baraitha states that when reciting the *shema* (daily, in the morning and in the evening), one must mention the division of the Red Sea (cf. n. 1 in 3.277). This shows how well-known the Song at the Sea was to the average Palestinian Jew.

[9] Cf. *Yalquṭ Ha-Makhiri on Isaiah* (Spira 37) on the "Song" of Isa 5:1, where the haggadic listing of the ten "songs" in the MT, including the Song at the Sea, is found.

[10] Cf. the sources mentioned by Safrai in *Die Wallfahrt* 262-263.

B. *Two Similar Tenant Parables.*

Before commenting on the relevance of expressions and motifs from Exod 15:1-18 in Judaic tradition to Mark 12:1-9, I would like to call attention to two important rabbinic tenant parables.

1) The first is related to Exod 13:17, the beginning of the section "Beshallaḥ," and part of that whole portion of Scripture read on the last day of Passover.

Exod 15:15 states that "all the inhabitants of Canaan have melted away," i.e. along with the Philistines, Edomites and Moabites they began to lose courage when they heard that the Israelites had left Egypt. According to Tannaitic tradition, the Canaanites thought the Israelites would utterly destroy them and take possession of / inherit (ירש) their land.[11]

Exod 13:17 says: "When Pharaoh let the (Israelite) people go, God did not lead them (to Canaan by the main direct route along the Mediterranean Sea,) by way of the land of the Philistines, although that was near." A now anonymous parable in *Tanḥuma* B Beshallaḥ 7 relates concerning this verse:

> "When (ויהי) Pharaoh let (the people) go." Who cried out "Woe!" (ווי)?
> The Canaanites (cried out) "Woe!" What is the matter like? Like a king
> who had a small son, and he (the king) had landed property (אוסיא). He
> intended to go off to a far-off country (מדינת הים). He told a tenant (אריס)
> that he should watch over it and that he might eat of its fruits (פירות)
> until his (the king's) son reached maturity. Afterwards he should hand it
> over to him (the son). When the king's son grew up, he requested the
> landed property. Immediately the tenant began to cry out "Woe!"

> Likewise, when the Israelites were in Egypt, the Canaanites lived there
> and watched over the Land of Israel and ate its fruits. When they heard
> that the Israelites had departed from Egypt, they began to cry out:
> "Woe!" "When (ויהי) Pharaoh let (the people) go."[12]

Rabbinic tradition maintained it was a rule of exegesis brought back to Palestine by the exiles in Babylon that "wherever Scripture uses the

---

[11] *Mek. R. Ish.* Shirata 9 on Exod 15:15 (Lauterbach 2.73).

[12] Buber 2.29a or p. 57; Bietenhard's Hebrew text, from a different MS, appears to be the same (1.350).

expression *wayehi* ('and it came to pass'), it presages trouble."[13] The phrase was broken up into וַי or וַוי, "woe,"[14] and הִי, "alas!"[15]

The term אוּסְיָא[16] (Greek οὐσία) is explained by S. Buber in his text as פַּרְדֵּס, an orchard.[17] This is correct, for the same term in *Tanh.* B Ki Thissa 19 on Exod 34:28 refers to a vineyard and a field of olive trees.[18] In Palestine at the time of Jesus there were very few pure vineyards. The great majority of them consisted of various fruit trees.[19]

In this parable the expressions "son," *'usiyya* (here as an orchard, most probably also including vines), "to go to a far-off country," "tenant" and "fruits" occur, which are all also found in Jesus' parable of the Wicked Tenants of the Vineyard.[20] In part the latter is also dependent on Judaic tradition regarding the same section, Exod 13:17-15:26, in the Torah lesson for the last day of Passover. This shows that Jesus was not the only early parable teller to employ these expressions and motifs in such a context. It also shows a possible source for his "tenant" background of the parable. The Canaanites as tenants are to watch over / care for the owner's land and enjoy its fruits until the Israelites, the son, come to inherit / take possession of it. Jesus needed tenants in order to portray the unfaithful keepers of the vineyard.

2)   The second relevant tenant parable is found in *Exod. Rab.* Bo 15/19 on Exod 12:1, the verse which begins the institution of the Passover feast in Egypt. The culmination of this is escape through the Red Sea, with the

---

[13] Cf. *Esth. Rab.* Proem 11 on Esth 1:1 (Soncino 9.11) in the name of R. Eleazar, probably R. Eleazar b. R. Yose the Galilean, a third generation Tanna and noted haggadist (Strack and Stemberger, *Einleitung* 83; he was forgotten in the English translation).

[14] Jastrow 373.

[15] *Ibid.* 343. Cf. also *b. Meg.* 11a (Soncino 61).

[16] Jastrow 30: substance, (landed) property, farm, estate.

[17] Cf. Jastrow 1216, with an example of gardens and "orchards."

[18] Buber 2.59b-60a, or pp. 118-119; Bietenhard 1.415. Cf. *Gen. Rab.* Vayera 49/2 on Gen 18:17 (Soncino 1.421) for an estate with fruit-bearing trees on it. References from Krauss, *Griechische und Lateinische Lehnwörter* 24.

[19] Cf. *Exod. Rab.* Mishpatim 30/9 on Exod 21:1 (Soncino 3.356); *b. Soṭa* 10a (Soncino 47); *Exod. Rab.* Beshallaḥ 20/5 on Exod 13:17 (Soncino 3.246-247); and other sources cited in Krauss, *Talmudische Archäologie* 204. See also his p. 228: "Vineyards in the present sense of the word did not exist in Palestine, only orchards (p. 205), in which all sorts of fruit trees stood next to each other...."

[20] P. Billerbeck had already called attention to it in Str-B 1.874-875. He does not analyze it, however, nor does he relate it to its context in Exod 13:17 – 15:26, the Torah lesson for the last day of Passover.

Song at the Sea. The parable is thus also directly related to the theme of Passover.

> For whose sake did the Holy One, blessed be He, reveal Himself in Egypt? For the sake of Moses. R. Nissim[21] related a parable. It is like a priest who had an orchard (lit. "garden") of figs. In the orchard there was an unclean field.[22] He wished to eat (of the) figs and said to one (of his servants): "Go, say to the tenant (אָרִיס) that the owner (בַּעַל) of the orchard told you to bring him two figs." He went and told him so. The tenant answered: "Who is this owner of the orchard? Go back to your work!" The priest said to him (the servant): "I (myself) will go to the orchard." They (his servants) said to him: "You're going to go to an unclean place?" He replied to them: "Even if there are 100 kinds of uncleanness there, I will go so that my messenger will not be put to shame (וְלֹא יִתְבַּיֵּשׁ שְׁלוּחִי)."
>
> Similarly, when Israel was in Egypt, the Holy One, blessed be He, said to Moses: "Come, I will send you (וְאֶשְׁלָחֲךָ) to Pharaoh (that you may bring forth My people, the sons of Israel, out of Egypt" – Exod 3:10). He went, and he (Pharaoh) told him: "Who is the Lord, that I should heed His voice (and let Israel go [lit. send away])? I do not know the Lord" (5:2). "Go back to your burdens!" (5:4). The Holy One, blessed be He, said: "I (Myself) will go to Egypt," as it is written: "An oracle concerning Egypt: Behold, the Lord is riding on a swift cloud and comes to Egypt" (Isa 19:1). The ministering angels said to Him: "You're going to Egypt, to an unclean place?" He replied to them: "I will go so that My messenger Moses may not be put to shame." Thus it is written: "The Lord spoke to Moses and to Aaron in the land of Egypt, saying..." (Exod 12:1).[23]

Here a later Palestinian rabbi narrates a parable with numerous similarities to Jesus' parable of the Wicked Tenants of the Vineyard.

1. The orchard of figs here is like the vineyard of Jesus' parable.

2. The owner (בַּעַל) is like the owner (κύριος) of the vineyard in Mark 12:9.

3. The owner wants to eat some of the figs from the orchard, as the owner wants to receive some of the fruit of the vineyard (Mark 12:2).

4. There is a tenant of the orchard, as there are tenants of the vineyard (Mark 12:1-2, 7, 9).

---

[21] Probably a third generation Palestinian Amora; cf. Str-B 5/6.124, and Strack and Stemberger, *Introduction* 98. He was also called Yose, Assa, Assi, Issi and Nissa.

[22] Cf. Jastrow 1233: "a field, of a square P'ras, declared unclean on account of crushed bones carried over it from a ploughed grave."

[23] Cf. Mirqin 5.183-184, and the English of Soncino 3.183-184.

5. The owner's attempt to send a servant to the tenant is unsuccessful. The tenant refuses to acknowledge the authority of the servant, humiliating / shaming the latter. This leads to the owner's going himself to collect the fruit. Mark 12:2-3, culminating in the owner's sending his own son (v 6), who alone can legally represent him fully, is similar.

6. "My messenger" is literally "my sent one." God tells Moses He will "send" (שלח) him to Pharaoh in Egypt. Pharaoh also refuses to "send away" Israel. This terminology of "sending" also occurs five times in Jesus' parable (Mark 12:2-6), each time of the owner of the vineyard sending a servant to the tenants. As I will show in section IV.1 below, those "sent" by God to His vineyard Israel are definitely the prophets. Moses too was considered a, if not the greatest, prophet in Judaic tradition, being sent by God to His people Israel.[24]

7. The owner of the orchard does not want his messenger to be "put to shame" again by the tenant. The hithpael of בוש means " to be put to shame, be insulted."[25] The owner of the vineyard in Jesus' parable also sent his second servant to the tenants, who wounded him in the head and "treated him shamefully" (Mark 12:4 – ἀτιμάζω),[26] the same type of behavior.

*   *   *

While there are also major differences between this later rabbinic parable and Jesus' much earlier narrative, the seven similarities described above show that Jesus stood in a definite line of tradition when he spoke of a vineyard let out to tenants, who refuse to grant the owner some fruit, shamefully treating his servant messengers, and forcing him to send them his own son, who alone can legally represent him fully. It is important to note that this line of tradition was associated with evil Pharaoh's refusal to allow Israel to leave Egypt; with God's messenger / sent one Moses, Israel's greatest prophet; and with the pilgrimage feast of Passover.

---

[24] Cf. the many early sources cited by Ginzberg in *Legends* 5.404, as well as the index in 7.324.

[25] Jastrow 151.

[26] BAGD 120: dishonor, treat shamefully, insult. The opposite is found in 12:6's ἐντρέπω, in the middle meaning "have regard for, respect" (BAGD 269).

C. *Expressions and Motifs from Judaic Tradition on Exod 15:1-18 in Mark 12:1-9.*

In the following I shall describe six expressions and motifs Jesus employed in the parable of the Wicked Tenants which he most probably derived from Judaic tradition on the Song at the Sea.[27]

1) *The Jerusalem Temple and a Vineyard.*

Except for the doxological phrase in Exod 15:18, the Song at the Sea concludes by stating in v 17a regarding God and His people, the Israelites:

Thou wilt bring them in, and plant them on the mountain of Thy inheritance,[28]
the place, O Lord, which Thou hast made for Thy abode,
the Sanctuary, O Lord, which Thy hands have established.

Tannaitic sources considered the mountain here to be Mount Moriah (Zion), the site of Jerusalem. The place which the Lord has made for His dwelling, the Sanctuary which His own hands established, is the earthly Temple, thought to be situated exactly opposite His heavenly Temple.[29]

The *Mekilta* of R. Ishmael on this verse interprets "Thou wilt bring them in and plant them" to mean: "like a vineyard that is planted in rows."[30] In addition, on v 18 it states that Israel is "the vine which Thou didst pluck up out of Egypt."[31] Israel is depicted several times as a vineyard or vine in Scripture, yet quite frequently as such in Judaic

---

[27] On this section of the *Mekilta*, see especially the valuable study by J. Goldin, *The Song at the Sea* (Philadelphia: Jewish Publication Society, 1990; original 1971). He states that Shirta contains "the familiar devices of haggadic Midrash, such as word plays, free association, exaggeration, imaginative dramatization and overdramatization" (p. 27). Much of this description also applies to Jesus' parable.

[28] The RSV translates "on thy own mountain," obscuring the motif of inheritance. The NRSV has "on the mountain of your own possession."

[29] Cf. for example *Tanh.* B Vayera 45 on Gen 22:2 (Buber 1.56b or p. 112; Bietenhard 1.118); *Mek. R. Ish.* Shirata 10 on Exod 15:18 (Lauterbach 2.77-79; *'Abot* 6:10 (Danby 461) on the Temple as one of God's five possessions; and *Num. Rab.* Bemidbar 4/13 on Num 4:5-6 (Soncino 5.110-111). See also Goldin, *The Song* 235.

[30] Shirata 10 in Lauterbach 2.10. The apportionment of the Land is meant, as indicated by references to Ezek 48:7, 1 and 3. In that chapter the portion of the Lord's sanctuary in the Jerusalem Temple is emphasized (vv 8-22, including Jerusalem's measurements). See also *Mek. R. Šim. b. Yoḥ.* on Exod 15:17 in Epstein and Melamed, *Mekhilta d'Rabbi Šim'on b. Jochai* 98. Goldin in *The Song* 231 refers to Isa 5:7.

[31] Cf. Lauterbach 2.80. Goldin in *The Song* 241 points out that this alludes to Ps 80:9 (Eng. 8).

sources in regard to its stay in Egypt, departure from there, journey through the wilderness, and entry into the Land.[32] Earlier in the *Mekilta*, Sages maintain that the Israelites would accompany God from the time of the exodus from Egypt until they brought Him with them to the house of His Sanctuary (in Jerusalem).[33] The prophet Jeremiah had already made "My house" (later considered the Sanctuary of the Temple in Jerusalem) and "My inheritance," and "My vineyard" parallel.[34]

The above shows that Jesus, in composing his parable of the Wicked Tenants of the Vineyard, could understandably have employed in it terminology and motifs not only from the Song of the Vineyard in Isa 5:1-7, but also from the Song at the Sea, also related in Judaic sources to the Temple vineyard in Jerusalem.

2) *Empty-handed.*

Mark 12:3 states that the owner of the vineyard sent a servant to his tenants to procure some of the fruit of the vineyard. Their reaction was to take him, beat him, and "send" him "away" (ἀποστέλλω) "empty-handed" (κενός). I suggest that Jesus employed this expression because of his consideration of Exod 15:9.

Exod 15:9, which early rabbinic tradition considered the real beginning of the section Shirata on 15:1-21,[35] had "the enemy," Pharaoh, say: "'I will draw' (אָרִיק) my sword." Some Sages maintained this does not mean "I will 'point' my sword," but "I will 'empty' my sword," a euphemism for Pharaoh's committing pederasty with the Israelite boys,

---

[32] Cf. Isa 1:8; 3:14; 5:1-7; 27:2; Jer 5:10 (her vine-rows); and Hos 10:1 ("Israel is a luxuriant vine that yields its fruit"). See also *Mek. R. Ish.* Shirata 6 on Exod 15:7 (Lauterbach 2.50) for the Egyptians as the "little foxes, that spoil the vineyard (Israel)" in Cant 2:15; *Gen. Rab.* Lech Lecha 42/3 on Gen 14:1, with Pharaoh plucking off single grapes from Israel (Soncino 1.343-344, with parallels); *Exod. Rab.* Mishpatim 30/17 and Exod 21:1 (Soncino 3.367); Ki Thissa 43/9 on Exod 32:11 (Soncino 3.504-506); and *Eccl. Rab.* 6:10 § 1 (Soncino 8.163-164). *Exod. Rab.* Beshallaḥ 20/5 on Exod 13:17 cites Ps 80:9 (Eng. 8), along with Isa 5:2 (Soncino 3.246-247).

[33] Cf. *Mek. R. Ish.* Shirata 3 on Exod 15:2 (Lauterbach 2.27). In a parable it is a king (God) who follows his son (the Israelites) to a "far-off country" (Egypt) and through the Red Sea and the wilderness until the Temple in Jerusalem. Before this, R. Yose the son of the Damascene woman, a second generation Tanna (Strack and Stemberger, *Introduction* 81), interprets the term "naveh" ("I will praise Him") of the Temple, as in Ps 79:7 and Isa 33:20 (Lauterbach 2.26).

[34] Cf. Jer 12:7-10.

[35] *Mek. R. Ish.* Shirata 7 (Lauterbach 2.54).

part of the "spoil" hoped for when the Egyptians pursue and capture the Israelites before they reach the other side of the Red Sea.[36]

The verb "to empty" here is רִיק, which in the hiphil means "make empty, empty."[37] It caused Jesus to think of the biblical phrase: "to 'send' someone 'away' (שלח) 'empty-handed' (רֵיקָם)."[38] It is found in Gen 31:42, Deut 15:13 and Job 22:9 of persons, and in 1 Sam 6:3 of the ark.[39] This suggestion is made more probable by Jesus' employing other terms from Exod 15:9 in his parable, as I indicate in 4) 2. and 6) below.

3) *Divine Forbearance, an Opportunity to Repent, and Destruction.*

In Jesus' parable of the Wicked Tenants, the owner of the vineyard performed four acts before letting it out to tenants and departing to a far-off country (Mark 12:1).[40] When the time came (τῷ καιρῷ), he sent a servant to these in order to receive some of the fruit of the vineyard (v 2). Him they beat; a second servant they wounded in the head and treated shamefully; a third they killed. Many other servants they either beat or killed, until the owner finally (ἔσχατον) sent his own son to them, yet they also killed him. The result is that the owner will come and destroy the tenants (vv 3-9).

In section IV.1 below I will suggest that these servants are the many prophets of Israel, calling the people, especially their leaders, again and again to repent. This culminates in the martyrdom of the beloved or favorite prophet, Isaiah, and the destruction of the Temple and its administrators. Here I shall point out how the motif of great patience was

---

[36] *Ibid.* (Lauterbach 2.56), where Ezek 28:7 is cited to support this interpretation. Cf. the sentence in 15:9, "my desire shall have its fill of them."

[37] BDB 937-938. R. Hezekiah b. Manoah, a thirteenth century French exegete, also understood the biblical phrase in this sense. Cf. Kasher, *Encyclopedia of Biblical Interpretation* 8.183.

[38] BDB 938.

[39] Cf. also Exod 3:21, where the Israelites shall not go out of Egypt "empty-handed," but with the "spoil" of the Egyptians (v 22). Although a different term, "spoil" is also found in 15:9. Ruth 1:21 and 3:17 speak of returning empty-handed. M. Hengel in "Das Gleichnis" 7, n. 31 "i" had noted the four biblical passages in the text as a Semitism in Jesus' parable. He does not, however, relate the expression "to send away empty-handed" to Exod 15:9.

[40] These activities are mentioned by Jesus to indicate how much effort God has invested in "cultivating" His people Israel. Cf. the statement of a tenant to a king who wants to cut down his vineyard, which only yields vinegar: "O my lord and king, consider what sums thou didst lay out before the vineyard was planted...." See *Exod. Rab.* Ki Thissa 43/9 on Exod 32:11 (Soncino 3.505, where n. 1 recalls Isa 5:1-7).

already associated with the first yield of a vineyard, and with the exodus
from Egypt.

1. The First Yield of a Vineyard.

The great patience or forbearance of the owner of the vineyard in
Jesus' parable is super-human. No normal owner would ever think of
sending more than a second servant to collect first-fruits from his
orchard or vineyard after learning how the first was treated. This clearly
informs Jesus' hearers that God is the owner of the vineyard. Only He
would show such great forbearance.

This is indicated, however, not only by the large number of
messengers the owner sends to the tenants. It is already shown in the
normal period of waiting for a vineyard to yield first-fruits.

Lev 19:23-25 prescribes a three-year period of waiting for the "fruit"
(פְּרִי) of fruit-trees. In the fourth year all their fruit is to be holy, "an
offering of praise to the Lord." The *Mishnah,* certainly reflecting pre-70
C.E. practice here, requires a vineyard owner who lives within a day's
journey of Jerusalem to bring his first grape clusters to the city.[41] In *b. Roš
Haš.* 31b it is stated that this was "to decorate the streets of Jerusalem
with fruit."[42] It was a privilege and honor for the owner, after waiting
three long years, to present the first-fruits of the vineyard in the fourth
year in Jerusalem. For this reason he was especially angry if a tenant
tried to foil this endeavor.[43]

Only in the fifth year was a vineyard owner allowed to partake of the
entire yield of his vineyard (Lev 19:25). This means that he needed a
great deal of patience before he could enjoy the fruits of his investment.
Even before sending off one servant after another to the tenants of his

---

[41] Cf. *Ma'aś. Š.* 5:2 (Danby 80).

[42] Soncino 151. If one lived outside the range of a day's journey, one could
exchange his first-fruits for money and spend this in Jerusalem. Cf. Deut 14:22-26,
and *b. Beṣa* 5a (Soncino 18, with notes).

[43] Cf. *Exod. Rab.* Bo 15/19 on Exod 12:1, cited above, with figs; *Gen. Rab.* Bereshith
22/5 on Gen 4:3 (Soncino 1.182: a bad tenant eats the ripe figs and honors the
king with late, less tasty figs); and *m. Bikk.* 1:2 (Danby 93): "They that lease the
land, or that hire it, a usurping occupant or a robber may not bring them (first-
fruits to Jerusalem)...for it is written, 'The first-fruits of *thy* land' (Exod 23:19)." As
I indicated above, the tenants of Jesus' parable are such "usurping occupants,"
who violently appropriate the property of a far-off owner. See also *Mek. R. Šim. b.
Yoḥ.* Beshallaḥ on Exod 15:1 (Epstein and Melamed 76-77) regarding two
watchmen, one lame and the other blind, who devoured the fine first-fruits of a
king's orchard. The text is translated by Goldin in *The Song* 105. A parallel is
found in *Lev. Rab.* Vayiqqra 4/5 on Lev 4:2 (Soncino 4.53-54) in the name of R.
Ishmael, a second generation Tanna (Strack and Stemberger, *Introduction* 79).

vineyard, the owner in Jesus' parable (God) had thus already demonstrated much patience in his hope for a good yield. This intensifies the significance of what follows.

2. God's Great Forbearance and Exod 15:6.

The Wisdom of Solomon, written by an Egyptian Jew in Greek, probably sometime during the first four decades of the first century C.E.,[44] deals in chapters 10-19 with the exodus of Israel from Egypt and how God punishes His adversaries there. The final section concerns the Egyptians' "pursuing" the Israelites at the Red Sea (19:2-3; cf. Exod 15:9). In 19:4 it is maintained that the fate they deserved drew the Egyptians to their end (drowning in the Red Sea), making them forget what had happened (for example, the death of all their firstborn at the tenth plague), "in order that they might 'fill up' (προαναπληρόω)[45] the punishment which their torments still lacked."

This motif of the Egyptians' "making their punishment complete" or "filling it up" is also found in early Palestinian comment on the same event. *Mek. R. Ish.* Shirata 5 on Exod 15:6, "glorious in power" (נאדרי בכח), states that God is both "fair"/"handsome" (נאה) and "mighty" (אדיר) in power. This is illustrated by the fact that God gave an "extension of time" (אָרְכָה)[46] to the generation of the flood for them "to perform repentance" (לעשות תשובה). However, they did not perform repentance. Yet He did not judge them yet, as Gen 6:3 is interpreted: "My Spirit shall not judge...." God did not definitely decree "destruction" (כְּלָיָה)[47] until "they made their wickedness complete" (השלימו רשען)[48] before Him. The same thing was true of the men of the tower (of Babel) and the men of Sodom,[49] who also refused to repent. The fourth and final example is that of the Egyptians, who pursued the Israelites to the Red Sea and wanted to destroy them all there (Exod 15:9). The *Mekilta* states regarding God at this point: "You brought ten plagues upon the Egyptians in Egypt, but

---

[44] Cf. Nickelsburg, *Jewish Literature* 184.

[45] Cf. LSJ 1501: fill up.

[46] Jastrow 121; cf. Dan 7:12. Goldin in *The Song* 147 speaks of "a grace period," which was extremely long (see also his commentary). On God's great forbearance, see also *b. Yoma* 69b (Soncino 329): "Therein lie His mighty deeds that He suppresses His wrath, that He extends long-suffering to the wicked."

[47] Jastrow 642.

[48] Jastrow 1585, hif.: to complete, finish.

[49] They are also castigated in Wisd Sol 19:14.

You did not definitely decree destruction upon them until they made their wickedness complete."[50]

I suggest that Jesus borrowed from this early motif complex for his parable of the Wicked Tenants. The owner of the vineyard (God) gave his tenants many chances ("extensions of time") to produce the fruits of repentance,[51] sending one servant (prophet) after another to them.[52] Yet they refused to perform repentance. Only after they finally filled up their wickedness by killing the owner's son and dishonoring his corpse, did he decide to come (in judgment) and "destroy" them. God's great forbearance had finally reached its limit.

4)   Seizing and Killing the Son.

The wicked tenants of Jesus' parable are represented as seeing the heir, the son of the vineyard owner, coming to them. They say to each other: "Come, let us kill him, and the inheritance will be ours" (Mark 12:7). Then they took him and killed him and cast him out of the vineyard (v 8). Before this, Jesus relates that after sending to no avail numerous servants to the tenants, the owner sent a "beloved son" (υἱὸς ἀγαπητός) to them, saying: "They will 'respect' (ἐντρέπομαι) my son" (v 6).

1.   Normally a tenant came to his employer to "pay him honor," to "show his respect to him" (לכבדו), as related in a rabbinic parable.[53] The exactly opposite behavior of the tenants in Jesus' parable shows their abject wickedness.

Israel in Egypt is frequently characterized in the MT as God's "son," and the Israelites as God's "sons" (= children). One example related to

---

[50] My translation of the Hebrew text in Lauterbach 2.39-41. Cf. also *Exod. Rab.* Mishpatim 30/1 on Exod 21:1 (Soncino 3.347, and n. 1: "But only when their measure of sin is full"). On the ten plagues, Goldin in *The Song* 148 states: "In this way God showed long-suffering toward the Egyptians, for not until after all these warnings and chastisements were they destroyed utterly in the Sea."

[51] Cf. Matt 3:8, "Bear fruit that befits repentance"; Luke 3:8 has "fruits." Isa 27:9 already points in this direction. The fruits of a vine(yard) are mentioned in 2 Kgs 19:29 (= Isa 37:30); Isa 65:21; Hos 10:1; and Zech 8:12. Cant 8:11 already notes that each keeper (tenant) of Solomon's vineyard was to bring for its fruit 1000 pieces of silver; see also v 12. *Gen. Rab.* Noah 38/9 on Gen 11:6 (Soncino 1.308) states that God gives people an opportunity to repent, but some say "No!" This is followed by the statement: "When a vineyard does not yield fruit, what does its owner do to it? He uproots it!"

[52] Regarding this phenomenon, E. Haenchen appropriately states in *Der Weg Jesu* 399: "Gott ist wirklich bis zum Alleräussersten gegangen mit seinem Werben."

[53] Cf. *Lev. Rab.* Tzav 9/4 on Lev 7:12 in Margulies, *Midrash Wayyikra Rabbah* 179-180, and in Soncino 4.110, where a tenant and a king are involved.

the exodus is Hos 11:1, "When Israel was a child, I loved (אהב) him, and out of Egypt I called My son."[54] Another is Exod 4:22-23, where Moses is to say to Pharaoh: "Thus says the Lord, 'Israel is My first-born son, and I say to you, Let My son go that he may serve Me.'" A third is Ps 80:16 (Eng. 15). After the psalmist states that God brought a vine out of Egypt, driving out the nations and planting it (v 9, Eng. 8), He is asked to have regard for this vine, "the stock which Thy right hand planted, and upon the son whom Thou has reared for Thyself."[55]

   Mek. R. Ish. Beshallaḥ 1 on Exod 13:21 ("And the Lord went before them [the Israelites] by day...to lead them along the way...") is a part of the reading for the last day of Passover.[56] After the citation of three scriptural passages with God's "glory" (כבוד), Rabbi or Judah the Prince, a fourth generation Tanna,[57] interprets the Exodus verse by relating a narrative regarding Antoninus. He took a torch and lit the way after dark for his sons, saying: "It is merely to show you 'how dear my sons are to me' (חבתם של בני), 'so that you should treat them with respect' (שתהיו נוהגים עמהם בכבוד)." Likewise the Holy One, blessed be He, showed the nations of the world how "dear" (חבתן) Israel was to Him by going Himself before them "so that they (the nations) should treat them (the sons of Israel) with respect" (שיהיו נוהגין עמהם בכבוד). It is not sufficient, however, that "they do not treat them with respect," they even put them to death in all sorts of cruel and strange ways.[58] On account of this terrible behavior, the Lord will judge them, as four verses from Joel 4 are then interpreted.

   Here God's sons are "dear" (חִבָּה)[59] to Him, just as the owner of the vineyard in Jesus' parable has a "dear" son (Mark 12:6). God wants others to "show them (His sons) respect" (היו נוהגים עמהם בכבוד), just as the owner stated: "They will respect my son." I suggest that the three terms in Jesus' parable, "dear," "respecting" a son, and "killing" by a cruel

---

[54] This is quoted in Matt 2:15 in regard to Jesus.

[55] Cf. also Deut 14:1 for the Israelites as "the sons of the Lord your God," and other references cited in BDB 120, 1.c.

[56] See above, section III.A, and the tenant parable on Exod 13:17, cited above in B. 1).

[57] Strack and Stemberger, *Introduction* 89; he probably died in 217 C.E.

[58] I slightly modify the translation of Lauterbach in 1.185-186. See also God's "honoring" (יקר; Jastrow 592, pa. 2) His people, Israel, likened to a vineyard, in Targ Isa 5:2. He honored them, but they nevertheless did evil deeds (Stenning 16-17).

[59] Jastrow 416: love, esteem, honor. It is the same root as חבב, to love, cherish (415-416) and חביב, beloved, dear, precious (418).

death were borrowed by Jesus from traditional comment on the exodus from Egypt on the part of the sons of Israel.

2. Seizing and Killing the Son.

Mek. R. Ish. Shirata 7, again on Exod 15:9, states that the Egyptians were divided into three factions at the Red Sea in regard to the Israelites. The third group, which proposed "Let us kill them (נהרגם) and take their money," said: "My (Pharaoh's) hand shall inherit them," as תורישמו ידי is here interpreted.[60] Pharaoh's evil boasting is illustrated by a parable of a robber who threateningly stood behind the king's palace, saying: "If I find the son of the king, I shall seize him (תופשו), I shall kill him (והורגנו), I shall crucify him, I shall make him die the most cruel death." This is wicked (רשע) Pharaoh, who threatened the Israelites with the words of Exod 15:9.[61]

I suggest that Jesus again borrowed from early Judaic interpretation of Exod 15:9 for terms and motifs in his own parable of the Wicked Tenants. Like the third group of Egyptians under "wicked" Pharaoh, they also propose regarding the "heir," the "son" of the owner of the vineyard: "Come, 'let us kill him' (ἀποκτείνωμεν αὐτόν),[62] and the inheritance will be ours" (Mark 12:7). "And having 'seized' (λαμβάνω) him, they killed him" (v 8), just as Pharaoh wanted to "seize" (תָּפַשׂ)[63] and "kill" (הָרַג)[64] the son (of the king, God). The "most cruel death" is described in terms of a vineyard, being cast out of it without proper burial (see the next section).

The concentration of all these terms and motifs makes it very probable that Jesus also borrowed from early Judaic interpretation of Exod 15:9 at this point.

---

[60] As I will elucidate below on the motif of "inheritance," the verb is here derived from יָרַשׁ, "to inherit" (Jastrow 598). See also Goldin's interpretation of the phrase in *The Song* 184.

[61] I again slightly modify Lauterbach's translation in 2.57-58. After Pharaoh's threatening words, *Mek. R. Šim. b. Yoḥai* adds: "When the king heard that, he was filled with rage at him" (Epstein and Melamed p. 90, where Melamed also corrects the "Arabian" robber of the text into "chief" robber, ἀρχιληστής, in his handwritten footnote; the "head" robber is Egypt's head of state, Pharaoh). On "dying the most cruel death," cf. a similar expression in Matt 21:41.

[62] Jesus may have added the "come" from Gen 37:20 regarding the intention of Joseph's brothers: "Now come, let us kill him...," as indicated in the margin of *Novum Testamentum Graecum* 1990[26]. "Let us kill" a son, and seize his inheritance, derives however from Judaic tradition on Exod 15:9.

[63] Jastrow 1687-1688.

[64] *Ibid.* 365.

5) *Corpse Desecration.*

Mark 12:8 relates that the wicked tenants of Jesus' parable took the vineyard owner's son, killed him, and "cast him out of (ἐξέβαλον αὐτὸν ἔξω) the vineyard." Both Matthew (21:39) and Luke (20:15) reverse the latter sequence, theologically reflecting Jesus' being crucified outside the city of Jerusalem (Mark 15:20 par.; John 19:17; Heb 13:12-13).[65]

There was nothing the wicked tenants could have done which would have better shown their despising the son, the only legal representative of his father, the owner. Proper burial, even of criminals[66] or of someone murdered by an unknown person,[67] was a major tenet of Israelite and Jewish religious practice. If possible, one was buried in one's family grave.[68] Joshua was buried within his own "inheritance" (Josh 24:30, נחלה), something the wicked tenants did not even allow the murdered heir to the vineyard. The proper anointing of the son in his tomb, and the mourning of him by his far-off family and friends, were made impossible.[69]

In addition, the (Jewish) tenants had acted like pagans, "casting out" the son and heir.[70] This was contrary to the Torah,[71] and on the level of the (non-) burial of an ass.[72] For a human corpse to be "cast out" (שָׁלַךְ), with none to bury and mourn it, was severe desecration.[73] Outside the guarded vineyard, the son's dead body would be food for the beasts of the earth and the birds of the air, a thought frequently expressed in the MT.[74] Such was the tenants' abject wickedness, certainly just as shocking to Jesus' hearers as the tenants' killing the heir.

---

[65] This was probably already available to them as a tradition developed within their respective communities.

[66] Cf. Deut 21:22-23.

[67] Cf. Deut 21:1-9, presupposing the victim's burial, and 1 Kgs 13:29, 24. See also Jastrow 823 on a מת מצוה, "the corpse of a person whose relatives are unknown and whose burial is obligatory on everybody."

[68] Cf. Gen 49:29, 32; Judg 8:32; and 1 Kgs 13:22.

[69] Cf. Mark 16:1-3 and 14:8, as well as John 11:19, 31 and 33.

[70] Cf. Tob 1:17, as well as Isa 34:3 on the fate of the nations' slain.

[71] Cf. *Lam. Rab.* 1:9 § 37 (Soncino 7.113), referring to Ps 79:3.

[72] Jer 22:18-19.

[73] Cf. Jer 14:16; 22:19; 1 Kgs 13:24; Isa 14:19; and 34:3.

[74] Deut 28:26; 1 Kgs 14:11; 21:24; 2 Kgs 9:34-37; Jer 7:33; Ezek 29:5; and Ps 79:2. Cf. also the articles on "Burial" by W. Reed and "Mourning" by E. Jacob in *IDB* 1.474-476 and 3.452-454, respectively. See also the reference in Golden (*The Song* 209) to D. Slotnick, *The Treatise "Mourning"* (New Haven: Yale University, 1966) 104-105.

In Jesus' parable the motif of corpse desecration, with none to bury it, also derives from Judaic comment on the Song at the Sea.

When the Israelites saw Pharaoh's troops approaching them at the Red Sea, they reproached Moses by asking him: "Is it because there are no graves in Egypt that you have taken us away to die in the wilderness?" (Exod 14:11). The Tannaitic *Mekilta* has the Israelites state their great fear here: "our brothers (who died in Egypt) were buried and mourned for, but we – our corpses will be exposed to the heat of the day and the cold of the night."[75] By God's leading them all through the Red Sea, they escaped this horrible fate. This was not true, however, of the Egyptian troops.

The pursuers all drowned in the Red Sea,[76] and the rescued Israelites saw them dead upon the seashore (Exod 14:28, 30). In the Song at the Sea, God is praised with the words: "Thou didst stretch out Thy right hand, the earth 'swallowed' them" (15:12). The term "to swallow down" (בלע)[77] is interpreted in Judaic sources as God's graciously burying the evil Egyptians. The *Mekilta* asks, for example: "By what virtue did they merit that a place of burial should be given to them (in the earth)? By virtue of (Pharaoh's) having said: 'The Lord is righteous, but I and my people are evil' (Exod 9:27). Said the Holy One, blessed be He, to them: 'You have accepted the judgment upon yourselves as righteous, and so I will not deprive you of your reward, but I will give you a place for burial,'" as Exod 15:12 states.[78]

Here God does not allow corpse desecration to occur, not even in regard to the enemies of the Israelites, who wanted to kill them. He provides a proper burial even for them. The wicked tenants of Jesus' parable, fellow Jews aware of the obligation to bury even a murdered person, show their contempt for the son of the owner of the vineyard not

---

[75] Beshallaḥ 3 (Lauterbach 1.210).

[76] Haggadic speculation on the number of those Egyptians who died in the Red Sea is very early. Jubilees, a Palestinian writing from the first half of the second century B.C.E., states for example in 48:14 that 1,000,000 perished (*OTP* 2. 140; on the dating and provenance, cf. 2.44-45). See also Josephus's numbers in *Ant.* 2.324.

[77] Cf. Ps 106:17 and Deut 11:6 on Dathan and Abiram, as well as Num 16:30, 32, 34 and 26:10 on Korah.

[78] Shirata 9 (Lauterbach 2.67). Virtually the same tradition is found in Beshallaḥ 1 on Exod 13:17 (Lauterbach 1.169). See also *Pirq. R. El.* 39 (English in Friedlander, *Pirke de Rabbi Eliezer* 309). Another interpretation has the sea and the land argue as to which shall receive the Egyptian corpses, which is settled by God's swearing by His "right hand" with an oath to the earth. See the *Mekilta* on 15:12 (Lauterbach 2.67-68); *Mek. R. Šim. b. Yoḥ.* (Epstein and Melamed 95); *Pirq. R. El.* 42 (Friedlander 334-335); all the targums except Onqelos on this verse; and *Lam. Rab.* 1:9 § 37 (Soncino 7.113), which calls the Egyptians "asses."

only by killing him, but also by refusing to bury him. They treat him like the carcass of an ass, simply casting him out of the vineyard.

I therefore suggest that Jesus also borrowed this motif from early Judaic interpretation of Exod 15:12.

6) The Heir, Inheritance.

In section 4) 2. above on "Seizing and Killing the Son," I called attention to *Mek. R. Ish.* Shirata 7 on Exod 15:9, including the expression "let us kill them," "My (Pharaoh's) hand shall inherit them," and a parable of a robber (Pharaoh) who wants to seize and kill the son (Israel) of the king (God). Here I wish to elucidate this inheritance motif.

The Hebrew phrase תּוֹרִישֵׁמוֹ יָדִי in Exod 15:9 is usually rendered "my hand shall destroy them" (RSV), certainly correct here.[79] Yet the *Mekilta* and other early Judaic sources interpreted the verb as "shall inherit them."[80] That is, by seizing and killing the son of the king, the robber hoped to inherit that which was due to the son.[81]

This is exactly the situation described in Mark 12:7, where the evil, usurping tenants say: "This is the heir (ὁ κληρονόμος, the beloved son of the owner of the vineyard). Come, let us kill him, and the inheritance (κληρονομία) will be ours."[82] Mark 12:7 par. is the only occurrence of the noun κληρονόμος in the four gospels, and except for Luke 12:13 the noun κληρονομία also only occurs here in the gospels. I suggest that Jesus derived his terms "seizing," "let us kill," the "heir" (יוֹרֵשׁ) and "inheritance" (יְרוּשָׁה)[83] from early Judaic interpretation of Exod 15:9.[84]

The linking of inheritance to the Jerusalem Temple was made via Exod 15:17, "Thou wilt bring them in and plant them on the mountain of

---

[79] Cf. BDB 439-440, hiph. 4 of ירשׁ. All the targums interpret similarly, which makes sense because of the preceding phrase: "I will draw my sword."

[80] Cf. BDB 440, hiph. 1. The *Mekilta* text is in Lauterbach 2.57.

[81] For sons as inheriting, cf. Jer 49:1, Ezra 9:12, *m. B. Bat.* 8:5, and Luke 12:13. Killing the heir is found in 2 Sam 14:7.

[82] For God's inheritance or heritage as parallel to His vineyard or vine in a Jewish Palestinian writing contemporary to Jesus' parable, see *Pseudo-Philo* 12:8-9; 18:10-11; 30:4; and 39:7 (*OTP* 2.320-321, 326, 343 and 352).

[83] For the latter two, see Jastrow 572 and 595 respectively.

[84] In addition to the Tannaitic *Mekilta*, see also *Lev. Rab.* Aḥare Moth 21/1 on Lev 16:3 (Soncino 4.265), where R. Samuel b. Naḥman, a third generation Palestinian Amora (Strack and Stemberger, *Introduction* 97), interprets Exod 15:9 as "shall give it unto them as an inheritance": "I shall give my wealth and glory to them as an inheritance."

Thy inheritance (נַחֲלָה,[85] LXX κληρονομία), the place, O Lord, Thou hast made for Thy abode, the Sanctuary, O Lord, which Thy hands have established." In rabbinic Hebrew נחלה can also mean the central sanctuary at Jerusalem.[86] The *Mekilta* also interprets "Thy inheritance" of Exod 15:17 as the Temple.[87]

This early association of the Temple and "inheritance" lends support to my proposal, to be made explicit in section IV.A. below, that in his parable of the Wicked Tenants Jesus threatened the Temple administrators and priestly aristocracy with judgment: the vineyard, God's Temple as His inheritance given to the Israelite / Jewish leaders to tend, would be given to "others" on account of their bad behavior.

*   *   *

In summary, Exod 15:6 in early Judaic tradition provided Jesus with the motif of God's great forbearance in regard to the opportunity to repent, which when rejected finally leads to destruction; 15:9 with the expressions "empty-handed," "seize," "let us kill the son," the "heir" and "inheritance"; and 15:12 with the motif of corpse desecration.[88] Terms such as "owner" of a vineyard, "tenant," "going off to a far-off country," "fruits," "treat shamefully" and "honor" a son are also found in other similar, early Judaic materials related to Exod 13:17 – 15:26, the reading for the last day of Passover.

The last major influence on Jesus' parable, the martyrdom of the prophet Isaiah in Jerusalem, remains to be analyzed.

IV. The Martyrdom of Isaiah and Isa 66:1.

Before discussing the great fame of the prophet Isaiah, his martyrdom and Isa 66:1 as related to the killing of the "beloved / favorite son" of Mark 12:6, it is helpful first to analyze the many "servants" of Jesus' parable.

---

[85] Cf. BDB 635, 1.e. end; "possession, property" is included in the term, as in the verb (qal 1., hiph. 2). As indicated in section C. 1., Jer 12:7 has God's "house" as parallel to His "inheritance" (see also vv 8-9, and God's vineyard in v 10); cf. also Ps 79:1, where "the inheritance" and "Thy holy Temple" are parallel.

[86] Cf. the examples in Jastrow 895, which in part refer to Deut 12:9 and Jer 12:7-9.

[87] Lauterbach 2.77-78, where it is one of four which are called "inheritance."

[88] In contrast to the clear allusions to the Song of the Vineyard, Isa 5:1-7, which Jesus' hearers in the Jerusalem Temple would have perceived, I doubt whether his use of the above motifs and expressions from the Song at the Sea were transparent enough to be recognized as deriving from Exod 15:1-18. My main point is rather that Jesus consciously borrowed them from this source, part of the Torah lesson for the last day of the Passover festival.

A. *The Servants as Prophets.*

In Mark 12:1-9, the owner of the vineyard "sends" (ἀποστέλλω) one servant after another, including his beloved son, to the wicked tenants in order to receive from them some fruit. This verb is repeated five times (vv 2, 3, 4, 5 and 6),[1] showing its great significance for Jesus' narrative. Its Hebrew or Aramaic equivalent is שלח.[2] Indeed, "one sent" or a "messenger" (שָׁלוּחַ)[3] is one of the ten names by which a prophet is called in Scripture, according to *'Avot R. Nat.* A 34.[4] An example of this is Isa 6:8 for Isaiah, who at his calling in the Jerusalem Temple hears the Lord ask: "Whom shall I 'send'?" The prophet replies: "Here am I! 'Send' me."

Another term for a prophet according to the same Judaic source is "servant" (עֶבֶד).[5] This stands behind the δοῦλος of Mark 12:2 and 4, and is assumed for "another" and "many others" in v 5, and "one other" in v 6. The latter is important, for the "beloved / favorite son" should first of all be viewed as one of the prophets from Scripture, and not as a veiled reference by Jesus to himself as the last prophet. I shall comment on the latter more extensively below in section V.

Standard references to God and the prophets in the MT are: "My servants the prophets" (9 times); "His servants the prophets" (6 times); and "Your servants the prophets" (2 times).[6] As in Jesus' parable, God "sends" them to Israel (2 Kgs 17:13; Jer 7:25; 25:4; 26:5; 29:19; 35:15; and 44:14). All the Jeremiah references add "persistently" (הַשְׁכֵּם),[7] which emphasizes God's great forbearance, as the owner sends an unexpectedly high number of servants to the tenants of his vineyard. The expression "'all' My servants the prophets" occurs in Jer 7:25; 25:4 (His); 35:15; 44:14; and 2 Kgs 17:23 (His).[8] This causes me to be very suspect of those exegetes who wish to excise Mark 12:5b, "and so with many others

---

[1] Some MSS add a sixth usage at the end of v 4; see the apparatus of Nestle-Aland.

[2] Jastrow 1579-1580. The assonance of "to cast out" in Mark 12:8 (hiph. of שָׁלַךְ, for ἐκβάλλω) should be noted. Jastrow 1585 notes that the hof. part., lit. "thrown," can mean "exposed" for a corpse, recalling the result of the tenants' action in Jesus' parable. Cf. *Sifre* Deut. 'Eqeb 43 on Deut 11:17 (Hammer 95), where King Jehoiakim of Judah was "buried with the burial of an ass" (Jer 22:19), "'exposed' to the heat of the day and to the chill of the night."

[3] Jastrow 1579.

[4] Schechter 102, Goldin 142.

[5] *Ibid.*

[6] Cf. the references cited in BDB 714, 4.

[7] BDB 1014 on שָׁכַם, "sending early and often."

[8] Cf. also 2 Kgs 17:13, with "every prophet."

(servants), some they beat and some they killed." Jesus is probably taking up a well-known biblical motif here.[9]

The object of God's sending His servants the prophets to Israel is that the latter "turn" or "repent" (2 Kgs 17:13; Jer 25:4-5; 35:15). This is what the owner of the vineyard (God) in Jesus' parable also desires, the fruits (of repentance): Mark 12:2; cf. Matt 3:8. If such are not brought, the prophet Jeremiah, speaking in the courtyard of the Jerusalem Temple shortly before his arrest, threatened: "If you will not listen to Me to... heed the words of My servants the prophets whom I send to you persistently, though you have not heeded, then I will make this house like Shiloh..." (26:5).[10] Jeremiah prophesied the destruction of the Jerusalem Temple if the priests, the (false) prophets and all the people refused to repent. For this he was seized and told he was deserving of the sentence of death. Jesus' parable is directed against the contemporary guardians or keepers, the tenants of God's vineyard, the Temple, who refuse to mend their ways. Rather, they consent to their predecessors' maltreating or killing one prophet after another sent to them by God.[11] For this attitude, Jesus threatens that they too will be "destroyed" (Mark 12:9).

It should also be noted that the prophet Isaiah is referred to by God in Isa 20:3 as "My servant Isaiah." In *'Avot R. Nat.* B 43, this verse is cited for Isaiah as one of the eighteen Scriptural persons or groups called "servants."[12] This supports my thesis below that the prophet Isaiah is the owner's beloved / favorite son, the "one more" servant he finally sent to the tenants of his vineyard (Mark 12:6).

Judaic interpretation of Isa 5:1-7, one of the major influences on Jesus' parable, may have affected his terminology of servants as

---

[9] V. Taylor in *The Gospel According to St Mark* (New York: St Martin's, 1966²) 475 is certainly also correct when he states: "5b heightens the tension" (of the parable), another reason for retaining it.

[10] Cf. also 2 Chron 36:16, with the prophets as God's messengers. When God's wrath was filled up, the Babylonians destroyed the Jerusalem Temple, fulfilling Jeremiah's prophecy (vv 17-21).

[11] On Jesus' associating the present leaders of the people with those who earlier murdered the prophets in Jerusalem, cf. Matt 23:31-32 and 37; and Luke 11:47-48. I accept the basic historicity of this particular strain of Jesus' prophetic criticism, even though the present context is secondary.

[12] Cf. Schechter 121, and Saldarini 263, with parallels in his n. 41. *Sifre* Deut. Wa'ethanan 27 on Deut 3:24 (Hammer 50-51) cites both Isa 49:5 and 20:3 for Isaiah. See also *Cant. Rab.* 1:6 § 1 (Soncino 9.56) with Isa 6:5. In 4 Ezra 2:18 God's servants are Isaiah and Jeremiah.

prophets. Aquila, a second generation Tanna,[13] interpreted Isa 5:6 regarding God's vineyard ("I will also command the 'clouds' [עָבִים] that they rain no rain upon it") as "I will also command the 'prophets' (וּנְבִיאִים) not to prophesy prophecies for them."[14] This tradition also entered the Targum, which reads: "and My prophets will I command not to utter a prophecy concerning them."[15] If this is very early, as Aquila's interpretation indicates, Jesus was probably already aware of prophets as connected to God's vineyard in Isa 5:1-7, to which he alluded five times in his parable.

Finally, Mark 12:4 begins by stating, "And again (καὶ πάλιν) he sent to them another servant." This Greek phrase can be וְשׁוּב in Hebrew. Since the verb שׁוּב also means "to repent,"[16] the hearer may have been reminded in this subtle way that God sent His servants, the prophets, one after another to the Israelites in order that they would "repent."

B. *The Prophet Isaiah's Great Fame.*

Before discussing Isaiah as God's "son" and the relevance to Jesus' parable of his martyrdom in Jerusalem, connected to Isa 66:1, it is helpful to describe his great fame.[17] This in turn led to his being viewed as God's son in the Judaic sources I cite below in section three.

Not divided up into two or more parts in the first century C.E. as in modern criticism, the prophetic book of Isaiah with its 66 chapters was longer than those of Jeremiah (52) and Ezekiel (48), and the twelve minor prophets, which all follow it in the Hebrew Bible.[18] This greater length and first position in Scripture alone afforded Isaiah precedence. Writing

---

[13] Strack and Stemberger, *Introduction* 80, noted for his translation of the Bible into Greek.

[14] Cf. *Eccl. Rab.* 11:3 § 1 (Soncino 8.292). This may be due to the fact that the usual term for "cloud" in Aramaic, עֲנָן, in its pa. verbal form (עֲנֵין) means "to augur from clouds"; an עֲנָנָא is an interpreter of clouds, or augur (Jastrow 1095-1096; cf. BDB 778).

[15] Stenning 16-17.

[16] For both terms, see Jastrow 1528.

[17] Cf. the articles "Isaiah," "In Rabbinical Literature," by I. Broydé in *JE* (1904) 6.636, and "Isaiah," "In the Aggadah," by E. Hallevey in *EJ* (1971) 9.67, as well as Ginzberg, *The Legends of the Jews* 4.262-263 and 278-279, with the relevant notes.

[18] Cf. the fact that the longest of the four gospels, that of Matthew, is also placed at the beginning. *Seder 'Olam* 20-21 in Milikowsky, *Seder Olam* 341-362 and 504-512, lists all the prophets and prophetesses in Israel, including the "former" prophets. *Eliyyahu Rabbah* 16 (Hebrew in *Seder Eliahu rabba und Seder Eliahu zuta,* ed. Friedmann 82; English in Braude and Kapstein, *Tanna debe Eliyyahu* 220) maintains there were 48 prophets all together. See also n. 101 below.

in Hebrew in Jerusalem at the beginning of the second century B.C.E., Sirach for example states that Isaiah was "great and faithful in his vision." "By the spirit of might he saw the last things, and comforted those who mourned in Zion. He revealed what was to occur to the end of time, and the hidden things before they came to pass."[19] The "last things" here certainly also refer to Isaiah's final chapter (66), dealing with the Lord's heavenly dwelling, His earthly Temple, the return of all Israel , with the nations, to Jerusalem, and new heavens and a new earth.[20] Verse one of this chapter plays an important role in the martyrdom of Isaiah.

The prophet's role as the primary "comforter" of Israel, shown in the repetition of the same verb in 40:1, is also emphasized in rabbinic sources.[21] In *b. Ber.* 57b "our rabbis taught," for example, that if one saw the prophet Isaiah in a dream, "he may look forward to consolation."[22]

Because Isaiah's prophecies regarding various events always came true according to Josephus, writing at the end of the first century C.E., this native of Jerusalem said that "he was acknowledged to be a man of God and marvelously possessed of truth."[23]

Traditions now only found in rabbinic sources also stress Isaiah's great fame. He it was who first reduced the 613 precepts communicated to Moses to 6, then to 2.[24] He was also one of thirteen mortals born circumcised.[25] Isaiah is labeled "our teacher,"[26] God's "holy one" of Isa 10:17,[27] "righteous,"[28] and God's "servant" (see section one above). He is

---

[19] Cf. the RSV of 48:22 and 24-25. Since πνεύματι μεγάλῳ probably represents רוח גבורה, the spirit of the "Mighty One," God, may be meant. For the dating, language and place of origin for Sirach, cf. Nickelsburg, *Jewish Literature* 64.

[20] For this chapter in Judaic tradition as the foundation for belief in the eschatological pilgrimage to Jerusalem, including gifts brought to the Messiah, see the articles in my *Barabbas and Esther and Other Studies in the Judaic Illumination of Earliest Christianity* (USFSHJ 54; Atlanta: Scholars, 1992) 125-191.

[21] Cf. for example *Pesiq. R.* 33/3 on Isa 51:12 (Braude 636).

[22] Soncino 355. See also *'Abot R. Nat.* A 40 (Goldin 167).

[23] *Ant.* 10:35. On the fulfillment of Isaiah's prophecies, cf. *Bell.* 7.432 and *Ant.* 9.276 and 13.64, 68 and 71; 10.12, 16, 27-28, 32; and 11.5-6.

[24] Cf. *b. Makk.* 24a (Soncino 172-173, referring to Isa 33:15-16 and 56:1); see also *Midr. Ps.* 17A 21 and 23 (English in Braude 1.228-229).

[25] *Midr. Ps.* 9/7, referring to Isa 49:1 (Braude 1.139).

[26] *Pesiq. Rav Kah.* 16/10 on Isa 40:1 (Braude and Kapstein 299); see also *Pesiq. R.* 29/30 A 10 (Braude 581).

[27] *Midr. Ps.* 22/2 (Braude 1.298).

[28] *Kallah Rabbati* 6, 54a in Cohen, *The Minor Tractates of the Talmud* 2.484, with "the rabbis taught."

also one of the four men in Scripture called "supremely perfect creatures whom God Himself formed."[29] Only Moses and Isaiah prophesied consciously,[30] and there were no greater prophets than these two.[31] Probably omitting the former prophets, including Moses, *Pesiq. R.* 33/3 says Isaiah was "foremost in rank among all the Prophets," attaining much "distinction and glory." God Himself had anointed him at his calling in the Jerusalem Temple (Isaiah 6). Isaiah's defense of his fellow Israelites caused David to say: "Therefore God, your God, has anointed you with the oil of gladness *above* your fellows" (Ps 45:8, Eng. 7). And the prophet could reply: "The spirit of...God is upon me, because the Lord has anointed me..." (Isa 61:1).[32] Isaiah's distinction of speaking mouth to mouth with God, and his stating at his calling his willingness to suffer, play a major role in his martyrdom, which I shall sketch below.

To conclude this short account of Isaiah's fame, however, it should also be noted that his was the only grave of a male prophet found within Jerusalem at the time of Jesus.[33] In the "Lives of the Prophets," most probably Palestinian, from the first part of the first century C.E., and originally written either in Hebrew or possibly in Aramaic, the author notes that Isaiah, a native of Jerusalem, was buried near the Pool of Siloam "with care and great honor." A description of the location of his tomb is then given.[34]

The above Judaic materials, from the beginning of the second century B.C.E. up into the later rabbinic period, show the great esteem in which early Jews held their greatest prophet, Isaiah. I shall now point out the relevance of his martyrdom in Jerusalem to the tenants' killing the "son" of the owner of the vineyard in Jesus' parable.

C. *The Martyrdom of Isaiah and Isa 66:1.*

As occurs in Jesus' parable in Mark 12:1-9, where the vineyard owner's servants (God's prophets) are beaten, wounded, treated shamefully and even killed, the prophet from Nazareth in the Jerusalem

---

[29] *Pesiq. R.* 26/1.2 (Braude 2.525, with Isa 49:5).

[30] *Midr. Ps.* 90/4 (Braude 2.88, with Isa 8:11 for Isaiah).

[31] *Deut. Rab.* Wa'ethanan 2/4 on Deut 3:23 (Soncino 7.32).

[32] Braude 636. The latter verse is applied to Jesus in the synagogue of Nazareth in Luke 4:18. See also Matt 11:5 and Luke 7:22. Cf. also *Pesiq. R.* 29/30 A 5 (Braude 577).

[33] *'Abot R. Nat.* B 39 (Schechter 107, Saldarini 236, with n. 48). The grave of Huldah the prophetess was found below the southern entrance to the Temple.

[34] Cf. *OTP* 2.385-386, and the introductory matter provided by D. Hare on pp. 380-381.

Temple elsewhere accuses the religious leaders there of "killing the prophets and stoning those who are sent to you!" (Matt 23:37; // Luke 13:34, spoken here however while "journeying toward Jerusalem"). This Jesus couples with a threat of the "house" (the Temple) becoming forsaken (Matt 23:38 adds "and desolate"; // Luke 13:35). There is no reason to doubt the basic authenticity of these statements, even if their present contexts are from the post 70 C.E. period.

Zechariah was one of the two prophets slain in Jerusalem according to Judaic tradition, and Jesus mentions him in Matt 23:35 (// Luke 11:51).[35] The other was Isaiah. On the basis of various Judaic writings, I shall now indicate the importance of his martyrdom for the killing of the "beloved / favorite son" of Mark 12:6.

1) *The Lives of the Prophets, and Hebrews.*

During the first quarter of the first century C.E. the author of "The Lives of the Prophets" began his entire description of twenty-three prophets by stating in 1:1, "Isaiah, from Jerusalem, died under Manasseh by being sawn in two...."[36] Heb 11:37 ("they were sawn in two") most probably refers to this event. The writing was composed sometime at the end of the first century C.E.[37]

2) *The Martyrdom of Isaiah.*

Referring to the latter verse in Hebrews, M. Knigg proposes that the narrative behind the "Martyrdom of Isaiah" (1:1 – 3:12 and 5:1-16), joined to a much later "Ascension of Isaiah," is "probably much older than this and goes back ultimately to the period of the persecution of the Jews by Antiochus Epiphanes in 167-164 B.C."[38] It was composed in Hebrew, in Palestine.[39]

---

[35] He was the son of Jehoiada the priest (2 Chron 24:20), not the son of Berechiah (Zech 1:1), as noted by Matthew or a later copiest. On Judaic lore regarding the blood of Zechariah, cf. Str-B 1.940-942 and *OTP* 2.398, with the relevant notes. His being stoned to death (2 Chron 24:21; cf. Matt 23:37) may be alluded to in Matt 21:35. Billerbeck states (1.943): "The rabbinic writings especially mention the killing of Isaiah and Zechariah..."; he then refers to Heb 11:37 regarding Isaiah (3.747). See also Ginzberg, *Legends* 6.396, n. 30. Only one late tradition says Jeremiah was stoned to death in the Temple (4 Baruch 9 in *OTP* 2.424-425; on the first third of the second century C.E. for the Jewish section of the writing, see 414).

[36] *OTP* 2.385.

[37] Cf. O. Michel, *Der Brief an die Hebräer* (Meyer 13; Göttingen: Vandenhoeck & Ruprecht, 1966[12]) 54.

[38] *OTP* 2.149.

[39] 2.150, 146-147.

In this early Judaic writing Isaiah is accused of prophesying against Jerusalem (thus also including the Temple) and the cities of Judah "that they will be laid waste" (3:6). In addition, he called Jerusalem "Sodom" and the princes of Judah and Jerusalem "the people of Gomorrah" (3:10; cf. Isa 1:10, connected to an anti-sacrificial stance). Presumptuously, Isaiah maintained: "I see more than Moses the prophet." While the latter stated, "There is no man who can see the Lord and live" (cf. Exod 33:20), Isaiah said, "I have seen the Lord, and behold I am alive" (3:8-9; cf. Isa 6:1). This led Manasseh to have Isaiah seized (3:12); he then "sawed Isaiah in half with a wood saw" (5:1). When the prophet began to be sawed in two, he "was in a vision of the Lord" (5:7). He "did not cry out, or weep, but his mouth spoke with the Holy Spirit until he was sawed in two" (5:14).[40]

3) *Rabbinic Traditions.*

Rabbinic traditions provided details for the above very early basic framework of the narrative of Isaiah's martyrdom in Jerusalem. This includes his being addressed by God as "My son," and his speaking Isa 66:1 at the very end of his life. While some of the rabbinic comments are patently late, others certainly also belong to the early core of the martyrdom.

The son of the good king of Judah, Hezekiah, was Manasseh. He surpassed all his predecessors in evil, even setting up the graven image of Asherah in the Jerusalem Temple (2 Kgs 21:7).[41] The Lord then warned Manasseh, Jerusalem and Judah "by His servants the prophets" (v 10) in regard to such "idols" (v 11). Judaic tradition often calls the prophet Isaiah the Lord's "servant," as noted above. It maintains that on this occasion, the 17th of Tammuz (only three weeks before the Ninth of Ab, the date on which the impending destruction of the Temple by Nebuchadnezzar was later commemorated),[42] Isaiah addressed the people for the last time, citing Isa 66:1. He here predicted the destruction of the Temple and the Babylonian captivity.

---

[40] Cf. M. Knibb's translation in *OTP* 2.160, 163-164. H.W. Surkau in *Martyrien in jüdischer und frühchristlicher Zeit* (Göttingen: Vandenhoeck & Ruprecht, 1938) 33 maintains that speaking with the Holy Spirit is foreign to Judaism, for which he offers no proof.

[41] Cf. *y. Ta'an.* 4:5, 68d (Neusner 18.270) on the statement of the Mishnah 4:6, "And he set up an idol in the Temple." A Tanna teaches this was a statue of Manasseh.

[42] Cf. *m. Ta'an* 4:6 (Danby 200) for the 17th of Tammuz and the 9th of Ab. On the three weeks between these events, see *y. Ta'an.* 4:5, 68d (Neusner 18.271).

This speech by Isaiah infuriated Manasseh so much that he "shed much innocent blood, till he had filled Jerusalem from one end to another (lit. 'from mouth to mouth')..." (2 Kgs 21:16). Judaic tradition maintains that this verse means only Isaiah, whom Manasseh "tried and then killed."[43] In *y. Sanh.* 10:2, 28c the question is asked, "Now is it possible for human beings to fill up the whole of Jerusalem with innocent blood from end to end (mouth to mouth)? But he killed Isaiah, who was equal to Moses, as it is written concerning him, With him I speak 'mouth to mouth,' (clearly, and not in dark speech; and he beholds the form of the Lord)" (Num 12:8).[44] Josephus comments on this biblical passage by stating that Manasseh "killed (a variant adds 'cruelly') all the righteous men among the Hebrews, nor did he spare even the prophets, some of whom he slaughtered daily, so that Jerusalem ran with blood." R. Marcus correctly considers it probable that the Jewish historian here alludes to the martyrdom of Isaiah.[45]

Isa 1:1 begins by stating, "The vision of Isaiah the son of Amoz, which he saw concerning Judah and Jerusalem...." Rabbinic tradition however, maintains that the prophetic book of Isaiah actually begins at 6:1, the Temple vision of Isaiah's calling[46]: "In the year that King Uzziah died I saw the Lord sitting upon a throne, high and lifted up; and His train filled the Temple." Isaiah is very afraid, "for my eyes have seen the King, the Lord of hosts" (v 5). After one of the seraphim removes his guilt, the Lord asks, "Whom shall I send, and who will go for us?" Isaiah replies, "Here am I! Send me" (v 8).

Manasseh killed the prophet Isaiah in part because he maintained that he had "seen" the Lord at his calling, but also at the moment of his death. (Below, I will show that the contents of Isa 66:1 are meant by the latter.) This "seeing" on the part of Isaiah is based on the expression בְּמַרְאֶה ("in seeing," "in a vision"), directly after "mouth to mouth" in Num 12:8.[47] Originally it referred to Moses,[48] but it was transferred in rabbinic sources such as *y. Sanh.* 10:2 also to Isaiah.[49]

---

[43] Cf. *b. Sanh.* 103b (Soncino 702). On the expression "brought him to trial and then slew him," see *b. Yebam.* 49b (Soncino 324). Only *Deut. Rab.* 'Eqeb (ed. Liebermann, *Midrash Debarim Rabbah* 74) refers it to Manasseh's killing the prophets.

[44] Neusner 31.335.

[45] *Ant.* 10.38, with n. "e" in the LCL edition.

[46] Cf. *Mek. R. Ish.* Shirata 7 on Exod 15:9 (Lauterbach 2.54), and Goldin's note in *The Song* 175.

[47] The MT now has וּמַרְאֶה, but as noted in Kittel's apparatus, 10 MSS as well as important versions also have בְּמַרְאֶה. They all agree with rabbinic interpretation. On מַרְאֶה, see BDB 909: "sight, appearance, vision." It can also be vocalized as מַרְאָה,

In *Sifre* Beha'alotekhah § 103 on Num 12:8, Exod 33:20 ("You shall not be able to see My face, for no man can see Me and live") is cited for Moses' seeing "in a vision." It agrees with the accusation made above against Isaiah in the Martyrdom of Isaiah.[50] R. Eleazar b. R. Yose, a fourth generation Tanna,[51] states concerning the latter verse: "When a person is alive, he cannot see God, but he sees God at the moment of death." Ps 22:30 (Eng. 29) is the proof text for this assertion.[52] In the parallel at *Sifra* Vayyiqra on Lev 1:1, pereq 2, J. Neusner cites the Jewish Publication Society's translation of this verse: "all those at death's door, whose spirits flag, shall bend the knee before Him."[53] This verse is also cited regarding R. Yoḥanan b. Zakkai, a first generation Tanna,[54] at the moment of his death, when he says he does not know whether he will enter Paradise or Gehenna.[55] Other rabbinic sources corroborate this view of one's seeing the glory of God at the moment of one's death.[56] They make it understandable that Judaic tradition could maintain Isaiah "saw" God not only at his calling (Isaiah 6), but also at the time of his death, when he uttered Isa 66:1 before being martyred. A passage now

---

BDB *ibid.*: "vision, as means of revelation." For the latter term as also meaning "mirror," see Exod 38:8 (BDB *ibid.*), and *Lev. Rab.* Vayyiqra 1/14 on Lev 1:1 (Soncino 4.17), where Moses saw through only one specularium (Num 12:8), and all the other prophets through nine, or Moses through one "polished" and the others through a "blurred" mirror (on this, see 1 Cor 13:12).

[48] *Pal. Targ.* Num 12:8 refers this expression to the calling of Moses at the burning bush of Exodus 3: "but in vision, and not with mystery, revealed I Myself to him at the bush, and he beheld the likeness of My Shekinah" (Aramaic in Rieder, *Targum Jonathan ben Uziel on the Pentateuch* 2.209, and English in Etheridge, *The Targums of Onkelos and Jonathan Ben Uzziel on the Pentateuch with the Fragments of the Jerusalem Targum* 377). Rieder has "mirror," חֵיזוּ, but see Jastrow 443 and 442 for "vision."

[49] Against Ginzberg, *Legends* 6.374, who refers to 2 Kgs 17:9 and not to Num 12:8.

[50] In Jerome's commentary on Isa 1:10, he notes that Hebrews (Jews) informed him that one of the two causes for Isaiah's being murdered had to do with Exod 33:20 and Isa 6:1. See Migne, *P.L.* 24.33, or *Corpus Christianorum*, Series Latina 73, p. 16.

[51] Strack and Stemberger, *Einleitung* 85; he is forgotten in the English translation.

[52] Cf. Neusner, *Sifre to Numbers* 2.124, and Kuhn, *Der tannaitische Midrasch Sifre zu Numeri* 269-270, with notes.

[53] Cf. *Sifra* 1.74. This is here spoken by R. Dosa, probably b. Arḥinos, a second generation Tanna (Strack and Stemberger, *Introduction* 77).

[54] *Introduction* 74-75.

[55] Cf. *'Abot R. Nat.* A 25 (Goldin 106, with n. 5 on p. 198).

[56] Cf. Str-B 1.208-209 on Matt 5:8.

found in *Pesiqta Rabbati* exemplifies these traditions and is worthwhile examining in detail.

Pesiq. R. 4/3[57] comments on 1 Kgs 18:31, "And Elijah took twelve stones, according to the number of the 'tribes' of the sons of Jacob...," with which he built an altar at his contest with the prophets of Baal on Mount Carmel. The unit also closes with an emphasis on the Temple's being rebuilt for the sake of the twelve "tribes" of Israel. In between, the story of Isaiah's martyrdom is related.

> This is what Scripture alludes to when it says, "The heavens are My throne, and the earth My footstool" (Isa 66:1). Isaiah prophesied this verse at the end of his life as a prophet. And when did he utter the prophecy? In the days of Manasseh. As soon as Manasseh brought the idol into the Temple (היכל), Isaiah began to prophesy to Israel, saying to them: "Of what do you boast to Me? Of this House which you have built for Me? The upper and the lower worlds cannot contain My glory. This House which you built for Me – do I need it? 'What is the House which *you* would build for Me?' (*ibid.*) Behold, Nebuchadnezzar will come up (from Babylon) and destroy it and exile you."

> Manasseh was immediately infuriated at him (Isaiah) and said to them (his Temple police): "Seize him!" (תפשוהו) They ran after him to seize him. As he (Isaiah) fled from them, a carob tree opened up and hid him. R. Ḥanina b. R. Isaac[58] said: And he (Manasseh)[59] brought carpenters and caused the carob tree to be sawed open, and blood poured out. This is what Scripture says: "Moreover Manasseh shed much innocent blood until he had filled Jerusalem from mouth to mouth" (2 Kgs 21:16). Is it possible to maintain that? Rather, it means that he slew Isaiah, who was of equal importance to Moses, since He spoke with him "mouth to mouth," as Scripture states: "With him I speak mouth to mouth..." (Num 12:8).

> (While being sawn in two,) Isaiah began to reprove[60] them (here Manasseh and his Temple police): "'The heavens are My throne, and the earth My footstool' (Isa 66:1). And in regard to this House, which will be rebuilt, do not think that it will be rebuilt for your sake, but for the sake of others (אחרים)."

---

[57] Friedmann 14a, Braude 1.88-89. Part of this is also found in *Yalquṭ Shem'oni*, Isaiah 510. I slightly modify Braude's English translation.

[58] Cf. the Parma MS cited and preferred by Braude, 1.88, n. 31. He was a fourth generation Palestinian Amora (Strack and Stemberger, *Einleitung* 98).

[59] Friedmann 14a, n. 35, notes that the language here is imprecise. Perhaps one should rather read: "And what did he do? He brought...." I thank Dr. N. Oswald of Berlin for discussing the Hebrew of this passage, especially Friedmann's notes, with me.

[60] This is the hiph. of the verb יכח, which in the qal means "to be firm, stand, be right" (Jastrow 577). It may be implied here in a subtle way that even at his martyrdom, Isaiah stood firm.

This is the end of the original narrative. It was then connected to 1 Kgs 18:31 by rabbinic comment on "others." R. Judah the Levite b. R. Shallum, a fifth generation Palestinian Amora,[61] suggests the Temple will be rebuilt for the sake of the Torah, which he sees alluded to in Isa 66:2. However, R. Joshua the priest b. Nehemiah, a fourth generation Palestinian Amora,[62] maintains it will be done for the sake of the tribes, which he derives by combining phrases from Isa 66:2 and Gen 49:28.

4) *The Dating of These Traditions.*

The date of this version of Isaiah's martyrdom, with Isa 66:1(-2), cannot be ascertained with certainty. The Amoraic comments were clearly added later to the earlier narrative.[63] *Eliyyahu Zuṭa* 9 also relates that God commanded Isaiah to quote Isa 66:1 to Manasseh when he defiled the Jerusalem Temple by setting up an idol in it.[64] In addition, the story of Isaiah's martyrdom is related in a targumic fragment from what P. Grélot calls an extract of a now lost Palestinian Targum on Isaiah.[65] In *Mek. R. Ish.* Pisḥa 16 on Exod 13:2, the Tannaite author also raises the question of why God asks the Israelites to build Him a sanctuary if He spoke Isa 66:1. He concludes that the fulfilling of God's commandment enables them to receive reward.[66] This text shows the early *Palestinian* use of Isa 66:1 in regard to a critique of the Jerusalem Temple.[67]

The earliest attestation of Isa 66:1-2 as Temple criticism, however, is in the martyrdom of Stephen in Acts 7.[68] According to the author of Acts,

---

[61] Strack and Stemberger, *Introduction* 106.

[62] *Ibid.*, 103.

[63] Cf. their employment in a very different context in *Gen. Rab.* Bereshit 12/2 on Gen 2:4 (Soncino 1.88-89). See also Friedmann's note 37 on his p. 14a.

[64] Friedmann 188, Braude and Kapstein 440-441.

[65] Cf. his article "Deux Tosephtas Targoumiques Inédites sur Isaïe LXVI" in *RB* 79 (1972) 511-543. He reproduces and translates the better MS, Codex Reuchlin, as well as Codex Vatican Ebr. Urbin. 1. Rashi (d. 1105 C.E.) was acquainted with this tradition on Isaiah and Manasseh, which he said was found in "Targum Yerushalmi" on Isa 66:1 (p. 535, n. 17). Grélot considers it almost certain that *Pesiq. R.* 4/3 presupposes a then current usage of Pal. Targ. Isa 66:1-2 (p. 535). Stenning in *The Targum of Isaiah* 226-227 reproduces an extract of Isa 66:1 from the "Targ. Yerush." of Lagarde's *Prophetae Chaldaicae.* B. Chilton has also translated the narrative of Isaiah's martyrdom from Codex Reuchlin in his *The Isaiah Targum* 126.

[66] Lauterbach 1.131. Isa 66:1 is also cited in *Mek. R. Šim. b. Yoḥ.* Beshallaḥ on Exod 15:17 (Epstein and Melamed 99) in regard to the earthly throne (of God in the Temple) as being opposite His heavenly throne. See Goldin, *The Song* 235.

[67] Cf. *b. Sanh.* 7a with Isa 66:1 (Soncino 27, especially n. 3).

[68] Braude also called attention to it in *Pesikta Rabbati* 1.88, n. 30.

the first Christian martyr was charged in Jerusalem with speaking words "against this holy place and the law," maintaining that Jesus would "destroy this place" and change Mosaic traditions (6:13-14). Stephen defends himself before the "council" (Sanhedrin) by extensively recounting the history of Israel from the time of Abraham. As of 7:44 he begins his critique of the Temple, God preferring the tent of witness in the wilderness, which He expressly directed Moses to have made. To emphasize that the Jerusalem Temple built by Solomon was wrong from the outset because God does nor dwell in houses made with hands (cf. Exod 15:17 for this "hands" imagery), Stephen quotes the prophet Isaiah (66:1-2, including "My hand") in 7:49-50. He then accuses the members of the council of acting like their fathers, who persecuted the prophets and slew those who announced the coming of the Righteous One, Jesus, whom they now also murdered. While they were enraged at him, Stephen was full of the Holy Spirit. He gazed into heaven and, like the martyr Isaiah, "saw the glory of God" (and Jesus standing at the right hand of God: vv 55-56). Because of this blasphemy, they cast him out of the city and stoned him (v 58).

While patently based in part on the trial of Jesus (cf. Mark 14:58 and 62 par.), the narrative of Stephen's martyrdom is in a major way also dependent on Judaic tradition regarding the martyrdom of Isaiah. He too was killed because of his Temple critique, including the explicit citation of Isa 66:1, and his "seeing" the glory of God.[69] Most commentators maintain that the Stephen speech is of Hellenistic Jewish Christian origin, primarily because of its Temple critique.[70] Yet the Hellenistic Jewish Christian community definitely received it from the Palestinian Jewish Christian community, as its very close connections with the Palestinian version(s) of the martyrdom of Isaiah show.

The Acts of the Apostles, a continuation of the Gospel of Luke, were written sometime after the fall of Jerusalem, probably between 80-90

---

[69] H. Conzelmann in *Die Apostelgeschichte* (HNT 7; Tübingen: Mohr, 1963) 51 notes on 7:55 *Asc. Isa.* 5:7 regarding the vision of a martyr. He also asks whether the use of Isa 66:1-2 is a topos, and he refers to Barn 16:2 with a major criticism of the destroyed Temple, and to Justin Martyr, *Dialogue with Trypho* 32 (in *The Ante-Nicene Fathers* 1.206), related to the original non-necessity of sacrifices in the Temple: they are only for Israel's sins, keeping the people from worshiping idols.

[70] Cf. Conzelmann, *Die Apostelgeschichte* 51, and E. Haenchen, *Die Apostelgeschichte* (Meyer; Göttingen: Vandenhoeck & Ruprecht, 1961) 241. Interestingly, W. Schmithals in *Das Evangelium nach Markus* (ÖTKNT 2/2; Gütersloh: Mohn; Würzburg: Echter, 1979) 515 considers the author of Mark 12:1-11 to be a Hellenistic Jewish Christian with thoughts akin to Acts 7:48ff. and Isa 66:1-2.

C.E.[71] The close associations of the martyrdom of Stephen with that of Isaiah corroborate an early date of the *core* of the rabbinic version of Isaiah's death. The same is true of Heb 11:37 and the "Martyrdom of Isaiah," noted above.

5) *"Others."*

If I am correct in viewing the prophet Isaiah as the final servant, the "beloved son" (see below) sent by the owner of the vineyard to his tenants in Jesus' parable, it is significant that this servant is also killed, like Isaiah. Because of their evil behavior, the owner will then "destroy" the tenants and give the vineyard (the Temple) to "others" (Mark 12:9). Jesus intentionally leaves the identity of these "others" open,[72] just as in the rabbinic version of the martyrdom of Isaiah the prophet just before his death states that the Temple will be rebuilt after its destruction by Nebuchadnezzar for the sake of "others." He does not state who they are. Both narratives end with the term "others," which leads me to believe Jesus appropriated it from an early core of the Isaiah narrative, known to him from popular tradition.

The prophet from Nazareth then very artfully employed the term "other" numerous times in his parable. The following table, with the Hebrew equivalents of five expressions, shows Jesus' narrative artistry. (I shall comment below in section VII. on the original Semitic language of the parable.)

Mark 12:4 –	"another servant,"	ἄλλον δοῦλον	:	עֶבֶד אַחֵר.
12:5 –	"he sent another,"	ἄλλον ἀπέστειλεν	:	שָׁלַח אַחֵר.
	"and many others,"	καὶ πολλοὺς ἄλλους	:	גַּם רַבִּים אֲחֵרִים.
12:6 –	"finally,"	ἔσχατον	:	בָּאַחֲרֹנָה.[73]
12:9 –	"to others,"	ἄλλοις	:	לַאֲחֵרִים.[74]

6) *Isaiah as "My son."*

In Judaic tradition God called the prophet Isaiah "My son" because he was willing to suffer at the hands of the Israelites when He called him in the Jerusalem Temple and Isaiah saw the Lord sitting on a throne

---

[71] Cf. A. Weiser, *Die Apostelgeschichte, Kapitel 1-12* (ÖTKNT 5/1; Gütersloh: Mohn; Würzburg: Echter, 1981) 40-41.

[72] E. Klostermann in *Das Markusevangelium* 122 does not interpret the vineyard as the Temple. Yet he correctly emphasizes that while the people are to receive "other" leaders, they themselves ("das Volk") are not rejected.

[73] Cf. this as a biblical form in BDB 31, b. β.

[74] On these phrases, cf. also the Hebrew New Testaments of Delitzsch and the United Bible Societies.

(Isaiah 6). As related above, Judaic tradition maintains that the book of Isaiah actually begins with this chapter. The narrative is related in *Pesiq. Rav Kah.* 16/4 as follows in regard to Isa 40:1 ("Comfort, comfort ye My people").[75]

> R. Azaraiah in the name of R. Judah b. Simon[76] interpreted the biblical verse (Ps 45:8, Eng. 7) of Isaiah. Isaiah stated, I was walking in my house of study[77] and I heard the voice of the Lord say: "Whom shall I send, and who will go for us?" etc. (Isa 6:8). He said: I sent Amos, and they called him "stammerer."[78] (R. Phinehas[79] said, Why was he named Amos? Because he stammered in his speech.)[80] They said, Did the Holy One, blessed be He, pass over the whole world and cause His Shekinah to rest only on this stammerer, this man with a crippled tongue? I sent Micah, and they smote[81] him on the cheek. "With a rod they strike upon the cheek the reprover of Israel" (Mic. 4:14).[82] Now "Whom shall I send, and who will go for us?" (Isa 6:8) Immediately (Isaiah) said, "Here am I. Send me!" (*ibid.*) The Holy One, blessed be He, said to him: "Isaiah, My son (בני), they are obstinate, they are troublesome. Are you willing to take it upon yourself to suffer[83] and to be despised[84] by them?" (Isaiah) replied to Him: Even under that condition. "I gave my back to the smiters, and my cheeks to those who pulled out the beard; I hid not my face from shame and spitting" (Isa 50:6). But am I worthy to go to Your sons (children) in Your commission?

The narrative then answers this positively, employing Ps 45:8 and the plural "My sons." As his reward, God anoints Isaiah above all his fellows (*ibid.*). In contrast to all the other prophets, he will prophesy from the

---

[75] The Hebrew is in Mandelbaum, *Pesikta de Rav Kahana* 269-270, and the English in Braude and Kapstein 293-294. Cf. also the parallels in *Pesiq. R.* 29/30 A 5 on Isa 40:1 (Braude 576-577, from the Parma MS, not available to me; see his 570, note), and *Lev. Rab.* Tsav 10/2 on Lev 8:1-4 (Margulies 197-199; Soncino 4.122-123).

[76] He was a fourth generation Palestinian Amora (Strack and Stemberger, *Introduction* 103).

[77] Here Isaiah is represented as walking in the Temple, his site of study, as it was for the major Sages of Jerusalem at the time of Jesus. See section III. A. above.

[78] Cf. Jastrow 1195 on פְּסִילוֹם as from ψελλός. See also *Eccl. Rab.* 1:1 § 2 (Soncino 8.3) on this.

[79] He was a fifth generation Palestinian Amora (Strack and Stemberger, *Introduction* 105).

[80] The pun is on "Amos" and עָמוֹס; see Jastrow 1089.

[81] This is a pun on "Micah" and מכים.

[82] Apparently the midrash reads the verb שפט here as "reprover" and not "judge"; cf. Braude 292.

[83] Cf. Jastrow 718 on לקה, לקי: to suffer, esp. to be smitten.

[84] Cf. Jastrow 153-154 on בזה, בזי.

mouth of the Mighty One (הגבורה), as Isa 61:1 is interpreted. In addition, Isaiah's reward is that his prophecies will be in double terms, as in "Comfort, comfort" (Isa 40:1) and other passages.

Here God addresses Isaiah as "My son" (בְּנִי), which is the more difficult reading and should be preferred to "My sons" (בני). The latter, occurring several times in the narrative, caused the earlier reading of Isaiah as "My son" to be adapted to it by the copyists.[85]

G. Vermes also points to two early rabbis whom God addressed as "My son." R. Ḥanina b. Dosa, a first generation Tanna,[86] is mentioned twice so in *b. Ber.* 17b: "Rab said, 'Every day a divine voice goes forth from Mount Horeb and proclaims: The whole world is sustained for the sake of My son Ḥanina, and Ḥanina My son has to subsist on a *kab* of carobs from one week end to the next.'"[87] The second rabbi labeled so is Meir, a third generation Tanna,[88] in *b. Ḥag.* 15b.[89] M. Hengel also calls attention to the designation "My son" for R. Ishmael b. Elisha, a second generation Tanna,[90] in *b. Ber.* 7a[91] and in 3 Enoch 1:8[92] ; R. Eleazar b. Pedath, a third generation Palestinian Amora,[93] in *b. Ta'an.* 25a[94]; and Moses in the "Midrash on the Death of Moses."[95] The rabbinic passages deal with visions of God.[96]

---

[85] Cf. the apparatus of Mandelbaum 270, who notes that the Safed MS (the basis for S. Buber's edition, employed by P. Billerbeck in Str-B 1.875), the shorter Oxford MS, and the Parma MS have the reading "My son." See also Margulies 108 on *Lev. Rab.* 10/2, with the MSS Oxford 1 and 2, Yalquṭ Makhiri, and Paris.

[86] Strack and Stemberger, *Introduction* 75.

[87] Soncino 104. There are parallels in *b. Ta'an.* 24b (Soncino 128) and *Ḥull.* 86a (Soncino 482).

[88] Strack and Stemberger, *Introduction* 84.

[89] Soncino 98. Cf. Vermes' *Jesus the Jew* (Philadelphia: Fortress, 1981) 206.

[90] Strack and Stemberger, *Introduction* 79.

[91] Soncino 30.

[92] *OTP* 1.256, which has God speak of "Ishmael my beloved son and honored friend...." The translator, P. Alexander, believes this work's final redaction occurred in Babylonia in the fifth and sixth centuries, but that it included some very old Palestinian material (1.229).

[93] Strack and Stemberger, *Introduction* 98.

[94] Soncino 130.

[95] Cf. Jellinek, *Bet ha-Midrasch* 1.121.

[96] See Hengel's *Der Sohn Gottes* (Tübingen: Mohr, 1975) 68-69. I thank Professor Hengel for calling my attention to the references in his work. See also "Jacob, My son" in Jellinek, *Bet ha-Midrasch* 6.XXII, last line; God's addressing Moses with "Take courage, son (ὦ παῖ), and listen to My words" in *Ezekiel the Tragedian* (*OTP* 2.813); *Test. Levi* 4:2 (*OTP* 1.789); the Logos as God's first-born son in Philo, *Agr.*

These Tannaitic and Amoraic references show how early Judaic tradition could also have God call Isaiah "My son," as in *Pesiq. Rav Kah.* 16/4 above. In turn, this supports my proposal that the owner of the vineyard in Jesus' parable, after sending many servants to the wicked tenants, sent yet one more (servant), a beloved / favorite son, to them (Mark 12:6). This is Isaiah, whom they also killed (v 8), just as Manasseh and his Temple police killed the prophet Isaiah in Jerusalem.

While the present form of the *Pesiq. Rav Kah.* 16/4 narrative, with parallels, is Amoraic, here too I consider it probable that the *core* of this episode is much earlier. If so, Jesus most probably appropriated the term "son" and "my / My son" for Isaiah from it.

7) *Micah and Amos.*

Also, the prophets Micah and Amos are probably meant by the first two servants in Jesus' parable, for Judaic tradition says they prophesied in the same period as Isaiah.[97] Mark 12:3 states that the evil tenants took the first servant sent by the owner, "beat" (δέρω)[98] him, and sent him away empty-handed. This is הכוהו or הכו אותו in Hebrew, from the verb נכה. By a word play, as in *Pesiq. Rav Kah.* 16/4, it can be associated with "Micah."[99]

The prophet Amos is probably alluded to by Jesus in Mark 12:4, where the evil tenants "wounded in the head" (κεφαλαιόω, only here in the NT) the second servant sent by the owner, i.e. the second prophet sent by God. According to the early first century C.E., Palestinian writing "The Lives of the Prophets" 7:1, Amaziah's son struck Amos on the temple with a club, which caused him to die several days later.[100] This is the only prophet known in Judaic tradition to have been beaten on the head, which makes it more probable the very rare Greek verb in Mark 12:4 refers to him.

51; Joseph as the first-born son of God in *Joseph and Asenath* 18:11 and 21:4 (*OTP* 2.233 and 235); and the sentence "He will be called son of God, and they will call him son of the Most High" in 4Q Aramaic Apocalypse (4Q246), col. II, 1 (Martínez 138).

[97] Cf. *Seder 'Olam* 20 (Milikowsky 341-343 and 505), which lists Isaiah, Hosea, Amos and Micah. See also *b. Pesaḥ.* 87a (Soncino 460), and other sources cited in *Legends* 6.355, n. 20.

[98] See also v 5, and BAGD 175.

[99] Cf. 1 Kgs 22:24, where Micaiah (the son of Imlah – v 8; he also saw the Lord sitting on His throne – v 19) is struck on the cheek by another prophet. For the identification of Micah and Micaiah in Judaic sources, see *Legends* 6.355, n. 20. See also *Mart. Isa.* 2:12, 16 (*OTP* 2.159).

[100] Cf. *OTP* 2.391 and n. "a." LSJ 945 can only refer to Mark 12:5 under κεφαλαιόω II.

If Micah and Amos are meant by the first two servants sent to the evil tenants, this in turn increases the probability that Isaiah, the most famous of all the prophets, with whom they prophesied in the same age, is meant by the one more (servant), a beloved / favorite son, in Mark 12:6.[101]

8) *Other Maltreated Prophets.*

In *Pesiq. R.* 33/3, a variant of the above narrative regarding Isaiah's calling, "our Masters" taught that not only Micah, later smitten, was sent by God. The Israelites also slew Zechariah (cf. 2 Chron 24:22 and Matt 23:35 // Luke 11:51) and threw Jeremiah into a cistern (Jeremiah 38). Then, when God asks whom He can now send, Isaiah proclaims his readiness. These and other maltreated prophets may be alluded to by Jesus in Mark 12:5b. This is one reason why I hesitate to doubt the verse's authenticity, which many scholars do.[102]

9) *Isaiah's Willingness to Suffer for Israel.*

In the above narrative from *Pesiqta de Rab Kahana* regarding the call of Isaiah, the prophet explicitly informs God, after Amos was ridiculed and Micah smitten, that he is nevertheless willing to take it upon himself to suffer and to be despised by the obstinate and troublesome Israelites. Even under those circumstances he will do so, for which Isa 50:6 is cited. This is also certainly meant in regard to Isa 6:8-9 in *Eliyyahu Rabbah* 16, which asks how Isaiah was distinguished from all the other prophets who comforted Israel. He "joyfully took upon himself the kingdom of heaven."[103]

Isaiah's willingness to suffer on behalf of his fellow Israelites is also reflected in his behavior at his martyrdom. While he was being sawed in

---

[101] We today tend to consider Isaiah, from the eighth century B.C.E., one of the first prophets. In the Hebrew Bible, however, the "former" or first prophets begin with those in the Book of Joshua and extend through Second Kings. Judaic tradition (cf. *Seder 'Olam* 20) lists many early prophets, from the Patriarchs to those in Egypt, including Moses. Significantly, Isaiah begins the section entitled the latter or "last" prophets: אחרונים. Isaiah was not *the* last prophet, but the first and most beloved of the last prophets. This helps to explain how Jesus could describe him as the servant whom the owner "finally" or "at last" (באחרנה – ἔσχατον) sent to his vineyard in Mark 12:6.

[102] Cf. Schmithals in *Das Evangelium nach Markus* 513, who, although he considers v 5b dispensable, says it "prevents the misunderstanding that only the concrete fates of three prophets are spoken of in vv 3-5a." He in turn relies here on A. Weiser.

[103] Friedmann 82; Braude and Kapstein 220. Cf. the following parable describing God's sending Isaiah to Israel to make it change its (evil) mode of life.

two, the early *Mart. Isa.* 5:14 says, "he did not cry out or weep...."[104] According to *b. Yebam.* 49b, Isaiah reasoned in regard to his persecutor Manasseh: "'whatever I may tell him he will not accept; and should I reply at all, I would only cause him to be a willful (homicide).' He therefore pronounced (the Divine) Name and was swallowed up by a cedar."[105] Here Isaiah even at his death thinks of the welfare of his persecutor.

If *Mart. Isa.* 1:13 has not been influenced by a Christian copyist,[106] Isaiah is also depicted here as being called to suffer. This is called his "inheritance." When the good King Hezekiah was informed by Isaiah that Manasseh would later kill the prophet, Hezekiah contemplated slaying his own son. Yet Isaiah countered: "The Beloved (God) has made your plan ineffective, and the thought of your heart will not come about; for with this calling have I been called, and the inheritance of the Beloved will I inherit." Isaiah's calling in chapter six of the prophetic book was linked in Judaic tradition to his willingness to suffer. This is the fate or inheritance given him by God, the Beloved.[107]

The motif of Isaiah's silence at his death may, of course, ultimately derive from Isa 53:7 ("he opened not his mouth").[108] This is part of the fourth "Servant Song" in the book of Isaiah. As noted in section IV.1 above, Isaiah is frequently described in Judaic tradition as a, or the Lord's, "servant." It is quite probable that many first century C.E. Palestinian Jews regarded the prophet himself, and not Israel or the Messiah, as being the so-called "Suffering Servant." If so, in Mark 12:6 Jesus means by "one other (servant), a beloved son,"[109] "my / My son,"

---

[104] *OTP* 2.164.

[105] Soncino 324. Pronouncing the "Name" was not always considered sacrilegious, as in Mark 14:61-64 par. (cf. John 19:7). In *b. Yoma* 69b on Neh 8:6, Ezra for example magnifies God by pronouncing the ineffable Name. This should be done, however, only within the Temple precincts (Soncino 327-328, with n. 2 on p. 327, and *b. Sanh.* 60a in Soncino 408, n. 1).

[106] *OTP* 2.157, notes a2 and b2.

[107] For God as the Beloved (ידיד; BDB 391) of Isa 5:1, cf. for example *b. Menaḥ.* 53a-b (Soncino 320), with parallels in *'Abot R. Nat.* B 43 (Schechter 121, Saldarini 265) and *Sifre* Deut. Berakah § 352 on Deut 33:12 (Hammer 364-365). While I do not deny that Jesus is meant by "the Beloved" elsewhere in *Mart. Isa.*, God seems more plausible here. On this inheritance, contrast that of "a beloved son" (Mark 12:6), whom I consider to be Isaiah. He is killed, and can thereby receive no inheritance.

[108] Cf. Mark 14:61 and 15:5 par.

[109] For a similar interpretation of this phrase, see Milavec, "A Fresh Analysis" 97. The son is also a servant.

the prophet Isaiah, well-known in Judaic tradition for his willingness to suffer and even to be killed. This is also the fate of the owner's son in Jesus' parable, who knows that other servants (prophets) have already been killed before him (12:5).

Isa 53:8 states that the Suffering Servant was "stricken (the noun נֶגַע) for the transgression of My people." The same term occurs in 2 Sam 7:14, where God says concerning "My son": "I will chasten him with the rod of men, with the 'stripes' (נִגְעֵי) of the sons of men."[110] While this passage in 2 Samuel refers to David's future offspring, the association of God's "son" and the "stripes" of suffering is noteworthy. In Judaic tradition, the latter are the fate of the prophet Isaiah, who could also be called God's "son."

This raises the question, finally, of whether Jesus meant himself as the "one other (servant), a beloved son," in Mark 12:6. Many commentators, especially of a conservative or evangelical bent, consider this to be the case. The prophet from Nazareth was simply referring to himself here in a veiled way.[111] It is incontestable that the earliest Palestinian Jewish Christians described Jesus in terms of the Suffering Servant.[112] Yet nowhere is it clear that he himself thought in these terms.

The parable of the Wicked Tenants does make it *possible*, however, that at the very end of his life Jesus felt he was following in the footsteps of the prophet Isaiah. The latter had delivered scathing criticism of the rulers of Israel (Isa 1:10), those who had severely misused the Lord's vineyard (3:14-15 and 5:1-7). He had prophesied against the sacrificial cult (1:11-20), of the imminent destruction of the Jerusalem Temple by Nebuchadnezzar (Judaic tradition; cf. 5:5, "My vineyard...shall be destroyed") and of the exile to Babylonia (Isaiah 39).[113] And he maintained that he had a very special relationship to God, even "seeing" Him (Isaiah 6, especially in Judaic tradition). Isaiah's willingness to suffer

---

[110] Cf. BDB 619 on this noun. See also Isa 53:4 for the verb: "we esteemed him 'stricken,' smitten by God, and afflicted."

[111] Cf. W. Grundmann, *Das Evangelium nach Markus* (ThHNT 2; Berlin: Evangelische Verlagsanstalt, 1977⁷) 322, without "beloved"; E. Gould, *The Gospel According to St. Mark* (ICC; Edinburgh: Clark, 1975) 221; C. Dodd, *The Parables* 97-98; and W. Lane, *The Gospel According to Mark* (NICNT 2; Grand Rapids: Eerdmans, 1974) 416 and 419.

[112] Cf. the art. *pais theou* by J. Jeremias in *TDNT* 5.677-717, as well as special studies on NT christology, for example R. Fuller, *The Foundations of New Testament Christology* (New York: Scribners, 1965) 43-46; O. Cullmann, *The Christology of the New Testament* (Philadelphia: Westminster, 1963) 51-82; and F. Hahn, *Christologische Hoheitstitel* (FRLAT 83; Göttingen: Vandenhoeck & Ruprecht, 1974⁴) 54-66.

[113] On this, see also the other references cited by Ginzberg, *Legends* 6.373-374.

for the sake of his people Israel also occurred in a context where God labeled him "My son." All this led to King Manasseh's seizing and killing him.

Jesus too delivered severe criticism of the current rulers of Israel (the parable of the Wicked Tenants; an earlier form of Matt 23:29-37 // Luke 11:47-52 and 13:34; the "cleansing" of the Temple in Mark 11:15-19). It is very probable that he too prophesied the destruction of the Temple by God if the rulers did not repent (Mark 13:2, with the divine passive, later transferred to Jesus in 14:58 and 15:29; Matt 23:38 // Luke 13:35). Jesus' very special relationship to his heavenly Father was expressed most clearly in the term "Abba" (Mark 14:36). This nearness in turn led to the special authority with which he spoke and acted (Mark 11:27-33). Jesus' outspoken criticism and deeds also finally led to the religious and secular authorities' seizing and killing him.

The more I examine the gospel reports, the greater my impression is that Jesus deliberately pursued a collision course during his final days in Jerusalem. This behavior closely resembled that of the prophet Isaiah, especially in Judaic tradition. *Perhaps* Jesus too hoped that by his own prophetic, Isaianic suffering, the kingdom would come. And he *may* have felt that his own death was inexorably imminent. This he then *may* have alluded to while in the Temple through the fate of the "beloved" prophet Isaiah in his parable of the Wicked Tenants. Mark 12:12 correctly states that the authorities "perceived that he had told the parable against them," therefore "they tried to arrest him." Only a few days later they were successful in their endeavor and had Jesus crucified. Like Isaiah in Judaic tradition, he was martyred. And like Isaiah, Jesus lived on in the hearts of those who loved, and still today love him.

V. The "Beloved" Son and Isa 5:1.

Mark 12:6 states that the owner of the vineyard had "yet one more (servant), a beloved (ἀγαπητός) son," whom he finally also sent to the evil tenants. He then calls him "my son" (τὸν υἱόν μου). Yet the wicked tenants seize and kill him too, as they had done with numerous other servants.

According to the proposal made above, the servants are the many prophets God sent to Israel in order that His people, especially the leaders, might repent. The final servant He sends, says Jesus, is the most famous or beloved of all the prophets, Isaiah, whom in Judaic tradition God could even call "My son." Primarily because he was willing to suffer on behalf of Israel, as shown in Judaic sources regarding his martyrdom, he was "beloved" by God and his fellow countrymen.

I suggest that Jesus' choice of the term "beloved" was not only influenced by the tradition behind the *Mekilta* on Exod 13:21 described above in section III.C.4) 1., with the term חִבָּה. Rather, a Hebrew expression in Isa 5:1 also played a major role here.

LXX Isa 5:1 has ἠγαπημένος twice for the Hebrew יְדִיד, referring to God. As shown above in section II.A, Jesus alluded five times to Isaiah 5 (vv 1-2 and 5) at the beginning and end of his parable. This makes it quite possible that he borrowed one more term from the Song of the Vineyard in Mark 12:6. The expression ידיד is poetic for "beloved," occurring five times in the MT of a beloved person.[114] Only Isa 5:1, however, has the male singular. Because of the poetic, archaic character of the term, the Targum first renders it of Abraham as God's "friend," lit. loved one or beloved (רחם). Then it uses חביב of Israel, God's "beloved one."[115] I suggest that this latter term, from the same root as חבה above,[116] was used by Jesus to describe the "yet one more (servant), a 'beloved' son," Isaiah.

If this is the case, the owner's son is "beloved" in the sense of "favorite," but he is not necessarily an "only" (יחיד) son.[117] The first meaning, however, does not exclude the second. By killing the beloved son of the owner, the wicked tenants hope to inherit the vineyard, especially if there is then no other legal heir.

VI. The Extent of the Narrative.

Jesus' parable of the Wicked Tenants now extends from Mark 12:1-11. To begin with the conclusion, in agreement with the majority of the commentators, I consider vv 10-11 a later addition.[118] My primary argument for this, however, is that I believe Jesus was acquainted with and employed a phrase from the end of an earlier form of the Judaic narrative regarding Isaiah's martyrdom described above. It closed with

---

[114] BDB 391; cf. Jastrow 564. Interesting in regard to the catchword "song" in Isa 5:1 and Exod 15:1, Ps 45:1 has "a song of love." Goldin in *The Song* 156 translates the Hebrew term as "favorite," referring to Judaic tradition on Abraham. See also the phrase "Ishmael My *beloved* son" in 3 Enoch 1:8 (*OTP* 1.256), if it has not been influenced by Christian copiests.

[115] Stenning 16-17. On the term, cf. Jastrow 418.

[116] Cf. Jastrow 415-416.

[117] The term ἀγαπητός in the LXX translates יחיד so in Gen 22:2, 12, 16; Judg 11:34; Jer 6:26; Amos 8:10; and Zech 12:10. Delitzsch has it, followed by "whom he loved," in his Hebrew New Testament. Jeremias in *The Parables* 75, n. 98, relying on C. Turner and C. Dodd, also preferred the meaning "only."

[118] Ernst, *Das Evangelium nach Markus* 340 and 343; Pesch, *Das Markusevangelium* 2.213, 222; Hengel, "Das Gleichnis" 36; Grundmann, *Das Evangelium nach Markus* 321; and Jeremias, *The Parables* 74; against Snodgrass, *The Parable* 63, 113-118.

the phrase "for the sake of 'others,'" who are not identified. The incident is thus open-ended. The same is true of Jesus' parable. At the end the owner of the vineyard will come (in judgment), destroy the tenants, and give the vineyard (the Temple, with its administration) to "others" (Mark 12:9).[119] Jesus deliberately does not relate who the "others" are. Leaving the story open-ended is a part of his narrative artistry.[120] The hearers of the parable were thereby forced to further concern themselves with its contents by asking whom Jesus actually meant. Also, by not identifying the "others," Jesus added to the ominous, threatening character of this judgment parable ("He [God] will come [in judgment] and destroy the tenants and give the vineyard to others"). Finally, if he had named the "others," Jesus' opponents, those meant by the "wicked tenants," may have persecuted them as probable supporters of his cause. This Jesus would have sought to avoid.

The introductory sentence in Mark 12:1a, "And he began to speak to them in parables," is clearly redactional.[121]

In addition, in section II.A. above I pointed out how important the setting of Jesus' parable in v 1b is. Alluding clearly to Isa 5:1-7, the Song of the Vineyard, especially as still reflected in Judaic tradition, it provided Jesus with the background for his critique of the high priestly, primarily Sadducean administrators of the Jerusalem Temple, the vineyard. My arguments above oppose an original formulation of v 1b in Greek, deriving from a Hellenistic Jewish Christian community.[122] The Gospel of Thomas, which omits v 1b entirely, has now clearly been shown to be a secondary, later development of the parable.[123]

---

[119] Snodgrass in *The Parable* 61 believes the phrase "given to others" "more likely reflects the wording of rental agreements." Jesus borrowed it, however, from Judaic tradition on the martyrdom of Isaiah.

[120] Cf. the open end of the parable of the Prodigal Son. No indication is given at Luke 15:32 whether the older son will accept his father's offer or not. Here too the hearer asks: How will the story end?

[121] Pesch in *Das Markusevangelium* 2.214 argues that the pleonastic ἄρχομαι is a stylistic mark of the pre-Markan Passion Narrative. At any rate, whether Markan or pre-Markan Christian, it does not belong to the original narrative. The same is true for 12:12, which, however, most probably retains the Temple leaders' authentic reaction.

[122] Cf. for example Jeremias, *The Parables* 71, who does not mention that a translator of the Semitic original recognized the clear allusions to Isa 5:1-7 and therefore employed LXX phrases from there, well-known to him. Schmithals in *Das Evangelium nach Markus* 514 and 522 considers the author of the entire parable to be a Hellenistic Jewish Christian; it is thus a "literary product" (513).

[123] Cf. the convincing arguments given by Snodgrass, *The Parable* 54. See also other authors cited by Gundry, *Mark* 683. Contrast J. Marcus, *The Way of the Lord*.

Some scholars have seen in v 5 a disturbance of the popular proclivity for triads.[124] Omitting it would make the beloved son of v 6 the last in the sequence. One argument in favor of this could be the fates of Micah ("beat" in v 3) and Amos ("wounded in the head" in v 4), contemporaries of Isaiah, who then followed in v 6. Yet as I indicated above, it was precisely the intention of Jesus to emphasize the great forbearance of God in persistently sending one prophet after another to Israel and their Jerusalem leaders in the hope that they would repent. The large number points to the fact that only when the measure is finally full does He come to judge and destroy. In addition, a variant of the Judaic narrative of Isaiah's calling, including his willingness to suffer on behalf of Israel, also mentioned Zechariah (killed) and Jeremiah (thrown into a pit). They may be included in the maltreated servant prophets of 12:5. There are therefore good reasons to retain the verse as it stands. It is always dangerous to press a "rule" by making it universally applicable.

This means that Jesus' original parable most probably extended from Mark 12:1 (after the introductory phrase) to v 9. It makes very good sense as a unit. In contrast to many other parables, it has been astonishingly well preserved.

VII. The Original Language.

In the course of this study I have cited almost exclusively Palestinian Judaic sources, which provide the background to the parable of the Wicked Tenants. They are all in Hebrew or, in exceptional cases, Aramaic (for example Targum Isaiah). In addition, I have called attention to a number of expressions which have direct Semitic equivalents. Other scholars have indicated Semitisms in the narrative.[125] This makes it all the more probable that Jesus composed the parable in Hebrew or Aramaic, his mother tongue.

Aramaic is possible because it would have allowed those people assembled in the Temple precincts who knew no Hebrew or could only read it, to understand the parable immediately. Yet the religious and secular leaders (cf. Mark 11:28) knew Hebrew very well, the language of

---

Christological Exegesis of the Old Testament in the Gospel of Mark (Louisville, KY: Westminster / John Knox, 1992) 112, who argues for a very short original parable (112-114).

[124] Cf. for example Hengel, "Das Gleichnis" 6.

[125] Cf. the still helpful list in Hengel, "Das Gleichnis" 7-8, n. 31, who refers repeatedly to the works of J. Jeremias and M. Black. Before him, W. Kümmel had noted a number of Semitisms in the pericope in "Das Gleichnis von den bösen Weingärtnern (Mark 12.1-9)" in *Aux sources de la tradition chrétienne*. Melanges offerts à M. Maurice Goguel (Neuchatel: Delachaux & Niestlé, 1950) 125, n. 20.

prayer, the academies and the Jerusalem Sages, who taught the people in the Temple area at the pilgrimage festivals such as Passover. If Jesus related the narrative in Hebrew, they would have easily understood it immediately also in this language as directed against them (12:12). D. Flusser has pointed out in a major study of the rabbinic parables that even if a rabbi was speaking Aramaic, he switched to Hebrew if he told a parable.[126] This is one argument for Jesus' relating the narrative of the Wicked Tenants originally in this language. Perhaps it was then translated immediately into Aramaic for those who did not understand spoken Hebrew. This phenomenon is known for the later rabbis.[127]

Whether in Hebrew or Aramaic, Jesus' parable was definitely delivered in one of these languages. This argues decisively against its being later composed in a Hellenistic Jewish Christian community.[128]

VIII. The Historicity.

The main argument against Jesus' telling the parable of the Wicked Tenants in Mark 12:1-9 is that the "beloved son" of v 6 recalls God's words to Jesus at the Baptism (1:11) and the Transfiguration (9:7). This leads many scholars to believe the narrative was composed in a Palestinian Jewish Christian community after Jesus, God's beloved Son, was crucified. The latter was alluded to by the wicked tenants' killing him. The vineyard would then be handed over to "others," either the disciples / apostles as Jesus' successors, or the "new" Israel, composed in turn of the Jewish Christian, or of a mixed Jewish and Gentile Christian community.

In spite of Jesus' very close relationship to the heavenly Father, he nowhere openly maintained that he was God's "son." Yet according to the proposal I have made above, based on Palestinian Judaic sources, the prophet Isaiah, so "beloved" by his people, was indeed called "My son." Him too the Jerusalem authorities killed according to Judaic tradition because he threatened them with the destruction of the Temple, and because he maintained a very special, "mouth to mouth" relationship with God.

---

[126] Cf. his *Die rabbinischen Gleichnisse und der Gleichniserzähler Jesus*. 1. Teil: Das Wesen der Gleichnisse (Judaica et Christiana 4; Bern: Lang, 1981) 18.

[127] Cf. for example the explanation of this phenomenon of an Aramaic interpreter or "meturgeman" given by H. Freedman on *b. Šabb.* 88a (Soncino 416, n. 12), and by D. Lazarus on *b. Ta'an.* 21a (Soncino 133, n. 10).

[128] Cf. G. Vermes, *The Religion of Jesus the Jew* (London: SCM, 1993) 104-105; Gnilka, *Das Evangelium nach Markus (Mk 8, 27 – 16, 20)* 144 and 148; R. Bultmann, *The History of the Synoptic Tradition* (New York: Harper & Row, 1963) 177; Haenchen, *Der Weg Jesu* 401; and Kümmel, "Das Gleichnis" 131.

Jesus did not mean himself, but Isaiah with the phrase: "he had yet one more (servant), a beloved / favorite son" in 12:6. This removes the main argument against the narrative as an authentic parable of Jesus. To what extent Jesus saw himself behind the figure of Isaiah, in Judaic tradition willing to suffer for, and be despised by, his own people Israel, is another, open question. Further research on Jesus as the (suffering) "servant of the Lord," who also threatened the Jerusalem hierarchy with the destruction of the Temple, should thus from now on include the parable of the Wicked Tenants.

IX. Mark's Understanding of the Parable.

The following six observations are intended to highlight how the Evangelist Mark understood the parable of the Wicked Tenants.

1) Mark very probably took over the parable of the Wicked Tenants from his source for the Passion Narrative, which already had it at this point. In the present context it is addressed to the chief priests, scribes and elders in the Temple (11:27), who question Jesus' authority. Mark makes the reference to these Temple leaders explicit by his own introductory words in 12:1, "And he began to speak to *them* in parables / by way of a parable." If Mark also composed v 12, his "they" also points back to the same leaders.

2) If Mark added 12:5b or even all of v 5, he intentionally intensified the motif of Israel's maltreating the prophets. As I have pointed out above, however, I consider all of v 5 to belong to the original parable. It is probable that Mark himself considered John the Baptist one of these maltreated prophets, who were even killed. This is indicated by the present context with 11:30-32, as well as Mark's great interest in the arrest and death of the prophet (1:14; 6:14-29; 8:28; and 9:13).

3) There are no indications that Mark, in addition to Greek, knew Aramaic or Hebrew. It is improbable that he understood Jesus' reference in 12:6, "the beloved / favorite son," as related to the prophet Isaiah. For the Evangelist, Jesus alluded to himself in a veiled way, as the "beloved son" of God at the Baptism (1:11) and the Transfiguration (9:7) clearly show.

4) In 12:8, the wicked tenants first kill the beloved son and only then cast him out of the vineyard. Further reflection on this motif in the earliest Christian communities, stressing Jesus as the beloved son, led to a reversal of this sequence. The reversal accentuated Jesus' being crucified outside the city of Jerusalem: Matt 21:39 and Luke

20:15.[129] While Mark already knew that Jesus was led out to be crucified (15:20b), his retention of the reading in his source (which may possibly have been oral) shows that he resisted the temptation to alter his source for theological reasons.

5)   For Mark, the wicked tenants who kill Jesus, the beloved son, are definitely the chief priests, elders and scribes of Jerusalem. Seeking to destroy Jesus, they hold a hearing regarding him and deliver him to Pilate to have him killed (11:18; 11:27 and 12:12; 14:53; 15:1,3; as well as the Passion predictions in 8:31; 9:31; and 10:33). The Evangelist also considers them to be the "builders" of 12:10, who reject Jesus, who became the head or corner stone of Ps 118:22-23. For Mark, this looks forward to Jesus' resurrection in 16:6.

6)   Finally, there are no signs that Mark understood the vineyard of the parable to be the Jerusalem Temple. He probably thought it signified God's election of, and covenant with, His people Israel. These were now superseded by a "new" covenant inaugurated by Jesus.[130] The "others," to whom the vineyard is to be given in 12:9, are consciously not spelled out by Mark. This is in contrast to Matt 21:41 and 43, which clearly allude to the kingdom of God as passing from the unbelieving Jews to Jewish and Gentile Christians.

Yet Mark himself probably thought primarily of the present leaders of the Christian churches, and of Gentile Christians as the "others," especially if he wrote his Gospel directly after the destruction of the Temple and Jerusalem in 70 C.E. by the Romans. Indications of this view are found in the narrative of the Syrophoenician woman (7:26-30), the phrase "a house of prayer for all the nations" (11:17), the thought that the gospel must first be preached to all the "nations" before the end will come (13:10), and above all the (Gentile, Roman) centurion at the Cross, who now believes in Jesus as the Son of God (15:39).

*   *   *

These six observations help to indicate how the Evangelist Mark himself understood the parable of the Wicked Tenants within the context of his Gospel. In retrospect, we must be grateful to him for making almost no changes in the account transmitted to him by his Passion Narrative source.

---

[129] Cf. Heb 13:12-13 and John 19:17, 20.

[130] Cf. Mark 14:24, where, however, only several textual witnesses have "new."

X. Concluding Remarks.

The members of the priestly aristocracy in Jerusalem were often large landowners, wealthy and almost exclusively Sadducees, known for their harsh judgments, and they were well represented in the Sanhedrin.[131] They would have combined Jesus' prophetic "cleansing" of the Temple,[132] his threat that if no repentance on their part came about God would destroy the Temple (the divine passive in Mark 13:2), and especially this parable as a devastating critique of their administration of the Temple, God's vineyard, and of them as the spiritual heirs of those who killed and continue to kill the prophets. They did not, for example, resist John the Baptist's being killed.[133] As his successor and with

---

[131] Cf. Schürer, *The history of the Jewish people in the age of Jesus Christ* 2.210-218, as well as the references I cite in *Barabbas and Esther* 26, to which should be added *t. Menaḥ.* 13:22 (Neusner 5.162, where the high priests "love money") and *Sifre* Deut. Ki Teṣe § 352 on Deut 33:11 (Hammer 364): "the Sages have said: Most priests are wealthy." See also *T. Levi* 14:2 – 15:1 (*OTP* 1.793), where the impieties of the chief priests are mentioned, including their "plundering the Lord's offerings," their "greed for gain," sexual immorality and inflated pride. These will lead to the Sanctuary's becoming "desolate," a threat similar in tone to Mark 12:9. H. Kee considers the Testaments of the Twelve Patriarchs to have originated in Syria in the Maccabean period (second century B.C.E.); see 1.778. B. Young, *Jesus and His Jewish Parables* (New York: Paulist Press, 1989) 290, calls attention to this and other texts. He also cites D. Flusser's assessment of the parable as directed against the "corrupt leadership" of the chief priests in his *Yahadut Umekorot Hanatzrut* (Tel Aviv: Sifriyat Poalim, 1979) 426-427. Finally, it may be noted that if someone made high priest was only of modest means, the "treasurers and administrators" of the Temple made him wealthy to fulfill Lev 21:10, which speaks of the priest who is "greater than his brethren" (also in wealth). See *t. Yoma* 1:6 (Zuckermandel / Liebermann 180; Neusner 2.186); *b. Yoma* 18a (Soncino 77, where his fellow priests endow him, showing their wealth); and *Sifra* on Lev 21:10 (Neusner 3.173). See also my n. 60 on p. 13 above.

[132] I intentionally omit the "triumphal entry into Jerusalem" of Mark 11:1-10 par. because I am undecided about its historical core. For the plausibility of its hardly being noticed because of Pilate's entry into Jerusalem directly before, cf. B. Kinman, "Jesus' 'Triumphal Entry' in the Light of Pilate's" in *NTS* 40 (1994) 442-448.

[133] When Herod Antipas had John killed (Mark 6:16), no critique of this came from Jerusalem. The moral complicity involved may indeed have infuriated Jesus. On John's being beheaded, cf. my essay in *Water into Wine and the Beheading of John the Baptist* (BJS 150; Atlanta: Scholars, 1988) 39-74. Representatives of the Sanhedrin may also already have been sent to Galilee to investigate reports concerning Jesus; see Mark 7:1. The role played in this by the "Herodians" unfortunately remains unclear (3:6; cf. 12:13). D. Stern in "Jesus' Parables from the Perspective of Rabbinic Literature: The Example of the Wicked Husbandmen," in *Parable and Story* 65, maintains Jesus implicitly accuses the Jewish leaders of killing John the Baptist. The same view is taken by M. Lowe in "From the Parable of the Vineyard to a Pre-Synoptic Source" in *NTS* 28 (1982)

language just as strong as his (cf. Matt 3:7 par.), Jesus threatened them with their own "destruction," including their being replaced by "others." This they perceived as blasphemy, directed against the national site of atonement, thought to be situated directly opposite God's heavenly throne, and against the worship services ordained by the heavenly Father, as they interpreted Holy Scripture. In addition, they allowed no challenge to their own power and prestige, or to their own positions in the "business" of the Temple. Dependent financially on the regular offerings and those made at the annual festivals, such as the current Passover celebration, and fearful of any disturbance leading to Rome's further intervention in their own affairs, they would have welcomed an opportunity to become rid of a provincial prophet who apparently presumptuously considered himself somehow to be God's final, definitive messenger to His people.[134] This particularly disturbed them precisely at the time of the Passover festival, when Israel's redemption took place in the past and, according to current belief, would take place again. For these reasons they demanded Jesus' death by the only one capable of pronouncing such a sentence, the Roman Pontius Pilate.

The parable of the Wicked Tenants thus played a much greater role in the arrest, "trial" and execution of Jesus than has been perceived up to now. The prophet from Nazareth's course of collision with the combined spiritual and secular leadership of his people ended in Jerusalem with his martyrdom, as did that of God's beloved son Isaiah in Judaic tradition.

257-263. Yet, as shown above, the beloved or favorite son is rather the prophet Isaiah, called "My son" in Judaic tradition.

[134] I basically repeat this from *Barabbas and Esther* 26. Yet Jesus did not characterize himself as the final servant / prophet in his parable, the "son" of Mark 12:6. That was Isaiah. On the *possibility* that Jesus considered himself to follow in the footsteps of Isaiah, see p. 55 above.

Chapter Two

Jesus in Gethsemane (Mark 14:32-42 par.): Psalm 116, Moses' Struggle with Death at the Very End of His Life, and The High Priest and the Day of Atonement

Introduction

The Gethsemane narrative in Mark 14:32-42, with Jesus praying three times that the hour (of his impending death) pass from him, the cup (of death) be removed from him, is one of the most moving in the Bible. Here, as a great exception, Jesus' deep emotions are openly described. He is not only greatly distressed and troubled, but also very sorrowful, even to death. This has made the account so attractive throughout the centuries, primarily for Christians trying to understand the great mystery of Jesus' death the next afternoon at Golgotha. God's apparent silence at this point, when Jesus could easily have avoided arrest and crucifixion by fleeing under the cover of night, has been difficult for many believers to comprehend. Jesus' own final subjection in prayer to the will of the heavenly Father, however, has also helped them to place their own confidence in God, especially in times of affliction.

V. Taylor speaks of Gethsemane as an "astounding narrative," and as "one of the most vivid in the Passion Narrative."[1] C. Mann thinks it is "the most dramatically articulated part" of the latter.[2] R. Feldmeier, the author of the most recent monograph on the pericope, notes its "terrific

---

[1] Cf. *The Gospel According to St Mark* 551.

[2] Cf. his *Mark* (AB 27; New York: Doubleday, 1986) 587.

tension."[3] These qualities have also recommended the scene to artists throughout the centuries. The present "Garden of Gethsemane," with its centuries-old, gnarled olive trees at the western base of the Mount of Olives, is also a must on the route of any Christian tour group visiting Jerusalem.[4]

In spite of countless studies of the Gethsemane narrative,[5] the account remains enigmatic in many respects. Much of the vocabulary occurs only here in Mark or in all the gospels. Apparent doublets have also led scholars to assume two (or more) possible sources to the narrative. Above all, the most difficult expression, ἀπέχει in 14:41, has up until now found no satisfactory solution.[6] In the following I propose solutions to most of the major difficulties sensed in the Markan Gethsemane account, including that of the term ἀπέχει. As a sidelight, I also comment on several aspects of the parallel narratives.

R. Feldmeier maintains that the Gethsemane scene is to be understood exclusively in light of the OT and Palestinian Judaism.[7] J. Gnilka says that its home is the Palestinian Jewish Christian community,[8] and J. Holleran speaks of the "Semitic and Palestinian character of much of the account...."[9] In light of my own analyses below, I can only agree with these opinions. The original narrator was an Aramaic- or Hebrew-speaking Palestinian Jewish Christian. This is shown primarily by his acquaintance with, and employment of, Judaic lore found almost exclusively in Hebrew or Aramaic on Psalm 116; the struggle of Israel's

---

[3] *Die Krisis des Gottessohnes.* Die Gethsemaneerzählung als Schlüssel der Markus-passion (WUNT 2.21; Tübingen: Mohr, 1987) 1.

[4] For a description of the site, including the "Rock of Agony" in the Church of All Nations, cf. Z. Vilnay, *Israel Guide* (Jerusalem: Daf-Chen, 1980[21]) 155-157.

[5] I count 114 entries in the bibliography of R. Brown, *The Death of the Messiah. From Gethsemane to the Grave* (New York: Doubleday, 1994) 111-115. Brown deals with the narrative on pp. 146-234, very ably summarizing the relevant secondary literature. For this reason I feel justified here in making primarily my own emphases concerning the account, referring the reader to Brown's exhaustive discussions for other possible viewpoints. See also the bibliography in Feldmeier, *Die Krisis* 260-271; in the monograph by J. Holleran, *The Synoptic Gethsemane. A Critical Study* (Analecta Gregoriana 191; Rome: Gregorian University, 1973) XI-XXXII; and in the recent commentary by R. Gundry, *Mark*, 863-877.

[6] Cf. the extensive special discussion in Brown, *The Death* 1379-1383.

[7] *Die Krisis* 4.

[8] *Das Evangelium nach Markus (Mk 8, 27 – 16, 20)* 258.

[9] *The Synoptic Gethsemane* 129. This view should be contrasted with that of R. Bultmann, *The History of the Synoptic Tradition* 306: "it could well have originated in an Hellenistic Christianity of a Pauline sort."

first redeemer, Moses, with the Angel of Death at the very end of his life; and the ritual involving the high priest in Jerusalem on the Day of Atonement (beginning the evening before). There is hardly a motif or expression in Mark 14:32-42 which does not derive from these Judaic materials. Except for very minor references, no one has pointed this out before.[10]

Since many of the sources I employ are not easily accessible, I cite them extensively for the convenience of the reader. Often I employ my own translation, which can be easily compared with those of the Soncino editions, J. Neusner, W. Braude, or others, when they are available.

Part I deals with the influence of Psalm 116 on the Gethsemane narrative, including fourteen comparisons between Jesus' struggle with death, and Moses' struggle with death. Part II concerns the relevance to Gethsemane of imagery and expressions regarding the high priest and the Day of Atonement. Before this I cite nine examples of high priest imagery elsewhere in the Passion Narrative in order to undergird my argument. Part III deals with the original language, Part IV with the extent, and Part V with the historicity and purpose of the original narrative. Two appendices are included, the first on Paul's calling and re-commissioning in 2 Cor 12:1-10 and Moses' calling and death scene, and the second on the contrast of God's taking away Moses' soul through a kiss, and Judas' handing Jesus over to certain death through a kiss in Mark 14:44-45 par.

The main object of my study is to recover as much as possible of the original narrator's oral account, and what it meant to the first Palestinian Jewish Christians who heard it. I gladly leave it to others to point out, for example, what rhetorical, reader response, structuralist, and feministic biblical criticism have to say about the narrative. It is my modest hope

---

[10] Cf. for example E. Lohmeyer, *Das Evangelium des Markus* (Meyer 1.2; Göttingen: Vandenhoeck & Ruprecht, 1963[16]) 315 on the high priest walking alone up the steps to the Holy of Holies, those accompanying him remaining before the curtain. Yet Lohmeyer cites this only after other examples of Abraham and Moses, names no sources, and does not pursue the tradition at all. After I finished this study, C. Wolff kindly called my attention to the short article by T. Pola, "Die Gethsemane-Perikope Markus 14, 32-42 im Lichte des Mischna-traktates Joma (m Yom I 4.6f)" in *TBei* 25 (1994) 37-44. He also notes the motif of "waking" in regard to the high priest in the night of the Day of Atonement, including Matthew's addition of "with me" in 26:38 and 40. He wrongly derives this in part, however, from the danger during the night of Passover outside the city of Jerusalem (40 and 43). The "Garden" of Gethsemane lay east of the Kidron Brook at the base of the Mount of Olives and was certainly included within the city limits of Jerusalem, extended at the pilgrimage festivals to include, for example, Bethphage on the Mount of Olives. See Str-B 1.839-840, as well as J. Jeremias, *Jerusalem in the Time of Jesus* 61.

that by helping to illuminate the Palestinian, Judaic background of the pericope, its later meaning(s) can also be better understood.

I
PSALM 116

1. The Use of the Psalter from Mark 11:1 to 15:41 par.

It has justifiably been maintained that the Psalter was the prayer book of early Jews. Since all the first Christians were also Jews, it is understandable that they continued this tradition and interpreted the final events in the life of Jesus in light of scriptural passages well-known to them. Specific Bible passages, when later considered in regard to the time after Jesus' entry into Jerusalem, now seemed to receive a new sense, even to be "fulfilled."[1] This was also an important means of gaining new members for the Christian church. If others could be convinced that Israel's Scriptures were fulfilled in Jesus of Nazareth, they would more easily become converts to the new fellowship of faith.

The Psalms, so popular among Palestinian Jews, indeed provided a major portion of the scriptural texts either quoted or alluded to in the Synoptic Gospels within the short period between Jesus' entry into the city of Jerusalem (as of Mark 11:1 par.) and his Crucifixion (15:41 par.). The following table provides an overview of the relevant psalms.

Mark	11:9-10 par.	Ps	118:25-26
Matt	21:16		8:2
Mark	12:10-11 par.		118:22-23
Mark	12:36 par.		110:1
Matt	23:39 // Luke 13:35		118:26
Luke	21:25		65:7 (allusion)
Mark	14:18		41:9 (allusion)
Mark	15:23 par.		69:21 (allusion)
Mark	15:24 par.		22:18 (allusion)[2]
Mark	15:29 par.		22:7
Matt	27:43		22:8
Mark	15:34 // Matt 27:46		22:1
Luke	23:46		31:5
Mark	15:36 // Matt 27:48		29:21
Luke	23:49		38:11 (allusion)

---

[1] Cf. Mark 14:49 par.; Matt 27:9; John 17:12; 19:24, 36; and 12:16.

[2] For an analysis of the use of Psalm 22 at the Crucifixion, cf. my volume *Barabbas and Esther and Other Studies* 11-14.

Passages similar to these may be added from the Fourth Gospel:

John	13:18	Ps	41:9
	15:25		35:19 and 69:4
	19:24		22:18
	19:28		69:21

The above table, including two independent borrowings from Psalm 118, makes it very understandable that the author of the Gethsemane narrative, Mark 14:32-42 par., may have also employed specific expressions and motifs from another psalm, 116. With it he described Jesus' great struggle as to whether or not to accept his upcoming fate as God's will for him.

Over forty years ago, A. Strobel pointed out how Heb 5:7-10, long before considered a parallel to the Gethsemane account, was dependent on Psalm 116 (LXX 114-115).[3] More recently M. Kiley in a five-page article has called attention to four motif parallels he sees from Psalm 116 in the Gethsemane narrative.[4] Unfortunately, he does not take any account whatsoever of Judaic interpretation of the psalm, which provides a major basis for my own analysis, which now follows.

2. Psalm 116 as Part of the Hallel Sung at the "Lord's Supper"

Psalms 113-118 were called the Hallel or Egyptian Hallel because they recalled the deliverance from slavery in Egypt.[5] R. Simeon b. Yehoṣadaq, a first generation Palestinian Amora,[6] noted that a Palestinian Jew completed the Hallel on eighteen days during the year, including the first day of Passover (the 15th of Nisan).[7] On the afternoon

---

[3] Cf. his "Die Psalmengrundlage der Gethsemane-Parallele Hbr 5, 7 ff." in *ZNW* 45 (1954) 252-266. He maintains that Psalm 116 "forderte das Erfüllungsdenken der Urgemeinde wie kein anderer heraus," and he points to the need for a study of the relevance of this psalm to the Synoptic Gethsemane scene (p. 265).

[4] See his "'Lord, Save My Life' (Ps 116:4) as Generative Text for Jesus' Gethsemane Prayer (Mark 14:36a)" in *CBQ* 48 (1986) 655-659.

[5] Cf. the art. "Hallel" by the editors of *EJ* (1971) 7.1196-1199. The "Great Hallel" was Psalm 136.

[6] Cf. Strack and Stemberger, *Introduction* 92.

[7] Cf. *b. Ta'an.* 28b (Soncino 150-151). The diaspora required this also on the second day of Passover. Parallels are found in *b.'Arak.* 10a-b (Soncino 56-57), and *Soferim* 20:9, 43a (Soncino, *The Minor Tractates* 314).

of the 14th of Nisan, the Levites also sang the Hallel while individuals slaughtered their Passover lambs in the Jerusalem Temple.[8]

Mark 14:12-25 par., just before the Gethsemane narrative, definitely portrays Jesus' last meal with his twelve disciples in Jerusalem as a Passover meal.[9] The lamb they shared will have been slaughtered by one of them in the late afternoon in the Temple (vv 12 and 16) on the 14th; when evening came, the beginning of the 15th, all ate it together (vv 17-18). Like all other participants in this festival meal, they will also have recited / sung the Hallel.[10] *Cant. Rab.* 2:14 ("Let me hear your voice") § 7 says "this refers to the melodious reciting of *Hallel*. When Israel recite *Hallel*, their voice ascends on high; and so the proverb says, 'The Passover in the house and the *Hallel* break the roof.'"[11]

Mark 14:26 then states: "And when they had 'sung a (NRSV the) hymn' (ὑμνήσαντες), they went out to the Mount of Olives," i.e. to Gethsemane (v 32).[12] This could refer to the benediction spoken at the end of the Hallel, called the "Benediction over Song" (בִּרְכַּת הַשִּׁיר).[13] Yet it more probably simply indicates the (completion of the) Hallel, described in one rabbinic source as a "'hymn' of praise" (הִימְנוֹן וְשֶׁבַח).[14]

---

[8] Cf. *m. Pesaḥ.* 5:7 (Albeck 2.158-159, Danby 142), which remarks that the Hallel was never completed a third time on this occasion.

[9] For compelling arguments for this as a Passover meal, cf. J. Jeremias, *The Eucharistic Words of Jesus,* available to me as *Die Abendmahlsworte Jesu* (Göttingen: Vandenhoeck & Ruprecht, 1967⁴) 9-82.

[10] The Mishnah at *Pesaḥ.* 10:6-7 (Albeck 2.178-179, Danby 151) describes when the various sections of the Hallel are recited / sung during the Seder meal.

[11] Soncino 9.133. Cf. the statement by R. Ḥiyya in *b. Pesaḥ.* 85b, "There was (only) as much as an olive of the Passover-offering (to eat), yet the Hallel split the roofs!" (Soncino 451, with n. 11: "It was sung with such gusto.") See also *y. Pesaḥ.* 7:12, 35b (Neusner / Bokser 13.377).

[12] Cf. John 18:1, "When Jesus had spoken these words (chapters 13-17), he went forth across the Kidron Valley, where there was a garden...."

[13] Cf. *m. Pesaḥ.* 10:7 (Albeck 2.179, Danby 151). See also the variant "with a new song" in R. Aqiva's version of the Benediction of Redemption spoken after reciting / singing the first part of the Hallel (10:6 in Danby 151, with n. 8). On the "song" of Isa 30:29 as interpreted of the Hallel, see *y. Pesaḥ.* 9:3, 36d (Neusner / Schiffman 13.448) and *b. Pesaḥ.* 95b (Soncino 510).

[14] Cf. *Pesiq. R.* 2/1 (Friedmann 5a, Braude 1.51). *Cant. Rab.* 4:4 § 6 (Soncino 9.193) speaks of the various "hymns" (psalms) the Levites chanted in the Jerusalem Temple on the seven days of the week. This example shows that the Hallel psalms could also be labeled a "hymn" (of praise). See also the parable regarding the redemption from Egypt in *Tanḥ.* B Beshallaḥ 13 on Exod 15:1. Only when the Israelites are safe on the other shore of the Red Sea will God allow the ministering angels to praise Him by singing a "hymn" (אימנון) to Him (Buber 30b or p. 60; German in Bietenhard 1.353). On this, see also the ὕμνησαν of Wisd 10:20.

The author of the Gethsemane account knew of the connection within the earliest Passion Narrative(s) of the Hallel recited / sung at Jesus' final Passover meal with the twelve, and his being arrested very shortly thereafter in Gethsemane on the Mount of Olives (Mark 14:43-50). Himself a Palestinian Jewish Christian, who like many others probably knew the entire Hallel by heart through repeated usage from childhood on, he logically applied motifs and terms from one of these psalms, 116, to flesh out his own portrayal of how Jesus already in advance wrestled in Gethsemane with his fate, or cup out of which he was to drink, the next afternoon at Golgotha.[15]

3. Expressions and Motifs from Psalm 116 in the Gethsemane Narrative

A) *The Prayer Setting.*

a) In Mark 14:32 Jesus reaches Gethsemane with the (eleven) disciples and tells them to sit there while he "prays" (προσεύχομαι). After taking Peter, James and John with him, he tells them to remain where they are while he goes off a little further, falls on the ground and "prays" (v 35). The content of this prayer is related in v 36. Jesus then returns to the three disciples, but goes off again and "prays" a second time with the same words (v 39). After returning to them again, he (prays a third time and)[16] returns to the disciples (v 41). He then announces the arrival of Judas to betray him.

Jesus is thus presented in this scene as asking God to remove the cup (of death at Golgotha the next afternoon) from him, in a prayer setting.

b) After a description of the author's acute distress in Ps 116:3, v 4 states: "Then I called on the name of the Lord: 'O Lord, I pray, save my

---

Numerous other occurrences of the Greek ὕμνος in Hebrew are cited by Krauss in *Lehnwörter* 2.227.

[15] The application of verses from the final Hallel psalm, 118, to Jesus at his entry into Jerusalem (Mark 11:9-10 par.), to the end of the parable of the Wicked Tenants (Mark 12:10-11 par.), and to the end of the woes to the scribes and Pharisees (Matt 23:39 // Luke 13:35), was most probably also partly due to this psalm's employment during the upcoming Passover festival. On the author's "filling in a gap," see section IV below. According to *b. Pesaḥ.* 117a (Soncino 599), the Hallel was to be recited in a time of distress. This fitted the Gethsemane situation very well.

[16] Recognizing Mark's somewhat rough style at this point, Matthew improved it for his readers by correctly adding: "he went away and prayed" for the third time (26:44).

life (lit. soul)'" (NRSV). The RSV has "I beseech Thee" for "I pray," a translation of the Hebrew אָנָּא.[17]

The NRSV translation of "I pray" is appropriate here since the author of the psalm is indeed uttering a prayer for deliverance from his negative fate. This is undergirded by the Targum, which reads: "And in the name of the Lord I call out בבעו: 'O Lord, save my soul.'"[18] The noun בָּעו means "prayer."[19] The phrase בבעו is literally "in prayer."[20] The Targum can thus also be interpreted as: "And in the name of the Lord I call out in prayer: 'O Lord, save my soul.'"

I suggest that this verse, as interpreted by the Targum,[21] and especially in connection with vv 3 and 13 (see below), was one important reason for the "prayer" setting for a Palestinian Jewish Christian's portrayal of Jesus' calling on the Lord "in prayer" in Gethsemane.[22] In some rabbinic sources David is represented as speaking Ps 116:4.[23] This may also have facilitated its being spoken in Gethsemane by the "Son of

---

[17] Cf. BDB 58: a strong particle of entreaty.

[18] Cf. the text in Merino, *Targum de Salmos* 90. With only very slight variations it is also found in de Lagarde, *Hagiographa Chaldaice* 69. I thank Dr. Niko Oswald for translating and discussing this targumic passage with me.

[19] Jastrow, *A Dictionary* 180.

[20] Cf. *ibid.* for "I pray."

[21] I do not propose, of course, an early date for the *present* form of the Psalms Targum. The fact that Psalms 113-118 were recited liturgically and by individuals so often during the year makes it probable, however, that these specific chapters received an Aramaic translation at a rather early date. On the problem of dating definite traditions within the targums, see the art. "Targums" by M. McNamara in *IDB Sup* 856-861. Haggadic interpretation of the Psalms must have taken place at a very early time. Cf. the statement in *y. Keth.* 12:3, 35a (Neusner 22. 348) that R. Ḥiyya the Elder, a fifth generation Tanna (Strack and Stemberger, *Introduction* 90), "was reviewing the aggadic traditions of the whole book of Psalms" in a bathhouse.

[22] To this extent M. Kiley (cf. n. 4) is partly correct when he describes Ps 116:4 as the "generative text" for Jesus' prayer in Gethsemane. In *'Avot R. Nat.* A 41 (Schechter 133, Goldin 173) R. Yose (b. Ḥalafta), a third generation Tanna (Strack and Stemberger, *Introduction* 84), interprets this psalm verse in regard to those who at the Final Judgment will be put through a purgatory in Gehenna. See also *b. Pesaḥ.* 118a (Soncino 608), where R. Naḥman b. Isaac, a fourth generation Babylonian Amora (*Introduction* 105), says (Hallel is recited) because it alludes to the righteous' being delivered from Gehenna, referred to in Ps 116:4. The "pangs of Sheol" in the preceding verse (3) probably influenced this idea.

[23] Cf. *Mek. R. Ish.* Baḥodesh 10 on Exod 20:20 (Lauterbach 2.277); *Tanḥ.* Jethro on Exod 20:2 (Eshkol 1.323); *Sifre* Deut. Wa'ethanan 32 on Deut 6:5 (Finkelstein 55, Hammer 60); as well as *Eliyyahu Rabbah* 20 (Friedmann 113, Braude and Kapstein 287, with n. 13); and (29) 27 (Friedmann 144, Braude and Kapstein 355).

David," Jesus.[24] Yet the main impetus for the prayer setting of Gethsemane probably derived from Judaic traditions on Moses' struggle with the Angel of Death, sent to him by God at the very end of his life. To this I now turn.

B) *Jesus' Struggle with Death, and Moses' Struggle with Death.*

In Judaic tradition Moses is considered the first redeemer of Israel because of his delivering the Israelites out of slavery in Egypt. The final or great redeemer of Israel will be the Messiah.[25] For this reason Palestinian Jewish Christians compared the birth of Jesus with Judaic lore regarding that of Moses.[26] The same was true for the impending death of Jesus. The Gethsemane scene was modeled to a great extent upon Judaic traditions regarding Moses' imminent death.[27] The following fourteen similarities in the setting, terminology and motifs speak very strongly in favor of this proposal.

1) THE SETTING.

a) After arriving at Gethsemane on the Mount of Olives with his (eleven) disciples, Jesus tells them to sit there while he prays. Then he takes with him Peter and the two sons of Zebedee, James and John. Going off a little further from them, he falls on the ground and prays by himself. Returning, Jesus finds the three sleeping. This sequence is then repeated two more times.

The basic pattern of going off to a mountain first with a larger group, then having an inner circle of three, and finally being alone, derives from Judaic haggadic tradition regarding Moses' impending death.

---

[24] Cf. Mark 10:47-48; 12:35, 37; as well as the implication of 11:10.

[25] Cf. the passages cited in Str-B 1.67-70.

[26] Cf. my study "Die Weihnachtsgeschichte im Lichte jüdischer Traditionen vom Mose-Kind und Hirten-Messias (Lukas 2, 1-20)" in *Weihnachtsgeschichte, Barmherziger Samariter, Verlorener Sohn* (ANTZ 2; Berlin: Institut Kirche und Judentum, 1988) 14-44, with many cross-references to the Matthean birth story.

[27] In *Legends* 3.417-473 and the respective notes, L. Ginzberg has an almost encyclopedic listing of Judaic sources dealing with Moses' impending death. The length of this material in *Legends* shows how much attention was attributed to it. See also K. Haacker and P. Schäfer, "Nachbiblische Traditionen vom Tod des Mose" in *Josephus-Studien*. Festschrift Otto Michel (Göttingen: Vandenhoeck & Ruprecht, 1974) 147-174, as well as E. Urbach, *The Sages* (Cambridge, MASS: Harvard University, 1987) 172-175.

b) Deuteronomy 34 has Moses ascend Mount Nebo, to the top of Pisgah, where he dies.[28] Josephus, a native of Jerusalem whose mother tongue was Aramaic, and who finished his *Antiquities* in 93-94 C.E.,[29] shows an acquaintance with Judaic expansion of this scene. In *Ant.* 4.320-331 he relates that all first follow Moses. Then only the elders (ἡ γερουσία) escort him, along with Eleazar and Joshua. When Moses arrives at Mt Abarim,[30] he dismisses the elders. Then he bids farewell to Eleazar and Joshua,[31] and disappears before them in a ravine.

The "elders" here are the representatives of the twelve tribes of Israel,[32] similar to the full number of Jesus' disciples. They accompany Moses to the mountain, where he dismisses them and proceeds with his own inner circle. The basic pattern recalls that in the Gethsemane narrative.

In Judaic haggada, Joshua is Moses' main "disciple" (תַּלְמִיד),[33] who after Moses' death assumes the leadership of the Israelites. The early Palestinian Jewish Christian describing Jesus' struggle with death in Gethsemane certainly thought here of Peter, Jesus' main disciple (μαθητής), who assumed the leadership of Jesus' adherents in Jerusalem some time after his death.[34] Therefore he had Peter accompany Jesus somewhat further when he prayed.

---

[28] Cf. also 32:48-52. It should be noted that Deuteronomy 34 was read in the Palestinian triennial lectionary system in the third year at the beginning of Adar, and that Moses is thought to have died on the 7th of Adar. See the art. "Triennial Cycle" in *EJ* (1971) 15.1389.

[29] Cf. *Vita* 7, *Ant.* 20.263, and 267 with note "c" in the LCL edition.

[30] Cf. Deut 32:49, where Mount Nebo is a mountain of the Abarim.

[31] A variant of this tradition may be found in the Greek fragments of the *Assumption of Moses*, where Joshua and Caleb are mentioned. Cf. R. H. Charles in *APOT* 408, bottom.

[32] Cf. Deut 31:28 ("the elders of your tribes"), and the blessing of the twelve tribes in chapter 33, after which Moses ascends Mount Nebo.

[33] Cf. for example *Tanḥ.* B. Wa'etḥanan 6 on Deut 3:23 (Bietenhard 2.454), where God tells Moses: "Now your task is finished, and the hour of Joshua, 'your disciple,' has come for him to serve Me." Bietenhard bases his translation on Codex Vaticanus Ebr. 34, which at this point varies slightly from the MS Oxford Opp. 20 employed by Buber, in Deuteronomy 12 ("your disciple" is the same, however). See also *Sifre* Num. Pinḥas 135 on Deut 3:26 (Horowitz 182, Kuhn 554), where Moses tells God he is even willing to enter the Land of Israel by becoming a "disciple" of Joshua. God replies: רב לך, "A teacher / master for you? A teacher cannot become the disciple of his disciple!" Philo in *Virt.* 66 also speaks of Joshua as Moses' "disciple" (φοιτητής) in this context.

[34] This begins already in Acts 1:13, where Peter, John and James are mentioned first among the eleven. It is probable that Peter, after fleeing to Galilee and

Josephus mentions only one other person, Eleazar (the son of Moses' brother Aaron). Since he and Joshua later distributed the land of Israel to the tribes,[35] his brother Ithamar was not as popular as he was in Judaic lore.[36] Yet the behavior of Joshua, Eleazar and Ithamar is described as being influential in finally making Moses resign himself to death.[37]

I suggest that the early Palestinian Jewish Christian author of the Gethsemane narrative mentioned not only Peter, but also the brothers James and John, because of his knowledge of the brothers Eleazar and Ithamar as present just before Moses' death. He intentionally chose Peter and the two brothers to make his original listeners aware of the similarities between the struggle with death on the part of the final redeemer of Israel, Jesus the Messiah, and that of Israel's first redeemer, Moses. This means, however, that the triad of Peter, James and John was not – as often maintained – appropriated by the Evangelist Mark from the scene of the transfiguration in 9:2. Rather, he took it over from his source.

2) INTENSE PRAYER BEFORE ONE'S IMMINENT DEATH.

a) In Gethsemane Jesus announces that he will pray ($\pi\rho\sigma\epsilon\acute{u}\chi\omicron\mu\alpha\iota$, in Mark 14:32); then he does so three times (vv 35, 39, 41 – assumed).[38] The prayer itself is related in vv 35-36. This intensity of Jesus' repeated praying also derives from Moses' doing so at the very end of his life.

---

receiving a vision of the resurrected Jesus (1 Cor 15:5; Mark 16:7; John 21), then returned to Jerusalem (Gal 1:18; Luke 22:32).

[35] Cf. Josh 14:1; 17:4; and 19:51.

[36] For the predominance of Eleazar's descendants over those of Ithamar, cf. 1 Chron 24:4, quoted in b. Ta'an. 27a (Soncino 143-144). For Moses, Eleazar and Joshua on Mount Nebo, see 1Q Words of Moses (1Q22 [1Q DM]), col. I, translated by F. Martínez in The Dead Sea Scrolls Translated 276. See also Num 27:12, 18-23.

[37] Cf. Tanḥ. B Wa'etḥanan 6 on Deut 3:23 (Buber 13, with "Eleazar and Ithamar"; Bietenhard 2.454, following Codex Vaticanus Ebr. 34, has "the sons of Aaron"); Tanḥ. Wa'etḥanan 6 (Eshkol 858); and Midr. Prov. 14 (Buber 77, Visotzky 74). Leviticus 10 deals with the death of Aaron's other two sons, Nadab and Abihu, leaving only Eleazar and Ithamar. Mek. R. Ish. Amalek 2 on Exod 17:14 (Lauterbach 2.153), a midrash also on Deut 3:23-27 here, has Moses ask Eleazar to pray for mercy on his behalf, i.e. that he not have to die. This Tannaitic tradition presupposes his presence at this point, an early attestation of the basic topos here. 4Q Psalms of Joshua[b] (4Q 379), fragment 17 (Martínez 283), interestingly lists: "Moses...Eleazar and Ithamar." The name Joshua probably originally stood in the blank space.

[38] Jesus' exhortation, that the disciples pray, is mentioned in v 38.

b) The following three examples show how strenuous and prolonged Moses' prayer was just before he died.

1. *Pseudo-Philo,* probably written in Hebrew in Palestine about the time of Jesus,[39] relates in 19:8 that "Moses ascended Mount Abarim as God commanded him, and 'he prayed,' saying, 'Behold, I have completed my lifetime....'"[40] Moses' praying is an haggadic addition, not found at Deut 32:49, 34:1, or Num 27:12.

2. Moses had been told by God that he may not go over the Jordan and see the good land beyond it before he dies (Deut 3:25-26; 31:2). Judaic tradition relates that he struggled greatly with God to obtain permission to go there and remain alive. R. Levi, a third generation Palestinian Amora,[41] comments in *Deut. Rab.* Wa'ethanan 2/7 on Deut 3:27, "You shall not go over this Jordan": "When Moses saw how emphatic (הֵיאָךְ...חֲזָקִים) God's words were, he began to plead strenuously (מְדַבֵּר דְּבָרִים קָשִׁים)."[42]

3. *Deut. Rab.* Vezot ha-Berakha 11/10 on Deut 31:14 ("And the Lord said to Moses, 'Behold, the days approach when you must die'") notes that Moses' "prayer" (תְּפִלָּתוֹ) "was like a sword which tears and cuts its way through everything, and spares nothing...."[43] The great intensity of Moses' prayer for (delivery from death and) permission to enter the Land is also expressed in its quantity. The same midrash maintains that Moses "prayed" (הִתְפַּלֵּל) at this point 515 times, the numerical value of the term *wa'ethanan* in Deut 3:25, "'And I besought' the Lord at that time, saying...."[44]

*   *   *

These three examples of Moses' prayer, strenuous and prolonged, are typical of the Judaic haggada which provided the Palestinian Jewish Christian author of the Gethsemane narrative with a model for portraying Jesus' intense, prolonged prayer that his life be spared.

---

[39] Cf. Harrington's remarks in *OTP* 2.298-300.

[40] *OTP* 2.327. The whole chapter deals with "Moses' farewell, prayer, and death," showing the importance attached by Pseudo-Philo to this topic. The Latin has *oravit* for "he prayed" in *Les Antiquités Bibliques,* ed. Harrington, 1.160.

[41] Strack and Stemberger, *Introduction* 98.

[42] Mirqin 11.33, Soncino 7.36.

[43] Mirqin 11.156, Soncino 7.182.

[44] *Ibid.*

3) JESUS' PROSTRATION IN HIS PRAYER.

a) In Gethsemane Jesus "falls on the ground" (ἔπιπτεν ἐπὶ τῆς γῆς – Mark 14:35), which should also be assumed for the second and third times he prays. This motif also derives from Moses' similar behavior while praying just before his death.

b) The following three examples show Moses' prostration at the point of his imminent death.

1. In *Deut. Rab.* Wa'ethanan 2/1 on Deut 3:23 ("And I besought the Lord"), R. Yohanan, a second generation Palestinian Amora,[45] states that prayer is known by ten different terms. One of them is *nippul*, as in Deut 9:18 and 25, "Then 'I lay prostrate' before the Lord," from the root נפל, to fall.[46]

2. In the same section, 2/3, R. Abin, a fourth generation Palestinian Amora,[47] states that Moses "supplicated and 'prostrated himself' (מִתְחַבֵּט)[48] to be permitted to enter the Land of Israel, yet it (his prayer) was not accepted (by God)." This is because Moses' hour was already past, as indicated by "And I besought the Lord 'at that time.'"[49]

3. Moses' falling on his face in prayer before God is also related in the "Midrash of Moses' Departure / Death." A voice from heaven asked Moses why he was so disturbed, for "the end of the hour has come." Moses then stood "in prayer" and asked the Lord of the world not to deliver him into the hand of Sammael (the Angel of Death). Having acknowledged that He has heard Moses' prayer, God then promised to concern Himself with his burial. When He then revealed Himself from heaven to take the soul of Moses, the latter "fell on his face" (נפל על פניו) and prayed.[50]

---

[45] Strack and Stemberger, *Introduction* 94.

[46] Mirqin 11.29, Soncino 7.29-30. On נִיפּוּל as "falling down for prayer," cf. Jastrow, *A Dictionary* 907, who calls attention to the Tannaitic midrash *Sifre* Deut. Wa'ethanan 26 on Deut 3:23, where the tradition is anonymous (Finkelstein 39, Hammer 48).

[47] Strack and Stemberger, *Introduction* 103.

[48] Jastrow 417, hithpael: "to prostrate oneself (in prayer, in deep commotion)."

[49] Mirqin 11.31, Soncino 7.32, with n. 2.

[50] Cf. Version A in Jellinek 1.128, and Version B in 6.77. A German translation is offered in A. Wünsche, *Aus Israels Lehrhallen* 1.160-161. See also Str-B 2.260-261 on different forms of falling down to the earth in prayer.

* * *

Moses' prostration or falling down to the earth on his face when praying that he may (be allowed to continue to live and) enter the Land of Israel, provides the background for Jesus' "falling upon the earth" and praying in Mark 14:35, then repeated twice. He too wishes to continue to live, if God will cause the hour to pass and remove the cup (of death) from him. Yet God does not accept Jesus' request, just as He rejected Moses'.

4) JESUS' THREEFOLD PRAYER.

a) In Gethsemane Jesus prayed the same prayer three times (Mark 14:35, 39 and 41 – assumed). This pattern of threefold prayer also derives from Moses' praying just before his death.

b) Early Judaic tradition describes Moses as praying three times that he may not die, but continue to live and enter the Land of Israel. God then rejects his request three times, and Moses must resign himself to his fate of dying. Four examples of this threefold prayer are the following.

1. A remnant of this motif is found in *Pseudo-Philo* 19:6, where at the end of Moses' life "God spoke to him *a third time*, saying, 'Behold, you are going forth to sleep with your fathers....'" (Deut 31:16).[51] Although God will show Moses the Land before he dies, he may not enter it (19:7; cf. Deut 32:52 and 34:4).

The origin of this motif is most probably 1 Sam 3:8, where only after the Lord's calling the boy Samuel "the third time" does Eli perceive that it is the Lord who does this. In the haggada on Moses' death, this means that only after God tells him three times that he must die and may not enter the Land, does Moses acknowledge this as God's will. The following texts demonstrate this.

2. *Mek. R. Ish.* Amalek 2 on Exod 17:14 states that on the very day Joshua became the successor to Moses, a hint of this was given to Moses, but he didn't comprehend it. Therefore at the end Moses continued to stand and beseech, as in Deut 3:23: "And I besought the Lord...."[52]

R. Joshua (b. Ḥananyah, a second generation Tanna[53]) then notes that "Let it suffice you" in Deut 3:26 means it is enough for Moses to have the world to come. "Still he was standing and making all these petitions / prayers (בקשות)."[54] He first requests permission to enter the Land as a

---

[51] *OTP* 2.327; Latin in Harrington, *Les Antiquités Bibliques* 1.158: *tercio*.

[52] Lauterbach 2.149.

[53] Strack and Stemberger, *Introduction* 77.

[54] The term בקשה means both desire / request, and prayer. See Jastrow 188.

private person, which God rejects. "Still he was standing and making all these petitions / prayers." Secondly, Moses requests permission to enter by way of the cave of Caesarion near Paneas, which God rejects with the words of Deut 34:4. Thirdly, Moses finally asks that at least his bones may go over the Jordan into the Land. This in turn God rejects in the words of Deut 3:27.[55] Only after the third request / prayer does Moses accept God's will for him.

3. In *Deut. Rab.* Vezot ha-Berakhah 11/5 on Deut 33:1 ("before his death"), R. Meir (a third generation Tanna[56]) says the Angel of Death came to Moses and informed him that God had sent him to him, for he is to depart this life today. Moses tells him to go away, for he wants to praise God, as in Ps 118:17. When the Angel of Death came to him a second time, Moses pronounced over him the Ineffable Name, whereupon the angel fled. Only when he came "a third time" did Moses acknowledge that this is from God, and that he must accept it as God's will.[57]

4. *Deut. Rab.* Vezot ha-Berakhah 11/10 on Deut 31:14 ("Behold, the days approach when you must die") states that Moses has only one or more hour to live. He says that if God will not bring him into the Land, He should leave him in this world so that he can live and not die. This God rejects. Secondly, Moses asks God to let him become like the beasts of the field. This God rejects with the words of Deut 3:26, "Let it suffice you." Then Moses, thirdly, asks God to let him become like a bird. Again He answers him with Deut 3:26. When Moses sees that no creature is able to save him from the path of death, in that hour he acknowledges God's justice by quoting Deut 32:4.[58]

---

[55] Lauterbach 2.151-152. Cf. also the parable in the same section of a king's son, who when he tries to enter the palace is rebuked by the guards "at the third" (בשלישי) gate (Lauterbach 2.149-150). A similar parable is related in *Sifre* Deut. Wa'ethanan 29 on Deut 3:27 (Finkelstein 48, Hammer 54).

[56] Strack and Stemberger, *Introduction* 84.

[57] Cf. Mirqin 11.152, and Soncino 7.176. This is anonymous in *Tanḥ.* Vezot ha-Berakhah 3 on Deut 33:1 (Eshkol 945). On the general phenomenon of struggling with the Angel of Death, see E. Diamond, "Wrestling the Angel of Death: Form and Meaning in Rabbinic Tales of Death and Dying" in *JSJ* 26 (1995) 76-92.

[58] Mirqin 11.157-158; Soncino 7.183-184. Moses' threefold prayer is thus the background of Jesus' prayer in Gethsemane, and not A. Loisy's proposal (*Marc* 416, as quoted in Holleran, *The Synoptic Gethsemane* 46) that Mark intends the three prayers to correspond to the three watches of the night.

*   *   *

The last three texts show that the motif of Jesus' praying "three times" in Gethsemane that his imminent death be averted, derives from the threefold request / prayer of Moses at the very end of his life. He wants to enter the Land and not die, but continue to live. This, however, God does not grant him, just as He does not remove the cup (of death) from Jesus in Gethsemane.

*   *   *

The pre-Markan, Palestinian Jewish Christian author of the Gethsemane narrative was not the only one to apply the "threefold prayer" motif from Judaic haggada on Moses' imminent death to a new situation. Although I shall analyze the entire pericope more extensively in Appendix One, the following remarks in regard to 2 Cor 12:7-9 are of relevance here.

Fourteen years before writing Second Corinthians, Paul was caught up to the third heaven, Paradise, where he experienced an abundance of revelations. To keep him from becoming too elated over this, a messenger of Satan, a thorn in the flesh, was given him. Paul besought the Lord "three times" (τρίς) that this should leave him, but He said to the apostle: "My grace is sufficient for you." The latter is a Judaic interpretation of Deut 3:26, applied above to Moses.[59]

Paul's beseeching the Lord three times (in prayer) that something very negative should be taken away from him corresponds to Jesus' threefold pattern of prayer in Gethsemane. Both Paul and the Palestinian Jewish Christian author of the Gethsemane narrative appropriated this motif from Judaic haggada on the end of Moses' life.[60]

5)   IF POSSIBLE.

a) In Mark 14:35 Jesus in Gethsemane falls on the ground and prays that "if it is possible (εἰ δυνατόν ἐστιν)," the hour should pass from him. The next verse (36) rephrases the petition: "Abba, Father, all things are possible (δυνατά) to You. Remove this cup from me. Yet not what I will, but what You (will)." The first expression, "if it is possible," (and indirectly also the second, together with "will") also derives from Judaic tradition on the last hour before Moses' death.

---

[59] For details of this, especially *Deut. Rab.* 2/1 on Deut 3:26, see Appendix One.

[60] According to C. Wolff, *Der zweite Brief des Paulus an die Korinther* (THNT 8; Berlin: Evangelische Verlagsanstalt, 1989) 248, n. 365, H. Windisch in 1934 had already called attention to the threefold prayer parallelism between Gethsemane and 2 Cor 12:8. Yet he was not aware of their mutual background.

b) In the Tannaitic midrash *Sifre* Deut. Wa'ethanan 28 on Moses' petition in Deut 3:25, "Let me go over, I pray, and see the good land," the commentator asks: "'Is it possible that' (אפשר ש) Moses could have asked God to let him (continue to live and) enter the land? Is it not stated elsewhere, 'you shall not go over this Jordan' (3:27)?" This situation is illustrated by a parable, in which a king decrees that his servant should be without wine for thirty days. The servant responds: "'Is it possible that' I can be without wine for even a single hour?" This was to show "how precious to him were the words of his master. So also Moses demonstrated how precious to him were God's words by asking Him to let him enter the land," as in 3:25.[61]

R. Hammer notes that this servant actually pleads against the king's decree. Because he wants to do the king's will, he emphasizes how precious the wine is which he is now giving up. Hammer remarks that "Moses' repeated pleading is...a demonstration of his full obedience."[62]

Here Moses, in the hour of his death, is likened to someone who asks that "if it is possible," he may not be without wine even for one hour, although his king decreed he should be without it for thirty days. That is, Moses pleads that the entire decree of the king (God) be taken from him. He wants to continue to live and to enter the Land.

Jesus' situation in Gethsemane is depicted as being similar. He prayed three times that "if it were possible," the hour should pass from him, the cup (of death) be removed from him. By praying to the Father repeatedly, he acknowledged that God's will alone was determinative for him.

Another example of the expression "if it is possible" is found in *Tanh.* B Wa'ethanan 5 on Deut 3:23 ("And I besought the Lord at that time").[63] It begins by asking: "Why (did Moses beseech the Lord)? So that he could enter the Land (of Israel)." Although God tells him, "Let it suffice you" (3:26), and "Die on the mountain which you ascend!" (32:50), Moses continues to beseech God, saying: "I do not want to go forth and die."[64] Later Moses says: "Now I pray, 'Hear my cry, O God' (Ps 61:2, Eng. 1), and hide not Yourself from my supplication' (Ps 55:2, Eng. 1). The Holy One, blessed be He, said to him: It is not possible (אי אפשר). 'Let it suffice you' (Deut 3:26). Your opponent in (the heavenly) court,[65] (the Angel of

---

[61] Finkelstein 44; I slightly modify the translation of Hammer, 52.

[62] Hammer 401, n. 1.

[63] Buber 10, Bietenhard 2.450.

[64] Buber's text omits "go forth," apparently found in Codex Vaticanus Ebr. 34, which Bietenhard follows.

[65] Cf. Jastrow 182 on בעל דין.

Death), has already issued a decree that you will die and all (human) creatures like you." Then "Let it suffice you" is quoted twice more.

In other words, in the "hour" when Moses besought the Lord[66] whether it was possible for him to remain alive and enter the Land, He responded: "It is not possible." The term אי here can be equivalent to אין, "not," certainly meant in this case.[67] Yet it can also be meant as אם, "if, whether."[68] I suggest that the Palestinian Jewish Christian author of the Gethsemane narrative was well acquainted with the haggada on Moses' resistance to death in his last hour, and borrowed the term אי אפשר from it. He then changed its meaning from "it is not possible" to "if it is possible," which was later correctly translated into Greek as εἰ δυνατόν ἐστιν. This agrees with the formulation cited in the *Sifre* text above: "Is it possible that...?"

The next section in *Tanḥ.* B, 6, also on Deut 3:23,[69] has R. Simlai (b. Abba, a second generation Palestinian Amora[70]) quote 3:26. Then God says: "Moses, I have sworn two oaths, one that you must die, and one to destroy Israel. To make both of them void 'is not possible' (אי איפשר). 'If it is your will' (אם תרצה אתה) to remain alive, Israel will be destroyed." Moses then accuses God of playing a trick on him. He states: "Moses and a thousand like him may be destroyed, but not one person from Israel should be destroyed!"

Here Moses is portrayed as sacrificing himself for the welfare of all Israel. His "will" may be to remain alive, but for him and Israel to do so "is not possible" according to the divine plan. Precisely these two expressions appear in Jesus' struggling with God in the face of death in Mark 14:35-36.

Finally, the same motif of "if it is possible" is reflected in *Sifre* Num. Pinḥas § 135, which deals with Deut 3:26 here, "Let it suffice you."[71] The background is again that Moses barters with God about entering the Land of Israel. He would prefer entering as Israel's leader, without placing the reins in Joshua's hands. The midrash states that he then tells God: "'If not' (אם לאו), I will enter as a plain man." This God rejects. The same is true for Moses' suggestions of entering as a disciple of Joshua, or

---

[66] Cf. MS "V" of *Frag. Targ.* Deut 3:23, "in that hour," for "at that time" in the MT (Klein 1.212; 2.170). See also *Targ. Neof.* 1 ad. loc. (Díez Macho 5.35 and 454).

[67] Jastrow 43, III.

[68] *Ibid.*, II.

[69] Buber 12, Bietenhard 2.453-454.

[70] Strack and Stemberger, *Introduction* 96.

[71] Horowitz 181-182, Kuhn 558-559.

through the air or a subterranean passage, or that at least his bones may cross over the Jordan.[72]

Here Moses means: "If it is not (possible) to enter the Land as I am, let me do so in a different way." As in the other haggadic passages cited above, this terminology is connected to Deut 3:26, "Let it suffice you." God informs Moses, who has prayed repeatedly to Him, that it is "not possible" to change His decision. Moses' death, like Jesus', has irrevocably come.

6) YOUR WILL / MY WILL.

a) In Mark 14:36 Jesus prays for God to remove the cup (of death) from him. "Yet not what I will (θέλω), but what You (will)." The contrast here between Jesus' will and God's will also derives from Moses' last hour, his own struggle with death.

b) The motif of the "will of God" at the time of Moses' impending death is already found in Josephus, *Ant.* 4.322. The Israelites' tears, their beating of the breast, grief, lamenting, sorrow, weeping and wailing on this occasion (321; cf. Deut 34:8) reduced Moses to tears. This was true although he had always been persuaded that one should not despair at one's approaching end because this fate befalls man "in accordance with 'the will of God' and by a law of nature." The first phrase in Greek is κατὰ βούλησιν...θεοῦ.

Here Josephus emphasizes that Moses' death at this point is a part of God's will.

Four occurrences of Moses' will or God's will when the hour of Moses' death has arrived are found in *Tanḥ.* B Wa'etḥanan 6 on Deut 3:23. After the citation of Deut 3:26, Moses continues to barter with God by saying: "Maybe the (coming) generations will maintain that I did 'Your will' (רצונך) in my youth, but in my old age (at the time of death) I did not do 'Your will' (רצונך). He spoke to him: I have already written, 'because you (pl.) did not revere Me as holy in the midst of the people of Israel' (Deut 32:51). (Moses) said before Him: If it is 'Your will' (אם רצונך), I will enter the Land and spend two or three years there, and afterwards I will die. He said to him: It is a decree before Me that you may not enter!"[73]

---

[72] Here Deut 31:2 is quoted by God. The same pattern of "if not" is found in *Deut. Rab.* Vezot ha-Berakhah 11/10 (Mirqin 11.157, Soncino 7.183-184).

[73] Buber 11, Bietenhard 2.452. I follow the Vaticanus MS of Bietenhard here. However, all the "will" phrases are the same.

Somewhat further on in the same section R. Simlai's exposition occurs, as described above in 5.b). There the expressions "it is not possible" and "if it is 'your will' to remain alive" are found together.

Finally, in S. Liebermann's edition of *Deut. Rab.* Wa'ethanan on Deut 3:26, Moses addresses God: "'And if it is not Your will' (ואם אינך רוצה), grant me permission, and I will go by the means I prayed for, on the condition that I not cross over the Jordan."[74]

The above five occurrences of Moses' will and God's will, once connected to "not being possible," all found in the context of the imminent death of Moses, make it very probable that the Palestinian Jewish Christian author of the Gethsemane narrative borrowed the expressions "my will" and "Your will" from this haggadic context.

7) SUBMISSION TO GOD'S WILL.

a) Connected with the above discussion of Jesus' will and God's will in Mark 14:36 is the fact that only after his threefold prayer with the same contents, does Jesus ascertain: "It is enough / sufficient for me. The hour has come. The Son of man is delivered into the hands of sinners. Rise, let us be going" (vv 41b-42a).[75] The Palestinian Jewish Christian author of this narrative creates the impression here of Jesus' submitting to God's will, his death at Golgotha the next afternoon, after struggling with God in prayer three times. This submission also derives from Judaic haggada on the imminent death of Moses.

b) In *Deut. Rab.* Vezot ha-Berakhah 11/5 on Deut 33:1 ("This is the blessing...before his death"),[76] R. Meir relates that the Angel of Death went to Moses three different times, informing him that God had sent him to him, for he was to depart from this life today. Only after the Angel of Death approached him a third time did Moses say: "Since this is from God, I must resign myself to God's will." The phrase צדק את הדין employed here means resigning oneself to the divine dispensation as just, submitting oneself to God's will.[77]

This is shown by the fact that Deut 32:4 is then quoted as a proof text: "The Rock (God), His work is perfect; for all His ways are justice. A God of faithfulness and without iniquity, just (צדיק) and right is He." A variant of this tradition is found in Vezot ha-Berakhah 11/10, where Moses

---

[74] Liebermann 47-48.

[75] See section 8 for my interpretation of "It is enough / sufficient for me."

[76] Mirqin 11.152, Soncino 7.176. A parallel is found in *Tanh.* Vezot ha-Berakhah 3 on Deut 33:1 (Eshkol 2.945).

[77] Cf. Jastrow 1263.

barters three times with God in order to remain alive, and God answers him with Deut 3:26. "When Moses saw that no creature could save him from the path of death, in that hour" he spoke Deut 32:4.[78] Finally, it should also be noted that Ḥananyah b. Teradion, a second generation Tanna who became a martyr during the Hadrianic persecution of 132-135 C.E.,[79] is described in *b. 'Abod. Zar.* 18a as also submitting to the divine judgment / will and quoting Deut 32:4 when he went out to his death.[80]

The Palestinian Jewish Christian author of the Gethsemane narrative knew of the Judaic haggadic tradition of Moses' submitting to the divine will that he must die, even after he prays to God three times. For this reason he has Jesus say "It is enough / sufficient for me" after praying to God three times. To this expression I now turn.

8) IT IS ENOUGH / SUFFICIENT.

a) After Jesus prays a third time in Gethsemane, he returns to the disciples and says to them: "Sleep from now on and rest! ἀπέχει. The hour has come. Behold, the Son of man is delivered into the hands of sinners" (Mark 14:41).[81] Neither Matthew (26:45) nor Luke (22:46) understood the meaning of ἀπέχει here; they therefore omitted the expression. In his recent exhaustive commentary on the Passion Narrative, R. Brown devotes a five-page appendix to the various possible meanings of it.[82]

Jerome, who had studied Hebrew extensively and had lived first in Antioch for some six years and then in Bethlehem from 386 until his death in 420, finished his translation of the New Testament into Latin, the "Vulgate," ca. 388 C.E. It is known that local Bethlehem Jews helped him to translate the Old Testament from the Hebrew and Aramaic, and he was also acquainted with many Judaic haggadic traditions.[83] Jerome translated the puzzling ἀπέχει as *sufficit*, "it is enough / sufficient."[84] There is no early lexicographical evidence for this interpretation.[85]

---

[78] Mirqin 11.157-158, Soncino 7.184. Cf. also the emphasis on God's justice in *Midr. Departure / Death of Moses* A (Jellinek 1.129) and B (Jellinek 6.78).

[79] Strack and Stemberger, *Introduction* 81.

[80] Soncino 91; here he speaks the first part of the verse, his wife the second. Cf. also *Sifre* Deut. Niṣṣabim 307 on Deut 32:4 (Hammer 312).

[81] For this interpretation of sleeping and resting, see below, section 9.

[82] *The Death of the Messiah* 1379-1383.

[83] Cf. Walker, *A History of the Christian Church* 159, as well as the many references to Jerome in Ginzberg's *Legends*, as shown in the index (7.591-593).

[84] Cf. BAGD 84-85 on the Greek verb.

[85] Cf. Brown, *The Death* 1381-1382.

Nevertheless, his interpretation has been adopted, for example, by the RSV ("It is enough"), NRSV ("Enough!"), and the 1985 Luther Bible ("Es ist genug"). Analysis of Judaic lore on the impending death of Moses, especially Deut 3:26 ("It is enough for you"), substantiates Jerome's translation, now adopted in many circles.

b) The Book of Deuteronomy closes by having God show Moses the Land from Mount Nebo, opposite Jericho. Before he dies, God tells him: "I have let you see it with your eyes, but you shall not go over there" (34:4).[86] This scene is adumbrated already in chapter three, where Moses "beseeches" (v 23) the Lord (in prayer) to allow him to go over and see the good land beyond the Jordan (v 25). Yet He tells him: "Let it suffice you (רַב לָךְ); speak no more to Me of this matter" (v 26). Moses is told to ascend the mountain and view the Land, but "you shall not go over this Jordan" (v 27).

As I have pointed out several times above, Judaic haggada bases Moses' threefold prayer just before his death on Deut 3:23's "beseeching." *Deut. Rab.* Vezot ha-Berakhah 11/10, for example, states that when only one hour remained to Moses, he asked God if He would not let him enter the Land, to allow him to live in this world and not die. This God rejects. Moses' second request, if entering the Land is not possible, is to become like the beasts of the field. This God rejects by stating: "Let it suffice you." Moses' third attempt involves his becoming like a bird which can fly anywhere. God again rejects this request with "Let it suffice you." The midrash then asks: "What does 'Let it suffice you' mean? God said to him: 'You have spoken sufficiently / enough.' When Moses saw that no creature could save him from the path of death, in that hour" he quoted Deut 32:4, acknowledging God's justice, i.e. he submitted to the divine will.[87]

The Tannaitic midrash *Sifre* Deut. Wa'ethanan 29 on Deut 3:26 explains Moses' words, "and did not hearken to me," as: "(God) did not accept my prayer."[88] *Sifre* then offers four different explanations of "Let it suffice you," showing how popular this motif was. The Palestinian Jewish Christian author of the Gethsemane narrative employed this motif by having Jesus pray three times to be allowed to continue to live, but God did not accept his prayer either. Therefore Jesus says precisely at this juncture: "It is enough for me; the hour (to die) has come" (Mark 14:41).

---

[86] Cf. also 32:52 and 31:2.

[87] Mirqin 11.157-158, Soncino 7.183-184.

[88] Finkelstein 45, Hammer 53.

In *'Avot R. Nat.* A 12, after Moses' persistent resistance to the Angel of Death's efforts to take his soul, God finally tells him: "Moses, 'you have had enough' (דייך) of this world; lo, the world to come awaits you."[89] *Mek. R. Ish.* Amalek 2 on Exod 17:14 has R. Joshua (b. Ḥananyah, a second generation Tanna[90]) say regarding Deut 3:26: "'Let it suffice you' means 'it is enough for you' (דייך) to have the world to come."[91] In *Sifre* Num. Pinḥas § 135, R. Ishmael (b. Elisha, a second generation Tanna[92]) also comments on this phrase with a parable, showing very early rabbinic reflection on its meaning as applied to Moses' death scene.[93] As noted above, *Tanḥ.* B Wa'etḥanan 5 has God reject Moses' prayer and supplication not to die with the words: "It is not possible; 'let it suffice you.'"[94] "If it is possible" is found in Mark 14:35, which strengthens my proposal for interpreting ἀπέχει in v 41 as deriving originally from "It is enough / sufficient (for me)."

In his Hebrew translation of the NT, F. Delitzsch rendered ἀπέχει as רַב לִי.[95] This is similar to the phrase found in Deut 3:26. The United Bible Societies' Hebrew New Testament has מַסְפִּיק! for ἀπέχει: "Enough!"[96] Both conform to Jerome's Vulgate translation of *sufficit*, "It is enough / sufficient."

Yet the Palestinian Jewish Christian author of the Gethsemane narrative most probably employed not the term רב, but דַי in Mark 14:41, as in *'Avot R. Nat.* A 12 and *Mek. R. Ish.* Amalek 2 above. It also means "enough, sufficient." The form דַיִ, pronounced almost the same, means: "It is enough for me."[97] In the context it means that, like Moses, after

---

[89] Schechter 50, Goldin 65.

[90] Cf. n. 53.

[91] Lauterbach 2.151. Before this another interpretation with דייך occurs.

[92] Strack and Stemberger, *Introduction* 79.

[93] Horowitz 181, Kuhn 556-557. In *b. Soṭa* 13b (Soncino 70) the "School of R. Ishmael" is cited. Cf. also the comments of R. Judah (b. Ilai) and R. Nehemiah, two third generation Tannaim (*Introduction* 84 and 85), on Deut 3:26 in the "Addition" to Deut 3:23 in Bietenhard 2.457, with n. 1.

[94] Buber 10, Bietenhard 2.450. The next section, 6, also deals with Deut 3:23 and 26; it mentions Moses' "will" and God's "will" several times, a term also found in Mark 14:36.

[95] *Ha-Berith ha-Ḥadašah* 93.

[96] Cf. *Ha-Berith ha-Ḥadašah* 135. On *maspiq*, see Alcalay, *The Complete Hebrew-English Dictionary* 1402: "sufficient, adequate, enough."

[97] Jastrow 293. Cf. the modern Hebrew expression דַי!, "Enough of that!" in Alcalay 427. It is also probably behind Matt 6:34, "Let the day's own trouble be 'sufficient' (ἀρκετόν) for the day." Both Delitzsch (344) and the United Bible Societies (466) have דַי לְךָ for ἀρκεῖ σοι in 2 Cor 12:9.

praying to God three times to be allowed to remain alive, Jesus finally
submits to His will and acknowledges the Lord's decision as just. His
strenuous struggling with his fate is now finished. Jesus resigns himself
to his imminent death, for, as with Moses, his hour has come.

The Hellenistic Jewish Christian translator of the originally Semitic
Gethsemane narrative[98] should have rendered רַד by ἀρκεῖ μοι, similar to
ἀρκεῖ σοι in 2 Cor 12:8. It too was based on Moses' death scene in Judaic
sources. The translator may have puzzled at its meaning, however,
considering it inappropriate on the lips of his Savior. He misunderstood
דַּיִּי, "It is sufficient / enough for me" as דַי, "Enough (of that)!" This was
for him another reproach to the disciples for their still sleeping and
resting instead of watching / keeping awake and praying. Not wanting
Jesus on the night before his death to again reproach his own disciples in
such a way, however,[99] he deliberately translated the term as ἀπέχει. To
him this probably meant: "full payment is being made."[100] That is, Judas
would now perform the deed necessary to receive the money promised
him (cf. Mark 14:11); he was already on his way to Gethsemane with a
crowd to betray and have Jesus arrested. Jesus' hour had thus come; he
was delivered into the hands of sinners (v 41). The translator's new term
fit the context well.

The above proposal has the major advantage that it derives directly
from early Judaic lore on Moses' imminent death in spite of his also
praying three times to God to allow him to continue to live. Jerome,
living near Antioch and in Bethlehem, may have corrected ἀπέχει back to
sufficit because he recognized Judaic motifs from the impending death of
Moses in the Gethsemane narrative. Or, more probably, he had contact
with Syrian or Palestinian Jewish Christians, a number of whom were
bilingual, who in spite of the Gospel of Mark in Greek retained at least in
oral tradition the earlier Syrian or Hebrew (possibly Aramaic) account of
the Gethsemane incident, including דַי. This he preferred and (partially)
correctly rendered as *sufficit*, which has been a favorite reading ever
since.

9) RESTING.

a) After praying for deliverance from death a third time, Jesus
returned to the disciples and said: "Sleep from now on (in the future, but

---

[98] See the discussion in section III below.

[99] The disciples' failure to watch with Jesus is nevertheless a major thrust in the
narrative. See section II.2.1) C. below.

[100] Cf. LSJ 188, IV; BAGD 84 for "the account is (now) closed"; Brown, *The Death*
1383, "The money is paid."

not now[101]), and take your rest! It is enough / sufficient for me. The hour has come. Behold, the Son of man is delivered into the hands of sinners" (Mark 14:41). Here the first clause is a reproach to the disciples similar to Jesus' question of Peter in v 37; the same is implied for the disciples in v 40. If one conceives v 41a as a question, the same reproachful tone is implied: "Are you still sleeping and taking your rest?"[102] I shall mention a third alternative at the conclusion of b) below.

It seems strange that "resting" (ἀναπαύομαι) is mentioned in addition to "sleeping" (καθεύδω) after the latter has occurred alone in vv 37 (twice) and 40. I suggest that "resting" has been mentioned here at the end of Jesus' praying three times because the Palestinian Jewish Christian author of the Gethsemane narrative knew of it in his Judaic model. There Moses, after praying three times before his imminent death, also spoke of "rest."

b) In *Pseudo-Philo* 19:12 God tells Moses just before he dies: "I will give you 'rest' (*requiem*) in your sleep / slumber (*dormitione*) and bury you in peace."[103] *Sifre* Num. Pinḥas § 135 also comments on Deut 3:26, "Let it suffice you," by stating: "You have toiled much, you have labored much. Depart, Moses, 'and rest' (ונח)."[104]

Here the emphasis is on Moses' resting. Yet the most important influence on Mark 14:41 derives from Moses' speaking the words of Ps 116:7 just before his death. As has been noted above, and will be noted below, this Psalm was very important in the fashioning of the Gethsemane narrative.

In *Deut. Rab.* Vezot ha-Berakhah 11/5 on "before his death" in Deut 33:1,[105] R. Isaac (probably II., a third generation Palestinian Amora[106])

---

[101] For this meaning of τὸ λοιπόν, see BAGD 480, 3.a.α.: "from now on, in the future, henceforth." See also Delitzsch's translation in his Hebrew New Testament (p. 93): מֵעַתָּה, "from now on" (Jastrow 1129).

[102] On this meaning of τὸ λοιπόν, see BAGD *ibid.* It has been preferred in the United Bible Societies' Hebrew New Testament (p. 134): "Are you still (עוֹדְכֶם) sleeping and resting?"

[103] Cf. *OTP* 2.328 and *Les Antiquités Bibliques* 1.162.

[104] Horowitz 181, Kuhn 558. The last verse in Daniel is then quoted (12:13): "But go your way till the end; and you shall 'rest'...." Delitzsch's Hebrew New Testament on Mark 14:41 (p. 93) has the word play נוּמוּ וְנוּחוּ, "(from now on) sleep and rest." The usual term for sleeping, however, is שׁנה.

[105] Mirqin 11.152-153, Soncino 7.176-177. A parallel is found in *Tanḥ.* Vezot ha-Berakhah 3 on Deut 33:1 (Eshkol 946). See also *Midr. Departure / Death of Moses* in Jellinek 6.77, which is anonymous. After this God takes Moses' soul with a kiss (Deut 34:5).

[106] Cf. Strack and Stemberger, *Introduction* 98.

says the soul of Moses severely resisted[107] departing (from his body), and Moses conversed with it, saying: "My soul (נַפְשִׁי), do you think that the Angel of Death seeks to rule over you?" It answered him: "God will not do so (allow it)!" The soul then quotes Ps 116:8. This type of question and answer sequence is repeated two more times, with different quotations from the same psalm verse. Then Moses asked his soul: "And where are you going to go?" It answered him: "I will walk before the Lord in the lands of the living" (Ps 116:9). When (Moses) heard this, he gave it permission (to depart), saying to it: "Return, O my soul, to 'your rest' (מְנוּחָיְכִי)," etc. (v 7).

Here Moses' soul struggles greatly with the prospect of death. Only when it is reassured of being with God in the future, i.e. at the Resurrection, can it depart. Only then can Moses die. In b. Pesaḥ. 118a it is stated that the fourth of five reasons for reciting the Hallel is the resurrection of the dead, as found in the above verse, Ps 116:9.[108] This thought is presupposed in the haggadic narrative above.

Moses is described here as saying to his soul at the very end of his life: "Return...to your rest." I suggest that this motif influenced the Palestinian Jewish Christian author of the Gethsemane narrative. He too has Jesus, who has just submitted to God's will for him to die, say to the disciples: "Keep on sleeping and 'resting'" (Mark 14:41).[109] This appears strange in the context, where Jesus tells his disciples in the very next verse (42): "Rise, let us be going." The reason for the strangeness of the clause is that it has been adapted from the scene of Moses' impending death. Without reflecting long, the author simply transferred it to Jesus' remarks to the disciples in the scene of his impending death. The proposal above also explains why the puzzling expression τὸ λοιπόν in v 41 has produced so many different modern interpretations.

10) THE HOUR (OF DEATH) HAS COME.

a) In the Gethsemane narrative Jesus tells three of his disciples that his soul is deeply grieved, even to "death" (Mark 14:34). He prays that this "hour" (ὥρα) may pass from him (v 35). It includes "this cup" (of death) in v 36. Jesus then reproaches Peter for not being able to watch / keep awake this "one hour" (μίαν ὥραν – v 37). Finally, Jesus submits to God's will for him that he should die, by saying: "It is enough for me" (see the interpretation of ἀπέχει above). This is immediately followed by:

---

[107] Cf. Jastrow 1430 on the hithpael of קשה.

[108] Soncino 608. Cf. the statement by Bar Qappara, a fifth generation Tanna (Strack and Stemberger, Introduction 90) in y. Kil. 9:3, 32c (Neusner 4.277), with parallels in y. Keth. 12:4, 35b (Neusner 22.352) and Pesiq. R. 1/4 (Braude 1.42).

[109] For "on and on," cf. BAGD 480, 3.a.α.

"The hour (ἡ ὥρα – of death) has come. Behold, the Son of man is delivered into the hands of sinners."

"The hour" is thus a major motif in the Gethsemane narrative. It too derives from the scene of Moses' impending death in Judaic sources.

b) *Deut. Rab.* Vezot ha-Berakhah 11/10 comments on Deut 31:14 ("Behold, your days have approached that you must die") up until the end of the biblical book with Moses' death in chapter 34. Examples from it show the major emphasis on the arrival of Moses' last hour.

"The wicked angel Sammael, the chief of the accusing angels (lit. 'Satans'), was awaiting the death of Moses 'every hour' (בְּכָל שָׁעָה), saying: 'When will the end (קֵץ) or the moment (רֶגַע) arrive (יַגִּיעַ) for Moses to die so that I can descend and take his soul from him?"[110]

"Meanwhile there remained unto Moses (only) 'one hour' (שעה אחת). 'In that hour' Moses said before God...." Moses then made three requests, ending with God's rejecting them with Deut 3:26, "Let it suffice you." "When Moses saw that no creature could save him from the path of death, he said 'in that hour'" Deut 32:4.[111] The "one hour" here before Moses is handed over to the Angel of Death should be compared with Jesus' asking his disciple Peter in Mark 14:37, "Could you not watch / stay awake 'one hour'?"[112] This means Jesus' final hour, which includes his being handed over to sinners to be killed by them.

"The moment for Moses' death then arrived. In that 'hour' (שעה) God said...."[113] Shortly after this a heavenly voice proclaims: "The end (סוֹף) has arrived, (the time of) your dying."[114] Then God tells Moses' soul: "Now your end has come (הגיע קצך), to depart (from this world)."[115] Here the term "end" (קֵץ)[116] is equal to "hour," which helps to explain the variant τέλος in several MSS of Mark 14:41, followed by "the hour has come / arrived."

---

[110] Mirqin 11.157, Soncino 7.183.

[111] Mirqin 11.157, Soncino 7.183-184.

[112] Contrast *b. Tem.* 16a (Soncino 109), where Joshua, Moses' disciple, replies to him when Moses is about to depart from the world: "My Master, have I ever left you for 'one hour' (שעה אחת) and gone elsewhere?"

[113] Mirqin 11.158, Soncino 7.184.

[114] Mirqin 11.159, Soncino 7.186.

[115] *Ibid.*

[116] On קֵץ, cf. Jastrow 1403-1404: end, term, designated time. See also *'Avot R. Nat.* B 25 (Schechter 51, Saldarini 149): "When the appointed time came (הגיע קצו) for Moses to depart from the world...."

These passages from *Deuteronomy Rabbah* could be supplemented by many others from the "Midrash on the Departure / Death of Moses." One example is the following: "When the hour arrived (הגיע שעה) in which he was to die...."[117] Another is: "The end has arrived (הגיע), the hour (שעה) for you to die."[118]

All of the above citations from Judaic haggadic material on the last hour of Moses make it very probable that they provided the background for a Palestinian Jewish Christian when he described Jesus' last "hour" (שעה) in Gethsemane, the hour of his impending death, in which Peter could not even watch / stay awake "one hour." After Jesus, like Moses, prayed three times to remain alive, but this prayer was rejected, he finally submitted to the will of God. This meant, as for Moses, that his hour had come / arrived (הגיע). This is also how the United Bible Societies' Hebrew New Testament translates Mark 14:41: הִגִּיעָה הַשָּׁעָה, "The hour has come / arrived."[119]

11) DELIVERED INTO THE HANDS OF....

a) After Jesus finally submits to the will of God in Gethsemane, he says: "The hour (of my death) has come. The Son of man is 'delivered into the hands' (παραδίδοται...εἰς τὰς χεῖρας) of sinners (Mark 14:41). Rise, let us be going. Behold, 'he who delivers / betrays' (ὁ παραδιδούς) me has arrived" (v 42). "He who delivers / betrays" Jesus is Judas (vv 43-44), who already before the Passover meal had gone to the chief priests in order to "deliver / betray" him to them (vv 10-11; cf. also 3:19). At the meal Jesus is recorded as predicting that one of those present would "deliver / betray" him (vv 18 and 21).

According to the Gospel of Mark, it was the chief priests who first "delivered" Jesus to the Romans to be tried and executed (10:33, with the scribes; 14:10-11; 15:1, with the elders and scribes, the whole council; 15:10). Yet the "Gentiles," i.e. the Roman occupational power, were the ones who in the person of Pontius Pilate actually "delivered" Jesus to be crucified (9:31 – "men"; 10:33 – the Gentiles; 15:10). In Judaic sources "sinners" is almost a technical term for Gentiles.[120] For this reason the "sinners" (ἁμαρτωλοί) into whose hands the Son of man is delivered in 14:42 are probably the Romans, and not just the (Jewish) troop sent by the Temple administration to arrest Jesus (v 43).

---

[117] Cf. Jellinek 6.75.

[118] Jellinek 6.77. Other examples are found on pp. 76-77, and on 1.127-129.

[119] In the 1979 edition, p. 135. Delitzsch has the simpler באה, "has come" (p. 93).

[120] Cf. the art. ἁμαρτωλός by K. Rengstorf in *TDNT* 1.325-326, as well as Gal 2:15, "Gentile sinners," with Str-B 3.537 on this.

"To be delivered 'into the hands of'" in 14:41 is also found in 9:31. A variant of this phrase may also lie behind the expression "through whom" (δι' οὗ) in 14:21: "through whose hand(s)."[121]

Jesus' being "delivered into the hands of..." in Mark 14:41, while also being a major topos of the entire Passion Narrative, at this point derives from Moses' being "delivered into the hands of" Sammael, the Angel of Death, at the very end of his life.

b) *Targ. Pseud.-Jon.* Gen 3:6 has Eve behold "Sammael, the Angel of Death."[122] *Deut. Rab.* Vezot ha-Berakhah 11/10 on the very end of Deuteronomy, including Moses' death, states that "the angel Sammael, the wicked (הרשע) – he is the chief of all the accusing angels (Satans) –, was awaiting the death of Moses every hour." It adds that "there is no one among the accusing angels so wicked (רָשָׁע) as Sammael."[123]

Tannaitic midrashim deal with Moses' final hour by describing it so: "In that hour God told the Angel of Death: 'Go and bring me the soul of Moses!'"[124] The *Deuteronomy Rabbah* passage above continues by saying that when Sammael came to Moses, the prophet told him: "'You shall not take away my soul!' He (Sammael) said to him: 'The souls of all who come into this world are 'delivered into my hand' (מְסוּרִין לְיָדִי)."[125]

A bit later, when the time of his death has come, Moses addresses God as follows: "I implore You, 'do not deliver me into the hand' (אַל תִּמְסְרֵנִי בְּיַד) of the Angel of Death!" God then promises that He Himself will attend to Moses and his burial.[126]

---

[121] Cf. Delitzsch's translation in his Hebrew New Testament (p. 92): אֲשֶׁר עַל-יָדוֹ. An extensive study of the term "to deliver" is found in W. Popkes, *Christus traditus. Eine Untersuchung zum Begriff der Dahingabe im Neuen Testament* (ATANT 49; Zurich and Stuttgart: Zwingli, 1967).

[122] Rieder 1.4. On Sammael, cf. Jastrow 998; the art. "Samael" by L. Blau in *JE* (1905) 10.665-666; "Samael" by G. Scholem in *EJ* (1971) 14.719-722; and Str-B 1.136-149.

[123] Mirqin 11.157, Soncino 7.183.

[124] Cf. *Sifre* Niṣṣibim 305 (Finkelstein 326, Hammer 296-297), and *'Avot R. Nat.* A 12 (Schechter 50, Goldin 65-66; see also B 25 in Schechter 51-52, Saldarini 149-153). The latter also has two occurrences of "handing over my soul to you," and one of "his soul to me."

[125] Mirqin 11.158, Soncino 7.185. Parallels are found in *Midr. Departure / Death of Moses* A (Jellinek 1.128) and B (Jellinek 6.76).

[126] Mirqin 11.159, Soncino 7.186. Parallels are found in *Midr. Departure / Death of Moses* A (Jellinek 1.128, with Sammael) and B (Jellinek 6.77). See also *Tanḥ.* B Wa'ethanan 6 (Buber 11; Bietenhard 2.452 – "Do not hand me over to the throes of the Angel of Death!"). Jude 9 has the Archangel Michael contend with the

The biblical expression for "give into the power of, deliver over to" is נתן ביד.[127] Rabbinic Hebrew, however, employs here מסר ביד.[128] The verb especially means "to surrender a person to the authorities," which admirably fits Mark 14:41.[129]

The Palestinian Jewish Christian author of the Gethsemane narrative again borrowed here from haggadic lore on the last hour of Moses. The prophet fears that his soul will be "delivered over into the hand of the 'wicked'" (רשע) Sammael. The author transferred this imagery to Jesus at the very end of his struggle with death. In the Septuagint, ἁμαρτωλός is most frequently a translation of רשע.[130] The Hellenistic Jewish Christian translator of the Gethsemane narrative thus most probably employed ἁμαρτωλοί in Mark 14:41 because he found רשעים in his source. The original Palestinian author, in turn, most probably employed the latter because Moses' soul was to be "delivered into the hands of 'wicked' (רשע) Sammael," the Angel of Death and chief "Satan."[131] To fit it into the new context, he simply changed the singular to the plural: "wicked men."

"Behold, he who delivers / betrays me has arrived" (= Judas) in Mark 14:42b continues the same thought as in v 41b. It probably derives from the Palestinian Jewish Christian author. "Rise, let us be going" (v 42a),[132] however, was part of an earlier tradition he incorporated into his narrative. This is shown by its odd occurrence in John 14:31.

"devil" (διάβολος) over Moses' body, not his soul. This Greek term already in the LXX translates "Satan"; see BAGD 182.

[127] Cf. BDB 390 on יד, 5.b.3).

[128] Jastrow 810-811; to hand over, to deliver. He cites *b. Giṭ.* 7a as one example: "It is within my hand (power) to deliver them to the kingdom" (= Roman government). Another is from the period of the (Hasmonean) war in *b. B. Qam.* 82b: "they will not be delivered into your hand."

[129] Jastrow 810.

[130] Cf. the concordance of Hatch and Redpath 1.64-65.

[131] In Luke 22:3 it is Satan who enters into Judas, who consults with others on how to "betray" Jesus (v 4). John 13:2 has the devil (διάβολος; see n. 126 for this as a translation of "Satan") put it into the heart of Judas to "betray" Jesus. In v 27 Satan then enters into him.

[132] The term ἄγωμεν is found once as a loanword in Hebrew. Cf. the parable by R. Levi, a third generation Palestinian Amora (see p. 76, n. 41), in *Gen. Rab.* Vayyishlaḥ 78/7 on Gen 33:1 (Theodor and Albeck 2.925, first line; Soncino 2.720). Here cattle and (other) animals say to a fox: "Let's go (to the lion)!" See Krauss, *Lehnwörter* 2.8. On the expression ἐγείρεσθε, said by Jesus to his disciples, cf. R. Aqiva's customary words to his disciples on the eve of Passover: "The time has come to rise (הגיע עת לעמוד)." This was spoken in the academy so that his disciples would not arrive home late and their children "fall asleep" (ישנו). Was it already a stock phrase at the time the Palestinian Jewish Christian author

* * *

(On the contrast between God's finally taking away Moses' soul with a kiss, and Judas' handing Jesus over to his certain death with a kiss in Gethsemane, see Appendix Two.)

12) PASS OVER.

a) After partaking of the "Passover" (פֶּסַח) meal with his disciples in Jerusalem, which commemorated God's "passing over" the houses of the Israelites in Egypt (Exod 12:12 and 23 – עבר), Jesus went with eleven of them to Gethsemane. Taking Peter, James and John with him, he told them to remain there and watch / keep awake. "Proceeding" (προελθών) somewhat further, he prayed that if it were possible, the hour might "pass" (παρέλθη) from him (Mark 14:35). "Going on / proceeding" here can be expressed in Hebrew by עבר. The same is true for "passing."[133]

In the next verse (36) Jesus prays to God: "'Remove' this cup from me." This too can be expressed by the hiphil of עבר: "to cause to pass, remove."[134]

The Palestinian Jewish Christian author of the Gethsemane narrative displays his artistic ability here. Assonance and a difference in meaning of the same root within two verses would have been appreciated by his original audience(s).

I suggest that the author employed the term עבר three times in his narrative not only because of the Passover festival, but also because it played such a major role in biblical and Judaic lore regarding the scene of Moses' impending death.

b) Almost all the haggadic sources which I have cited in sections 1) to 11) above deal primarily with Moses' resistance to God's telling him he may not "pass over" (עבר) the Jordan and enter the Land of Israel (Deut 3:25, 27; 31:2; 34:5; cf. 32:52). Instead, Moses is to ascend Mount Nebo and die there.

It seems probable, then, that the Palestinian Jewish Christian author of the Gethsemane account, which took place on the first evening of the "Passover" Festival, also borrowed the term from this and haggadic

---

composed the Gethsemane narrative? See *b. Pesah.* 109a, a baraitha (Soncino 563), as well as *b. Sukk.* 28a (Soncino 123, with notes 1-2) on Yoḥanan b. Zakkai.

[133] Cf. Delitzsch's Hebrew New Testament, p. 92. For עבר as also "pass on, go on, proceed," see BDB 718, 5. For "passing a little" (further on), see עֹבֵר מְעַט in 2 Sam 16:1. Reference from A. Schlatter, *Der Evangelist Matthäus* (Stuttgart: Calwer, 1948³) 751.

[134] Cf. Delitzsch as in n. 133. On the verb, see Jastrow 1038.

development of the above texts from Deuteronomy dealing with the impending death of Moses. He then employed it three times.

13)   THE CUP OF DEATH.

a) In Gethsemane Jesus told the inner circle of three disciples that his soul was very sad "unto death" (ἕως θανάτου; Mark 14:34). Then he fell on the earth and prayed that if possible, the hour (of his death) might pass from him (v 35). This Jesus made into a direct request in v 36: "Remove / cause this 'cup' (ποτήριον) to pass from me." Every Palestinian Jewish Christian hearer acquainted with even the simplest form of the gospel message knew this was the "cup of death" which Jesus was to taste at Golgotha the next afternoon. When Judas arrived in Gethsemane to deliver him, Jesus knew: "the hour (of death) has come" (v 41).

The "cup (of death)" also plays a role at the very end of Moses' life.

b) Before analyzing the "cup of death" as associated with Moses, it will be helpful to make several other observations about the use of "cup" in the Hebrew Bible: כּוֹס.

Lam 4:21 states that "to you (Edom) also the cup shall 'pass.'" Here the same verb, עבר, occurs for a cup as in the Semitic original (hiphil of עבר) of "'removing' this cup" in Mark 14:36.

Cups of judgment, wrath, staggering, horror and desolation occur numerous times in the MT, but not a cup of death.[135] It is another use of "cup" which is the general background for Jesus' cup and Moses' cup of death.

Ps 11:6 speaks of "'the portion' of their cup." Ps 16:5 also notes that "The Lord is my 'chosen portion' and my cup; You hold my 'lot.'" Here cup means the same as one's "fate": portion or lot.[136] When Jesus asks God in Gethsemane to remove "this cup" from him, it is not one of His negative judgment or wrath. Rather, it is Jesus' portion or lot, i.e. to die the next afternoon by crucifixion. For him it is "the cup of death."

The latter very rare expression is found in regard to only two biblical passages in Judaic sources. One of them is Deut 32:1, the beginning of the "Song of Moses," recited directly before he ascends Mount Nebo to die. *Targum Neofiti 1* on this verse reads:

> When the appointed time (קצה) of Moses the prophet arrived to be gathered in peace from the midst of the world (= to die), Moses thought in his heart and said: "Woe now is me, since I am being gathered from the midst of the world and I have not borne witness against the children

---

[135] Cf. BDB 129.

[136] Cf. BDB on מנת, חלק and גורל, respectively.

of the Lord. If I bear witness against them before the sons of man who die and taste 'the cup of death,' the people die and their decrees are void; I shall bear witness against them, however, before the heavens and the earth, who never die and who do not taste 'the cup of death,' but whose end (סוף) is (that) they wear out in the world to come...."

Here "the cup of death" (כסא דמותה)[137] is repeated twice in connection with the imminent death of Moses. "Tasting the cup of death" is synonymous here with dying. It is emphasized that (all) the sons of man die / taste the cup of death. This also included Moses, who very shortly thereafter in fact does die.

Again, it is the Judaic haggadic description of the scene of Moses' imminent death, as still found in *Targum Neofiti 1* on Deut 32:1, which most probably inspired the Palestinian Jewish Christian author of the Gethsemane narrative to describe Jesus as asking God to remove "this cup (of death)" from him. The cup imagery itself, however, was probably inspired by Ps 116:13 (cf. section "C" below).

14) GREAT GRIEF.

a) After taking Peter, James and John with him, Jesus in Gethsemane began to be greatly distressed and troubled. Then he said to them: "My soul is 'very sorrowful' (περίλυπος), even to death" (Mark 14:34). At this point Jesus began to pray that death might pass by him (vv 35-36: the hour, this cup).

I suggest that the Palestinian Jewish Christian author of the Gethsemane narrative also borrowed the expression of Jesus' being "very sorrowful" or "greatly grieved" from Judaic haggada on Moses' great grief at the time of his impending death, when he too prayed that the Angel of Death should depart from him.

---

[137] Cf. Díez Macho, *Neophyti 1*, vol. 5.265, English 558. S. Speier in "'Das Kosten des Todeskelches' im Targum" in *VT* 13 (1963) 344-345 correctly defends the authenticity of these readings in Neofiti 1 over against R. Le Déaut, "Goûter le calice de la mort" in *Bib* 43 (1962) 82-86. The only other occurrence of the expression "the cup of death" is found in *Targ. Neof.* Gen 40:23 (Díez Macho 1.269, English 609) in regard to "flesh that tastes the cup of death." The same is found in the Fragment Targum on the same verse (Klein 1.62 and 152, English in 2.26 and 114). The latter was pointed out by M. Black in "The Cup Metaphor in Mark xiv. 36" in *ExpT* 59 (1957) 195. On "drinking the cup" that Jesus drinks, see Mark 10:38-39 par., and Acts 12:2 on the martyrdom of James the son of Zebedee. "The cup" and martyrdom are also related in *Mart. Isa.* 5:13, where Isaiah, while being sawed in two, says: "for me alone the Lord has mixed the cup" (*OTP* 2.164). I suspect Christian influence in the "Testament of Abraham," which speaks of the "bitter cup of death" in regard to Abraham in 1:3 and 16:11-12 (*OTP* 1.882 and 892).

b) In *Deut. Rab.* Wa'ethanan 2/7 on Deut 3:24, Moses pleads with God to be able to enter the Land of Israel for the sake of His mercy. God replies in the words of v 27: "for you shall not go over this Jordan." R. Levi, a third generation Palestinian Amora,[138] then comments: "And when Moses saw how emphatic God's words were, he began to plead strenuously," i.e. to speak v 24: "O Lord God, You have only begun to show Your servant...."[139] The Hebrew for "to plead strenuously" is "he spoke hard / difficult (קשה) words." The English translator in the Soncino edition, J. Rabbinowitz, correctly renders this as "to plead strenuously," for the phrase is designed to express Moses' strong inner feelings in light of his impending death.

In the same midrash, Wa'ethanan 2/3 on Deut 3:23 ("And I besought the Lord at that time"), R. Abin, a fourth generation Palestinian Amora,[140] noted that Moses now "supplicates and 'prostrates himself' to be permitted to enter the Land of Israel, and his prayers are not accepted. His hour is past," (as is indicated by) Deut 3:23.[141]

The Hebrew for "prostrates himself" is the hithpael of חבט: "to prostrate one's self (in prayer, in deep commotion)."[142] The expression seeks to describe Moses' deep, inner feelings when he prays to (escape death and) be able to enter the Land.

Most importantly, the Tannaitic midrash *Sifre* Deut. Niṣṣabim § 304 on Deut 31:14 ("And the Lord said to Moses: 'Behold, the days approach when you must die'") has Moses respond to this statement by replying: "Master of the world, since I am departing from the world 'in great grief,' show me a trustworthy man who can take charge of Israel...."[143] This is his disciple Joshua.

The Hebrew for "in great grief" is בנסיס גדול. The Hebrew noun נְסִיס means "falling away, grief," the Aramaic "evil, trouble."[144] I suggest that this expression lies behind the term περίλυπος in Mark 14:34. Moses' "strenuous pleading," his prostrating himself in prayer, in deep inner commotion, were a part of his "great grief." Jesus was "greatly grieved" or "very sorrowful" in light of his upcoming death, so he, like Moses, prayed that his "hour" might pass by him.

---

[138] See p. 76, n. 41.

[139] Mirqin 11.33, Soncino 7.36 (cf. n. 2).

[140] See p. 77, n. 47.

[141] Mirqin 11.31, and Soncino 7.32 (cf. n. 2).

[142] Jastrow 417.

[143] Finkelstein 323; Hammer 293; Neusner 2.289.

[144] Jastrow 917. Hammer has "in great agony," Neusner "with great anguish." Cf. Luke 22:44, "And being in an agony, he prayed more earnestly."

For the above reasons I do not believe that the Palestinian Jewish Christian author of the Gethsemane narrative alluded in Mark 14:34 to the phrase "Why are you cast down/ despairing, O my soul...?" in Ps 42:6, 12 and 43:5, as maintained by the commentators.[145] The Hebrew verb in these psalm passages is the hithpoel of שׁחח,[146] which was not so employed in later Hebrew.[147] The Hellenistic Jewish Christian translator of the original Semitic "my soul has great grief, unto death," could have employed λύπη πολλά or λύπη μεγάλα.[148] Yet he may also have been acquainted with the term περίλυπος in connection with both one's soul and prayer in Tob 3:1 (S), as well as with one's soul in LXX Ps 41:5, 11 and 42:5. They then encouraged him, the translator, to prefer the latter Greek term for "great grief." The origin of the term, however, lies in Judaic lore on Moses' departing from this world "in great grief."

* * *

The above fourteen similarities in regard to the setting, a threefold prayer pattern, and numerous expressions and motifs, are found in the Markan Gethsemane narrative and Judaic lore on the scene of Moses' impending death. While one may question the relevance of an individual comparison, the cumulative argument is very strong that the Palestinian Jewish Christian author of Jesus' last hours in Gethsemane borrowed extensively (and creatively) from traditions available to him regarding the last hours of Israel's first redeemer, Moses.

Other terminology in the Gethsemane narrative also derives from Judaic interpretation of Psalm 116, to which I now return.

C) *The Cup.*

In addition to the remarks found above in B) 13) on "the cup of death" related to the end of Moses' life, the "cup" of Ps 116:13 very probably played a major role for the Palestinian Jewish Christian author of the Gethsemane narrative, who mentioned it in Mark 14:36.

The MT of Ps 116:13 states: "I will lift up the cup of salvations (pl.), and I will call on the name of the Lord." This specific cup (כּוֹס) was

---

[145] Cf. the margin of the Nestle / Aland Greek New Testament; Feldmeier, *Die Krisis* 156-162; Gundry, *Mark* 867; and Brown, *The Death* 154.

[146] BDB 1006.

[147] Jastrow 1546.

[148] For "great grief" in the LXX, cf. Jonah 4:1, Tob 3:6, and 1 Macc 6:4, 9 and 13. Sir 37:2 somewhat recalls the betrayer Judas: "Is it not a grief to the death when a companion and friend turn to enmity?"

associated in Judaic sources with the cup used for grace after meals,[149] and with two of the four cups of salvation in the time to come,[150] including that of the days of the Messiah.[151] More important for the Gethsemane narrative, which immediately follows the "Lord's Supper," a Passover meal, is the fact that the Sages maintained that the four cups of wine to be drunk (at the Seder meal) on the eve of Passover fulfilled the verse Ps 116:13.[152]

In addition, the Targum of Ps 116:13a can be read as: "I bear / endure the cup of redemption (sing.) leading to the world to come" (כסא דפורקנא אסובר לעלמא דאתי).[153] If at least this form of the Targum was early and thus already known to the Palestinian Jewish Christian author of the Gethsemane narrative, it also would have motivated him to apply the term "cup" to Jesus in Mark 14:36. The cup (of death) which Jesus asks his heavenly Father to take away from him is the cup he "endures" on the Cross. Paradoxically, it leads to "redemption" for him (the Resurrection on Easter Sunday) and for those who believe in him as the Messiah, the second or final redeemer of Israel.

D) *Being Greatly Distressed and Troubled.*

a) Mark 14:33 states that Jesus in Gethsemane began to be "greatly distressed and troubled" (RSV), or "distressed and agitated" (NRSV). The two Greek verbs employed here are ἐκθαμβέομαι and ἀδημονέω.

The verb ἐκθαμβέομαι occurs elsewhere in the NT only in Mark, and only in the passive. In 9:15 it describes a crowd's being "greatly amazed" at Jesus' arrival. The same translation is appropriate for the women on Easter Sunday morning, who see an angel in Jesus' tomb (16:5-6). The cognate adjective ἔκθαμβος[154] is found in the NT only in Acts 3:13, where it applies to people who are "greatly astonished" at seeing in the Jerusalem Temple the healed man who had been lame from birth.

---

[149] Cf. *b. Ber.* 51b (Soncino 309); *Pesaḥ.* 119b (Soncino 616); and *Eliyyahu Zuṭa* 20 (Friedmann 32, Braude and Kapstein 501).

[150] Cf. *Midr. Pss.* 11/5 on Ps 11:6 (Buber 100: literally "many," but only two of the four mentioned are left; Braude 1.163).

[151] Cf. *Gen. Rab.* Vayesheb 88/5 on Gen 40:11 (Theodor and Albeck 3.1083, Soncino 2.816-817).

[152] Cf. *Exod. Rab.* Va'era 6/4 on Exod 6:6 (Soncino 3.108-109), as well as *y. Pesaḥ.* 10:1, 37c (Neusner / Bokser 13.478).

[153] Cf. the Aramaic in Merino, *Targum de Salmos* 90. In his Latin translation on p. 300, he forgets the phrase "to the world to come." See Jastrow 952 for סבר II as "to carry, bear, endure," and the Hebrew of the MT, נשא, as "to bear, carry" (BDB 671).

[154] Cf. BAGD 240 and LSJ 506.

The verb ἀδημονέω is also rare. Elsewhere in the NT it occurs only twice: once in the parallel passage Matt 26:37 (where the Evangelist substitutes λυπεῖσθαι for Mark's ἐκθαμβεῖσθαι),[155] and once in Phil 2:26 of Epaphroditus' being "distressed" because the Philippians had heard that he was ill.[156] The cognate noun ἀδημονία ("trouble, distress")[157] occurs three times in Philo together with "affliction" (ἄση).[158] In *Flacc.* 167 it is employed, as in Gethsemane, in a context of solitary prayer, with "endless and boundless" distress. In 166 Flaccus is prostrate on the ground, like Jesus.

I suggest that the two verbs of Mark 14:33, both describing Jesus as being inwardly "greatly distressed and troubled / afflicted," also derive from Psalm 116.

b) Ps 116:10 has the author say: "I am greatly afflicted." The next verse (11) repeats this mental anguish: "I said in my consternation / trepidation."

Verse 10 in Hebrew is: אֲנִי עָנִיתִי מְאֹד. The verb ענה means "to be bowed down, afflicted."[159] I suggest that the Palestinian Jewish Christian author of the Gethsemane narrative described Jesus in Mark 14:33 as לַעֲנוֹת מְאֹד, (he began) "to be greatly distressed / afflicted." He borrowed the expression from Ps 116:10. The Hellenistic Jewish translator of this episode later attempted to render the adverb "greatly" here not by employing the simple form θαμβεῖσθαι,[160] but rather the compound ἐκθαμβεῖσθαι.[161]

"In my consternation / trepidation" in Ps 116:11 is the Hebrew בְחָפְזִי. The verb חפז basically means "to be in trepidation, hurry or alarm."[162] The Targum renders it with the verb עוק, "to be narrow, pressed," to be in distress / anxiety.[163] In Deut 16:3 the noun חִפָּזוֹן, "trepidation, hurried

[155] Cf. Sir 30:9, where ἐκθαμβέω is parallel to λυπέω.

[156] Cf. BAGD 16 and LSJ 21 ("to be sorely troubled or dismayed, be in anguish").

[157] LSJ 21.

[158] LSJ 255, 2: "distress, vexation." See *Det.* 98, *Ios.* 90, and *Mos.* 1.120.

[159] BDB 776. See Qal 3 on this passage, Ps 119:67, and Zech 10:2 for being afflicted.

[160] Cf. Mark 1:27 and 10:32.

[161] He also avoided the LXX reading: ἐταπεινώθην σφόδα, for it conveys being greatly humbled / humiliated / shamed, in contrast to the intended meaning in the Gethsemane setting.

[162] BDB 342. Here the infinitive construct is employed.

[163] Cf. Merino 90, as well as Jastrow 1056 on עוק (note its close relationship to the Hebrew צר, and מעיק as "troubled, feeling dread"). See also Jastrow 1109 on עקת:

flight,"[164] is employed of the exodus from Egypt, including eating the Passover with the bread of "affliction" (עֹנִי). The latter recalls the related verb ענה in Ps 116:10, part of the Hallel recited at the Passover Seder meal.

I suggest that the Palestinian Jewish Christian author of the Gethsemane narrative described Jesus' inner trepidation by employing the verb חפז from Ps 116:11.

Most important for this theory concerning the verbs ἐκθαμβεῖσθαι and ἀδημονεῖν in Mark 14:33 is the fact that Symmachus renders the verb חפז of Ps 116:11 (Greek 115:2) by ἀδημονεῖν, and the noun חפזון in Isa 52:12 by (the passive of) ἐκθαμβεῖν.[165] Aquila also translates the verb חפז of Ps 116:11 by the simple form θαμβεῖν, and the noun חפזון in Isa 52:12 by the cognate noun θάμβησις.[166]

The Hellenistic Jewish Christian translator of the Gethsemane narrative avoided the expression ἐν τῇ ἐκστάσει μου of the LXX of Ps 116:11 (115:2) as meaning "distraction, confusion, astonishment, terror."[167] This was inappropriate for Jesus' state of deep mental anguish. Instead, like Symmachus, he rendered the term חפז which he found in his "Vorlage" by ἀδημονεῖν. He knew that ἐκθαμβεῖσθαι conveyed basically the same meaning, as shown by the passages from Symmachus and Aquila cited above. This encouraged him to employ this Greek verb for the expression ענה מאד, which itself ultimately derived from the neighboring verse, Ps 116:10.

If this proposal is basically correct, it shows that the Palestinian Jewish Christian author of the Gethsemane narrative gives one more sign in Mark 14:33 of his dependence on Psalm 116. His final borrowing from this important Passover Hallel psalm is found in the expression "heavy eyes."

E) *Heavy Eyes.*

a) Mark 14:40 says that after Jesus prayed a second time, he returned and found them (Peter, James and John) sleeping, "for their eyes were very heavy" (ἦσαν γὰρ αὐτῶν οἱ ὀφθαλμοὶ καταβαρυνόμενοι). Matthew at 26:43 changes the latter participle into the simpler βεβαρημένοι.

"anguish, trouble, distress." The same root is employed twice in the Targum of Ps 116:3, where the RSV has: "The pangs (מְצָרֵי) of Sheol laid hold on me; I suffered distress and anguish (צָרָה וְיָגוֹן)."

[164] BDB 342; it occurs elsewhere only in Exod 12:11 and Isa 52:12.

[165] Cf. the LXX concordance of Hatch and Redpath, 24 and 431.

[166] Cf. Hatch and Redpath 623 (note also 4 Kgdms 7:15 with θαμβεῖσθαι for חפז).

[167] BAGD 245; LSJ 520, II 2.

The verb καταβαρύνω, "to weigh down, burden, oppress,"[168] occurs only here in the NT. LXX Joel 2:8 has the same participial form as in Mark: "'weighed down' by their weapons." In both 2 Kgdms 13:26 and 14:26 the verb translates the Hebrew כבד.[169] At the transfiguration scene in Luke 9:32, Peter, James and John, as in Gethsemane, are described as "heavy" (βεβαρημένοι) with sleep. Yet their "eyes" are not specifically mentioned. The verb βαρύνω in the LXX also usually translates כבד. The same is true for the adjective βαρύς, "heavy."[170] Both LXX and Theod Dan 2:11, however, translate יקיר with βαρύς.

Gen 48:10 states that "the eyes of Israel were dim / heavy (כָּבְדוּ) with age." The LXX translates this by employing a compound with the root βαρυ: βαρυωπέω.[171] Philo in *Ebr.* 131 remarks that one who wishes to serve the Lord in the Temple should not have "his eyes heavy with wine" (βεβαρημένος τοὺς ὀφθαλμοὺς ἀπ' οἴνου). *Leg. Gai.* 269, however, is the closest passage in Philo to the condition of the disciples in Gethsemane. King Agrippa I, in Rome in 40 C.E., heard from Gaius Caligula of the latter's plan to erect a statue of himself as a god within the Jerusalem Temple. Philo says that greatly distressed, Agrippa "lay sunk in profound coma and knew nothing of what went on. But about the late afternoon he lifted his head slightly and just managed to open his eyes a little, 'weary as they were' (βεβαρημένους)...." Then he fell asleep again (270).[172]

I suggest that the imagery of the "eyes" of the disciples in Gethsemane as "very heavy" derives not from Gen 48:10, overeating or overdrinking from the cups of wine at the Passover meal,[173] or the lateness of the hour,[174] but from Ps 116:15.

b) Ps 116:15 reads, "Precious in the sight of (בְּעֵינֵי יְקָר) the Lord is the death of His saints" (RSV). The adjective יְקָר can mean "precious, rare,

---

168 Cf. BAGD 408, LSJ 884.

169 The only other occurrence is Sir 8:15, without a Hebrew equivalent. Other MSS omit the κατα-. Joel 2:8 is a paraphrase, also without a Hebrew equivalent.

170 Cf. Hatch and Redpath 191.

171 LSJ 308 cites only this passage; no other occurrences are known.

172 Cf. the LCL translation of F. Colson, as well as Schürer, *The history* 1.395-396 for a description of the historical situation.

173 Cf. *m. Pesaḥ.* 10:8 (Albeck 2.179, Danby 151), which speaks of participants falling asleep, dozing, or falling into deep sleep already at the meal. See also Philo, *Leg. All.* 183, and *Spec. Leg.* 1.98-99.

174 In *m. Pesaḥ.* 10:9 (Albeck 2.180, Danby 151; cf. *Zebaḥ.* 5:8 in Albeck 5.26, Danby 475), the Passover offering must be consumed by midnight.

splendid, weighty," and the basic meaning of the root is "to be heavy, weighty, precious."[175] It is frequently synonymous with כבד.[176] This is best shown in Gen 48:10, quoted above in a): "the eyes of Israel 'were heavy' (כבדו) with age." *Targum Pseudo-Jonathan* here has יקרין.[177]

I suggest that the Palestinian Jewish Christian author of the Gethsemane narrative continued to employ imagery from Psalm 116 by appropriating the terms יקרות and עינים from v 15. Mark 14:40 would then be in Hebrew: כִּי עֵינֵיהֶם הָיוּ יְקֵרֹות, "for their eyes were heavy." Both Delitzsch and the United Bible Societies in their Hebrew New Testaments employ the synonym כבדות here for "were heavy," without מְאֹד, "very."[178] The Hellenistic Jewish Christian translator of this narrative probably himself wished to emphasize the disciples' eyes as "very" heavy. He therefore chose the term καταβαρυνόμενοι, which Matthew again reduced to βεβαρημένοι in 26:43.

Assonance between "their eyes" (עֵינֵיהֶם) and "they should answer" (לַעֲנוֹת or יַעֲנֻהוּ – him, from ענה, "to respond, answer"[179]) may be intentional in Mark 14:40. In section D) b) above I also suggested לענות מאד for Jesus as having begun "to be greatly distressed / afflicted" in v 33. One verbal root with different meanings would have appealed to the original hearers.

Finally, if the Palestinian Jewish Christian author of the Gethsemane narrative was aware of Ps 116:15 as applied to the first redeemer Moses, this may also have encouraged him to borrow the imagery "heavy eyes" from it and to apply this imagery to the disciples of the final redeemer, the Messiah Jesus. This is indicated in *Deut. Rab.* Vayelech 9/1 regarding the impending death of Moses:

> The Rabbis say: God finds it hard to decree death upon the righteous. Whence this? For it is said, "'Precious' in the sight of the Lord is the death of His saints" (Ps 116:15). And this is the proof. God should have spoken to Moses thus: "Behold, you are about to die." He, however, did not speak in this way, but He left him alone, and He attached "death" to the days. Whence this? From what we read in this matter: "Behold, your 'days' approach that you must die" (Deut 31:14).[180]

---

[175] BDB 429-430, Jastrow 591-593.

[176] BDB 457-459, Jastrow 606-607.

[177] Rieder 1.76.

[178] Cf. pp. 93 and 134 respectively.

[179] As in the Hebrew New Testaments of the United Bible Societies (p. 134) and Delitzsch (p. 93), respectively. On the verb, see Jastrow 1093.

[180] Mirqin 11.134; I slightly modify the Soncino translation in 7.157 (see n. 1). Cf. *Midr. Pss.* 116/6 on 116:15, including the death of Moses (Buber 477-478, Braude 2.225-226). See also the words of R. Meir, a third generation Tanna (see p. 79, n.

F) *The Shema', Psalm 116:13 and 3-4, and the Night and Morning Prayers.*

According to Mark 12:28-30, Jesus maintained that the "first" of all the commandments is Deut 6:4-5. These verses are the beginning of the Shema', the so-called Jewish confession of faith, which extended to v 9.[181] It was to be recited both at night, and in the morning, which was based on Deut 6:7 ("when you lie down, and when you rise").[182]

It is significant that the Mishnah in *Ber.* 9:5 codifies a long accepted practice, which was buttressed by part of the Shema'. It states: "Man is bound to bless (God) for the evil even as he blesses (God) for the good, for it is written, 'And you shall love the Lord your God with all your heart and with all your soul and with all your might' (Deut 6:5)." Then the phrase "and with all your soul" is interpreted to mean: "even if He takes away your soul."[183]

The Jerusalem Talmud at this point (*Ber.* 9:5, 14b) asks why one is obliged to say a blessing over bad fortune as well as over good fortune. After the opinions of three individual rabbis, the general consensus is stated: "And Sages say, 'I will lift up the cup of salvation and call on the name of the Lord' (Ps 116:13). 'I suffered distress and anguish. Then I called on the name of the Lord' (vv 3b-4a). For both (salvation and distress) he 'called on the name of the Lord.'"[184]

In the same section R. Aqiva's martyrdom by the Romans is given as an example. It was the time to recite the Shema'. Aqiva smiled because he now realized the time had finally come for him to also fulfill (by being killed) the phrase "and with all your soul."[185]

The above shows how the Palestinian Jewish Christian author of the Gethsemane narrative, which took place in the late evening, when the Shema' was usually recited, could think of Jesus' bearing the cup of salvation (Targum) through his death the next afternoon, and his calling on the name of the Lord in prayer in a situation of deep distress and

---

56), in *Tanh.* Vayechi 4 (Singermann 283). Ben Azzai, a second generation Tanna (*Introduction* 82), comments on Ps 116:5 in *Exod. Rab.* Pequde 52/3 on Exod 39:33 (Soncino 3.576); a parallel is found in *Gen. Rab.* Hayye Sarah 62/2 on Gen 25:8 (Soncino 2.550).

[181] The Shema' later also included Deut 11:13-21 and Num 15:37-41. See the art. "Shema'" by J. Eisenstein in *JE* (1905) 11.266-267, as well as "Shema" by L. Jacobs in *EJ* (1971) 14.1370-1374.

[182] For the opinion of the Sages, "until midnight," cf. *m. Ber.* 1:1 (Albeck 1.13, Danby 2).

[183] Albeck 1.32, and Danby 10, which I have slightly modified.

[184] Neusner-Zahavy 1.344, which I slightly modify.

[185] *Ibid.*, 1.346.

anguish (Ps 116:13, 3b-4a). Precisely these psalm verses were associated at a very early time.[186]

In *m. Ber.* 9:3 it is also stated, as in 5, that one "should say the benediction for misfortune regardless of (any consequent) evil."[187] This shows that other materials relevant to the topic of thanking God also for evil could be adduced in this general Mishnah section, now "nine," long before the individual passages were given specific numbers such as 3, 4 and 5. In *b. Ber.* 60b on the end of *m.* 9:4 and just before 5, for example, the prayers are stated which are to be said on going to bed and upon waking in the morning, especially when washing one's face.[188]

Before gong to bed, one is first to recite the Shema' from Deut 6:5 to 7:12. Then one says: "Blessed is He who causes the bands of sleep to fall upon my eyes and slumber on my eyelids, and gives light to the apple of the eye. May it be Thy will, O Lord, my God, to make me lie down in peace.... And bring me not into sin, or into iniquity, or into temptation.... And enlighten my eyes lest I sleep the sleep of death."[189]

The terms "sleep" (ישן and שינה), "eyes" (עינים), "May it be 'Your will'" (יהי רצון מלפניך), and "lie down / rest" (שכב) all occur also in the Gethsemane narrative in Mark 14:37, 40, 41 (sleeping), 40 (eyes), 36 (will), and 41 (rest). The Night Prayer, in addition to the other sources already analyzed above, may thus also have encouraged the Palestinian Jewish Christian author to use this terminology in his account of Gethsemane, the incident also occurring at night.

I suggest that another motif now found in the Gethsemane account was suggested by the Night and Morning Prayers.

After Jesus returns to the disciples and finds them sleeping, he tells them to watch / stay awake and pray "lest you enter into temptation" (ἵνα μὴ ἔλθητε εἰς πειρασμόν : Mark 14:38). This seems rather strange in the context. The disciples can hardly imagine what their temptation / trial should be here. The narrative would thus make quite good sense even if v 38 were omitted. I propose that the author has paraphrased a

---

[186] Cf. *b. Ber.* 60b (Soncino 380); *Mek. R. Ish.* Baḥodesh 10 on Exod 20:20 (Lauterbach 2.277); *Sifre* Deut. Wa'etḥanan 32 on Deut 6:5 (Finkelstein 55-56, Hammer 60); *Lev. Rab.* Qedoshim 24/2 on Lev 19:2 (Soncino 4.305); and *Midr. Pss.* 101/1 on Ps 101:1 (Buber 427, Braude 2.150).

[187] Albeck 1.31, Danby 9.

[188] Soncino 378 and 379, respectively. Cf. the art. "Night Prayer" by H. Blumenthal in *EJ* (1971) 12.1157-1158. On the present night prayer, see *The Authorized Daily Prayer Book*, trans. S. Singer, revised and enlarged by J. Hertz (London: Eyre and Spottiswoods, 1954[23]) 293-297.

[189] With the exception of the last clause, all these phrases are also found in the Morning Prayer.

petition from the Night Prayer at this point. There the speaker says: "Bring me not...into (lit. the hands of) temptation" (וְאַל תביאני...לידי נסיון). The term נִסָּיוֹן, "temptation,"[190] corresponds exactly to πειρασμός in Mark 14:38. In the Night Prayer the speaker prays that he not enter into temptation, especially at night while sleeping. The disciples' temptation is the opposite; they are tempted to fall asleep while he prays, even though Jesus has asked them to watch / stay awake with him and thus not to leave him alone in his darkest hour. The failure of the disciples to do so is the temptation into which they have fallen.

Another motif from the events surrounding the Gethsemane narrative is also found in the Morning Prayer, spoken when one washes one's face. This basically repeats the Night Prayer, but adds: "and remove me far from an evil person and a false friend" (ורחקני מאדם רע ומחבר רע). Here the Palestinian Jewish Christian author of the Gethsemane narrative could easily have thought of the betrayer Judas, Jesus' disciple and "false friend."[191] While not specifically mentioned in Mark 14:32-42, (except for the "sinners" in v 41, who can be "evil ones" in the Semitic), this motif may have encouraged the author to apply the above expression, "to enter into temptation," from the Night and Morning Prayers to the account in v 38.

Finally, the problem of the dating of the above Night and Morning Prayers should be mentioned. I. Elbogen points out that the origin of the Night Prayer, and individual prayer, was in the Shema' verse Deut 6:7, "and when you lie down (to sleep)." He states that "The prayer was already in general use at the beginning of the Common Era."[192] He also calls attention to the statement in Josephus, *Ant.* 4.212: "Twice each day,

---

[190] Jastrow 916, who translates here: "suffer me not to come within the power of sin, iniquity, or temptation." Cf. also the petition of the "Lord's Prayer" in Matt 7:13 // Luke 11:4. Feldmeier, *Die Krisis* 201, also called attention to not falling into temptation in *b. Ber.* 60b.

[191] For the term "evil companion / false friend," cf. for example *m. 'Avot* 2:9 (Albeck 4.360, Danby 449).

[192] Cf. his *Der jüdische Gottesdienst in seiner geschichtlichen Entwicklung* (Frankfurt / Main, 1931[3]; Darmstadt: Olms, 1962) 100. See also J. Heinemann, *Prayer in the Talmud.* Forms and Patterns (SJ 9; Berlin: de Gruyter, 1977) 157 regarding "Private and Non-statutory Prayer": "The work of establishing norms in this area began at a relatively early date – at the outset of the Tannaitic period or perhaps even before ...." Also, "it would seem that only the benedictions to be recited before partaking of some material enjoyment and before performing a ritual commandment achieved a kind of obligatory status (apparently at a relatively early stage)" (p. 158). See also the statement of L. Jacobs, art. "Shema" 1370, regarding the Shema', recited together with the Night Prayer: "it was a long established practice at the beginning of the present era to read the *Shema* in the evening and morning...."

at the dawn thereof and when the hour comes for turning to repose, let all acknowledge before God...." The latter very probably alludes to the Night Prayer, at the end of the first century C.E. It seems reasonable to assume that the basic forms of the Night and Morning Prayers as now preserved in *b. Ber.* 60b already prevailed in the first century C.E. so that the Palestinian Jewish Christian author of the Gethsemane scene could have been influenced by them.

*   *   *

Sections two, and three A, B9, and C-F above have described the role of Psalm 116 as part of the Hallel sung at the "Lord's Supper," but especially the psalm's great influence on the Gethsemane narrative in Mark 14:32-42. Connected to this complex is Moses' struggle with death, which influenced Jesus' struggle with death in Gethsemane in a major way. There is one more important source of imagery for the latter account, the situation of the high priest, especially on the Day of Atonement. To this I now turn.

II
THE HIGH PRIEST AND THE DAY OF ATONEMENT
Introduction

Acts 6:7 states that "the number of the disciples multiplied greatly in Jerusalem, and a great many of the priests were obedient to the faith." While this is a typically Lukan summary statement, there is no reason to doubt its basic content. Many of the priests, who served on a rotational basis in the Temple and had intimate, personal knowledge of its rites, including the Day of Atonement, became Christians.[1] It is understandable that they too would exert influence on the ways in which the final evening and day of Jesus' life were described.

Lev 4:3 and 5 speak of the high priest as "the anointed priest" (הַכֹּהֵן הַמָּשִׁיחַ; cf. 16:32),[2] which enabled the earliest Palestinian Jewish

---

[1] On the twenty-four courses of priests from both Judea and Galilee, who in rotation served for a week and at the three pilgrimage festivals, see Jeremias, *Jerusalem* 198-207, and Schürer, *The history* 2.245-250. Jerusalem itself had a course (cf. for example the baraitha in *y. Pesaḥ.* 4:1, 30c [Neusner / Bokser 13.149]), and those priests with a permanent function certainly lived in the city or nearby. On the latter, see *The history* 275-291.

[2] It should also be noted that the former high priest, who had "passed" from his office, was called מָשִׁיחַ שֶׁעָבַר, "the anointed one who has passed." Cf. *b. Sanh.* 19a, a baraitha (Soncino 97, with n. 2). This is important in regard to Jesus' first being taken from Gethsemane to Annas, the former high priest, in John 18:13. He too was thought to be an "anointed one."

Christians to think of Jesus, their Messiah / Anointed One, also as the high priest. In *Bell.* 4.318 Josephus calls the Jews' high priest "the captain of their salvation." The same writer, a native of Jerusalem, maintained that after the death of Herod's son Archelaus (6 C.E.), "the high priests were entrusted with the leadership of the nation" (*Ant.* 20.251).[3]

Only the high priest was allowed to function in the Holy of Holies of the Jerusalem Temple on the Day of Atonement (Leviticus 16). On this day the decree concerning the judgment of man made on New Year's was thought to be finally sealed.[4] The high priest secured atonement for himself, his house, the holy place, and the transgressions of the people of Israel, indeed, for "all" their sins, iniquities and transgressions (Lev 16:16, 21-22, 30, 34).

Philo of Alexandria, who was born ca. 20 B.C.E.,[5] could describe the high priest as having a nature on the borderline between the divine and the human. This allows men to have a mediator, and God a servitor (*Spec. Leg.* 1.116).[6] The high priest for the Alexandrian is a divine Word (λόγος), whose father is God (*Fug.* 108).[7] Especially when he enters the Holy of Holies, he is "less than God, (but) superior to man," as Philo interprets LXX Lev 16:17 in *Som.* 2.188 and 231.[8] There he pours as a libation the blood of the soul (*Leg. All.* 2.56); there the truly great high priest "pours that potent undiluted draught, the libation of himself" (ἑαυτόν: *Som.* 2.183). Indeed, he is "none other than the draught which he pours" (2.249).[9]

These descriptions of the high priest's sprinkling the blood of the he-goat and bullock near (and sometimes onto) the veil / curtain of the Holy of Holies as the high priest's "pouring out himself" come very close to the thoughts contained in the Book of Hebrews, certainly written by a Jewish Christian (of priestly descent, living in the diaspora?), who was

---

[3] Cf. E. Hirsch in the art. "High Priest" in *JE* (1904) 6.393, who states that "in the post-Maccabean period the high priest was looked upon as exercising in all things, political, legal, and sacerdotal, the supreme authority...."

[4] Cf. *t. Roš Haš.* 1:13 (Zuckermandel / Liebermann 210, Neusner 2.252). On the great importance of this day, "the most important day in the liturgical year," see M. Herr, art. "Day of Atonement," in *EJ* (1971) 5.1376-1384, quotation col. 1376.

[5] Cf. the LCL edition of Philo, I ix.

[6] Cf. *Mos.* 2.135 and *Som.* 2.231-232 for the latter, and *Quaes. Exod.* 2.118 (the divine Logos as a mediator) for the former.

[7] On the first, cf. also 110 and 117.

[8] Cf. also *Her.* 84.

[9] I employ here the English translations of F. Colson and G. Whitaker in the LCL edition.

very well acquainted with the rites of the Day of Atonement. For him Jesus is the great high priest (4:14), who makes expiation for the sins of the people (2:17); he offered himself up (7:27). Also, he "entered once for all into the Holy Place, not through the blood of goats and calves but his own blood, thus securing an eternal redemption" (9:12; cf. v 26, and 10:12).

As I noted in section I.1 above, the author of Hebrews in 5:7-10 most probably also described Jesus in Gethsemane in terms of Psalm 116 (LXX 114-115).

The Apostle Paul also represents Jesus' Crucifixion in terms of his offering himself as an expiation, which is reminiscent of Philo's interpretation of the high priest in the Holy of Holies. Gal 1:4 speaks of "our Lord Jesus Christ, who gave himself for our sins." In addition, Rom 3:25 has God put forward Christ Jesus "as an expiation by his blood," through which we are justified (5:9), enabling us to become reconciled to God (vv 10-11).

This borrowing from Hellenistic Jewish thought regarding the role and nature of the high priest on the Day of Atonement, as seen in Hebrews and the diaspora Jew Paul of Tarsus, may also have influenced Hebrew- or Aramaic-speaking Palestinian Judaism. There was not only a synagogue of the Alexandrians in Jerusalem (Acts 6:9).[10] Various craftsmen were also summoned from the city to offer their expertise in the Temple.[11] M. Hengel has even estimated that between 10-15% of the Jerusalem population at the time of Paul consisted of Greek-speaking Jews.[12] Certainly much more theological dialogue between Palestinian and Hellenistic Jews took place than was earlier thought. For this reason it is quite possible that the Palestinian Jewish Christian author of the Gethsemane narrative could also have been influenced by Hellenistic Jewish thought in regard to the high priest, who on the Day of Atonement "pours out the libation of himself."

Whether the latter was the case or not, the author definitely described Jesus in Gethsemane not only in terms of Psalm 116. He also described him by means of the typology of the imminent death of Israel's first redeemer Moses (also thought of as a high priest up until his death),[13] and its last or great redeemer, the Messiah. Finally, the author

---

[10] Cf. the sources cited by Str-B 2.663-665 on this.

[11] Cf. *t. Yoma* 2:5-6 (Neusner 2.193-194) and *b. Yoma* 38a (Soncino 176). See also the sources mentioned in n. 62.

[12] Cf. his *The Pre-Christian Paul*, in collaboration with Roland Deines (London: SCM, 1991) 55.

[13] Cf. the statement by R. Yehoshua b. Qorḥa, a third generation Tanna (Strack and Stemberger, *Introduction* 85), in *Lev. Rab.* Shemini 11/6 (Soncino 4.141):

also pictured Jesus in terms of the high priest on the (evening and) Day of Atonement. Before analyzing the Gethsemane account in light of the latter, it will be helpful to note that the author was not the only one to describe an episode within the Passion Narrative in such terms. There are nine other such occurrences. If the author was aware of any such endeavors, this too may have encouraged him to paint his picture in the colors he chose. (The reader who wants to concentrate only on the Gethsemane narrative can proceed to section 2.)

1. **Other High Priest and Day of Atonement Imagery in the Passion Narrative.**

1) *The Anointing at Bethany.*

a) Directly before Judas went to the chief priests in Jerusalem in order to betray Jesus (Mark 14:10-11), two days before Passover (v 1) an unknown woman in the house of Simon the leper at Bethany east of Jerusalem broke an alabaster jar of ointment / oil (ἡ ἀλάβαστρος)[14] of pure nard and poured it over Jesus' head (v 3). This he interpreted as her having "anointed" (μυρίζω)[15] his body beforehand for burial (8).

While Matt 26:7 also has the woman pour the oil onto Jesus' head, Luke 7 reports this incident already during the Galilean ministry. There she anoints Jesus' feet with the ointment (vv 38 and 46). The Evangelist

---

"Throughout the forty years spent by Israel in the wilderness Moses did not refrain from ministering in the High Priesthood," which he bases on Ps 99:6. (A parallel is found in *Pesiq. Rav Kah.* 4/5, in Mandelbaum 70, Braude and Kapstein 76.) See also the following opinions in the section (Soncino 4.142, and n. 1, which explains how Moses was thought to be a high priest until his death), which are also found in part in *y. Yoma* 1:1, 38b (Neusner 14.17). In *Midr. Pss.* 99/4 on Ps 99:6 (Buber 424, Braude 2.145), R. Eleazar b. Yose, a fourth generation Tanna (*Einleitung* 85; he was forgotten in the English edition), taught that "On each of the seven days of consecration, Moses, wearing a white linen garment that had no seam, ministered as high priest." See also the discussion below of Jesus' seamless robe, as well as the fact that in Judaic thought Moses descended a second time from Mount Sinai with the Tables of the Law on the 10th of Tishre, thought to be the Day of Atonement (*Seder 'Olam* 6, with Exod 34:9 and Lev 16:34, in Milikowsky 252-253 and 467; see also b. *Ta'an.* 30b in Soncino 162).

[14] BAGD 34. It is found in the NT only at this point in the Synoptics. In his Hebrew New Testament (p. 91), Delitzsch has here: פַּךְ~שֶׁמֶן, "a jar of oil," and the United Bible Societies (p. 132): פַּךְ וּבוֹ שֶׁמֶן, "a jar, and in it was oil." A פַּךְ is a flask or jar with a narrow neck (Jastrow 1173, who cites an example from the Jerusalem Talmud with "were anointed out of a flask").

[15] BAGD 529. The verb is only found here in the NT. In his Hebrew New Testament (p. 91), Delitzsch has here: לִמְשׁוֹחַ, and the United Bible Societies the same (p. 132).

John has Mary, the sister of Martha and Lazarus at Bethany, also anoint the feet of Jesus with her ointment (12:3). However, as in Mark and Matthew, for him the event also takes place before Passover. For John, it was six days before this pilgrimage festival (v 1).

I suggest that the interpretation of Jesus' head as being anointed by oil is the earliest version of the narrative. Only later, in retrospect, was this motif applied to the burial of his body (cf. Mark 16:1). This anointing, just before his death, took place to represent Jesus as the high priest, who offered himself at Golgotha.

b) According to Leviticus 8, Moses took the anointing oil and poured some of it onto Aaron's head to anoint and consecrate him (v 12). This ordination lasted seven days (vv 33, 35).[16] In Judaic thought, Aaron thus became the high priest, and all high priests after him were to have the same anointing for seven days.[17] This is based on Exod 30:31, "This shall be my holy anointing oil 'throughout your generations.'"[18] The high priest was thus "the priest, the anointed one."

However, when King Josiah feared that the Babylonian Nebuchadnezzar would conquer Jerusalem, he had the Levites hide the ark, the bottle containing the manna, the jar of anointing oil, and other things "in the house of the Most Holy of Holies."[19] This meant that the high priest could no longer be anointed.[20] R. Eliezar (b. Hyrcanus) maintained that the jar of anointing oil is one of the three things which Elijah will restore to Israel in the future.[21]

Since the first Palestinian Jewish Christians believed Elijah had already returned in the form of John the Baptist,[22] I suggest that because the Baptizer did not get to anoint Jesus before Herod Antipas had him killed, they created the narrative of an unknown woman in Bethany

---

[16] Cf. Exod 29:7, 29-30, 35.

[17] Cf. for example *b. Yoma* 5a (Soncino 19, with n. 2, and 20).

[18] Cf. *'Avot R. Nat.* A 1 (Schechter 1, Goldin 4) in the name of R. Eliezer (b. Hyrcanus), a second generation Tanna (Strack and Stemberger, *Introduction* 77).

[19] Cf. *t. Yoma* 2:15 (Zuckermandel / Liebermann 186 as 3:7, Neusner 2.198). On this whole issue see Ginzberg, *Legends* 3.48 and 6.19, n. 112.

[20] Cf. Schürer, *The history* 2.244, n. 28, however, for the historical discontinuance of the anointing of the high priest as probably much later. Yet see p. 108, n. 2.

[21] Cf. *Mek. R. Ish.* Vayassa' 6 on Exod 16:33 (Lauterbach 2.126). On the dating of Eliezer, see n. 18. See also *t. Soṭa* 13:1 (Zuckermandel / Liebermann 318, Neusner 3.200-201).

[22] Cf. for example Mark 9:13. See also Justin Martyr, *Dialogue with Trypho the Jew* 49, where Trypho states that Elijah when he comes will anoint (the Christ): *The Ante-Nicene Fathers* 1.219.

doing so. She took an alabaster jar of oil, like that used to anoint the high priest, and poured it over Jesus' head two days before his death. The Evangelist John, who knew that the high priest was anointed for seven days and alone could serve in the Holy of Holies on the Day of Atonement,[23] may have changed this date to six days before Passover to emphasize the high priest imagery. For him, Jesus' death was his high priestly offering of himself.

2. *Jesus' Supposed Blasphemy.*

a) Immediately after Jesus' prayers in Gethsemane, according to the Evangelist Mark he was taken captive there by representatives of the "chief priests, scribes and elders" (14:43). At this time one of (Jesus' adherents) drew his sword and cut off the ear of the high priest's slave (v 47). Then he was taken to the high priest, where all the chief priests, elders and scribes were assembled (v 53). At a "hearing" of Jesus, the high priest asked him if he was the Christ, the Son of the Blessed, to which Jesus answered: "I am." Jesus then said that "you (pl.) will see the Son of man sitting at the right hand of Power, and coming with the clouds of heaven" (vv 61-62).

Although Jesus does not utter the Ineffable Name (יהוה) here, but, like the high priest ("the Blessed") employs a substitute for it ("Power"),[24] the latter tears his mantle, required at hearing blasphemy.[25] He then tells the others present that they have heard Jesus' blasphemy, and they all maintain it deserves death (vv 63-64).[26]

According to *m. Sanh.* 6:4 the Sages say only the blasphemer (המגדף) and the idolator are hanged. The transgressor, however, must be taken down the same day, as Deut 21:23 is interpreted.[27] This "hanging" on a beam was easily associated with Jesus' Cross, as in Gal 3:13.

I suggest that Jesus is represented here at his hearing as presumptuously taking upon himself a prerogative especially of the high priest, that of openly pronouncing the name of the LORD, especially on the Day of Atonement. This (falsely) led to the accusation of blasphemy, punishable by death.

---

[23] Cf. *b. Yoma* 5a (Soncino 19-20), which is related to *m.* 1:1, where the high priest is removed from his house seven days before the Day of Atonement.

[24] For a list of such substitutions for the divine Name, cf. *b. Šebu.* 35a (Soncino 204).

[25] Cf. *m. Sanh.* 7:5 (Albeck 4.191, Danby 392) and the other sources cited in Str-B 1007-1008.

[26] For declaring the blasphemer "guilty" (of death), cf. the term חַיָּב in *m. Sanh.* 7:5 (see n. 25).

[27] Albeck 4.187-188, Danby 390.

b) Priests were allowed to say the Aaronic benediction (Num 6:24-26) outside the Jerusalem Temple with a substitute for "the LORD"; there they pronounced the Name as it was written.[28] Yet on Sabbaths and festival days, including Passover, it was the high priest who did this, raising his hand(s) up to his "frontlet" (ציץ).[29] The latter was a plate of gold, fastened to the turban over his forehead, and on it was an inscription: "Holy to the LORD" (Exod 28:36-38; 39:30-31).[30]

One major Judaic stream of thought considered precisely this frontlet to atone for blasphemers.[31] The nocturnal "hearing" of Jesus took place at the high priest's home (Mark 14:53), where the latter of course did not wear his eight high priestly garments. Nevertheless, the first Palestinian Jewish Christians would have thought of him as wearing them, including the frontlet, both on the same afternoon before the first day of Passover (starting at sunset) in the Temple, and on the next morning there. He openly pronounced the name LORD on these occasions in the Temple. It was precisely this person who is represented as accusing Jesus of blasphemy, although the Galilean prophet used a substitute for the Name, making him inculpable.[32] The contrast could not have been greater.

The occasion on which the high priest pronounced the divine name LORD the most, however, was the Day of Atonement. The Tosefta at *Yoma* 2:2 states in this respect: "Ten times that day he expresses the Divine Name, six in regard to the bullock, three for the goat, and one for the lots."[33] The Mishnah at *Yoma* 3:8 and 6:2 notes that when the high

---

[28] Cf. *m. Soṭa* 7:6 (Albeck 3.250, Danby 301).

[29] *Ibid.* On this, cf. Lev 8:9; Exod 28:36; and 39:30 in BDB 847 and Jastrow 1279.

[30] Cf. Josephus, *Bell.* 5.235 and *Ant.* 3.178, as well as Sir 45:12 regarding this. On the high priest's frontlet captured by Titus in Jerusalem in 70 C.E. and brought to Rome, see *y. Yoma* 4:1, 41c (Neusner 14.110).

[31] Cf. *y. Yoma* 7:3, 44c (Neusner 14.201), and *Lev. Rab.* Tzab 10/6 on Lev 8:2 (Soncino 4.130). The "forehead" of (the blasphemer) Goliath in 1 Sam 17:49 and the "forehead" of the high priest Aaron in Exod 28:38 are connected here.

[32] Cf. again *m. Sanh.* 7:5 in n. 25. This hearing, often called the "trial" of Jesus, is basically unhistorical. While the high priest and the rest of the Temple aristocracy certainly wanted to get rid of someone who challenged their administration of the Temple, the Lord's Vineyard (see Chapter One), a nocturnal, preliminary hearing was impossible according to what is now known of contemporary Judaic legal procedure (see for example the end of *m. Sanh.* 4:1 in Albeck 4.180 and Danby 387).

[33] Zuckermandel / Liebermann 183, Neusner 2.192. Cf. also *b. Yoma* 39b (Soncino 187), which adds from *m. Tam.* 3:8 (Danby 585) that the voice of the high priest could even be heard in Jericho when he pronounced the Name on the Day of Atonement.

priest spoke the divine name in Lev 16:30 over the bullock and the scapegoat, the priests and the people who were assembled in the Temple Court "used to kneel and bow themselves and fall down on their faces and say, 'Blessed be the name of the glory of His kingdom for ever and ever.'"[34]

Palestinian Jewish Christians, in meditating on the passion of Jesus, thus not only may have thought of his innocence in regard to blasphemy of the divine Name, atonable through the frontlet of the high priest. They also probably thought here of the high priest on the Day of Atonement, when he himself pronounced the Name a total of ten times, including the occasions over the scapegoat.

3. *Peter's Threefold Denial.*

a) Simultaneous to Jesus' open acknowledgment of who he really is at a hearing before the high priest, Mark 14:66-72 relates the incident of Peter's threefold denial of his master.[35] Jesus had already predicted it in v 30 with the expression "before" (πρὶν ἤ; πρίν in v 72). The denial itself then took place in the "courtyard" (αὐλή) and "forecourt" (προαύλιον) of the high priest (vv 54, 66 and 68), and it included the "cock's crowing" (ἀλέκτωρ ἐφώνησεν in v 72). The latter three expressions, as well as other imagery such as "warming oneself at a fire," "taking an oath," and "going away and weeping," plus the more general setting, derive from Judaic traditions regarding the high priest and the Day of Atonement.

b) Of the four occurrences of "cockcrow" in the Mishnah, two are found in *Yoma* 1:8.[36] This is stated after the "elders" (זְקֵנִים) of the court "delivered" (מסר) the high priest to the "elders" (זְקֵנִים) of the priesthood, who then brought him up to the "upper chamber" (עֲלִיָּה)[37] in the house of Abtimas (1:5).[38]

---

[34] Albeck 2.231 and 240, Danby 165 and 169. On "concealing" the divine Name, cf. *y. Yoma* 3:7, 40d (Neusner 4.96).

[35] On recent bibliography on this pericope, cf. Brown, *The Death* 564-565, and his analysis on pp. 587-626.

[36] Albeck 2.225, Danby 163. The other two occurrences are *Tam.* 1:2 (Danby 582), which also deals with the ashes of the altar, as in *Yoma* 1:8a, and *Sukk.* 5:4 (Danby 180). In the latter, trumpet blasts in the Temple are described as taking place at cockcrow during the festival of Booths (Tabernacles).

[37] Jastrow 1082. It also means "upper story" (of a building). Cf. the ἀνάγαιον or upper room in which Jesus celebrated the "Lord's Supper" with his disciples in Mark 14:15 // Luke 22:12, the only occurrences of the term in the NT.

[38] Albeck 2.224, Danby 163. The House of Abtimas was in charge of preparing the incense in the Temple (cf. *m. Šeq.* 5:1 and *Yoma* 3:11). The Chamber of Abtimas

I suggest that the Palestinian Jewish Christian author of Peter's threefold denial thought here of Jesus as the Christians' high priest, who just before at the "Lord's Supper" in Mark 14:18 and 21 predicted that one of his disciples would "deliver" or "hand (him) over" (παραδίδωμι). This then in fact took place in Gethsemane, through Judas ("he who delivers" – v 44). A crowd with swords and clubs, from the chief priests, scribes and "elders" (πρεσβύτεροι – v 43), then led Jesus to the (residence of the) high priest, where all the chief priests, "elders" and scribes were assembled (v 53).

Mark 14:66 says Peter was "below" (κάτω) in the courtyard of the high priest. That is, Jesus is pictured as now being given a hearing before the high priest in an upper chamber or story of his residence, corresponding to the "upper chamber" in the house of Abtimas.

In *m. Tam.* 1:1 it is stated that the Chamber of Abtimas in the Temple was on the "upper story" (עליה).[39] In this connection it is related that if one of the young priests on watch there had a seminal emission at night, he went down, immersed, dried himself off, and then "warmed himself before the fire" (וְנִתְחַמֵּם כְּנֶגֶד הַמְּדוּרָה). The nithpael of the verb חָמַם means "to

---

was one of the three sites over which the priests watched in the Temple (*Midd.* 1:1 and *Tam.* 1:1).

[39] Albeck 5.293-294, Danby 582, with notes 2 and 5. The passage is connected to *m. Yoma* 1 through the catchword "cockcrow" in 1:2. Earlier, of course, there were no numberings of the individual sections, so that "warming himself before the fire" and "cockcrow" were considered to be part of one complex. The Jerusalem Talmud at *Yoma* 1:5, 39a (Neusner 14.40) states that (the chamber of Abtimas) "was over the water gate, and near his (the high priest's) chamber." In *m. Midd.* 5:4 (Albeck 5.334; Danby 597-598), Abba Saul (a third generation Tanna: Strack and Stemberger, *Introduction* 86) states that the Wood Chamber was the actual chamber of the high priest, (one of six chambers of the Temple Court – 3); it was on the south side and next to the Chamber of Hewn Stone, where the Great Sanhedrin met for judgment (see also *m. Sanh.* 11:2). On the somewhat complicated topography, cf. the Soncino edition of the Babylonian Talmud, *Yoma* 1, n. 1; 11a (Soncino 46); and 19a (Soncino 81) on the two cells (chambers) of the high priest: the Chamber of the Councillors, and the Chamber of the House of Abtimas. See also Ezek 41:6 and 42:3-6; Josephus' "turret-like chambers" and "numerous chambers, in three stories," in *Bell.* 5.203 and 220, respectively; the Temple Scroll (11Q Temple Scroll[a]), col. 38:12 (Martínez 164); T. Busink, *Der Tempel von Jerusalem von Salomo bis Herodes.* 2. Von Ezechiel bis Middot (Leiden: Brill, 1980) 1556-1557; and W. Stinespring, art. "Temple, Jerusalem. C. The Temple of Herod" in *IDB* 4.554.

The Palestinian Jewish Christian narrator of Peter's denial could thus easily picture Jesus as if he were in the House (upper Chamber) of Abtimas, one of the high priest's official chambers. Near it was the site of the Sanhedrin.

warm oneself."[40] The noun מְדוּרָה means a row or pile of wood, a fire.[41] It is this imagery, connected to the Chamber of Abtimas, which the Palestinian Jewish Christian author of Peter's denial applied to him in the courtyard of the high priest. There Jesus' main disciple was "warming himself" (Mark 14:67 – θερμαινόμενον). Earlier in v 54 the narrator had related that Peter was sitting in the courtyard of the high priest with the guards, "warming himself at the fire" (θερμαινόμενος πρὸς τὸ φῶς).[42]

Now the author described Peter in imagery applied to the high priest in the upper chamber of the House of Abtimas. In *m. Yoma* 1:5 the elders of the priesthood there made him "take an oath" (hiphil of שָׁבַע)[43] by the name of God that he would not change anything of what they told him.[44] This provided the background for Peter's "taking an oath" (ὀμνύω)[45] in Mark 14:71, "I do not know this man of whom you speak."[46]

Immediately after this in *Yoma* 1:5 it is related that the high priest "turned aside and wept" (הוּא פוֹרֵשׁ וּבוֹכֶה, with the present participle). The Tosefta in *Yoma* 1:8 explains this as the high priest's reaction to the necessity of imposing an oath on him.[47] This phrase provided the Palestinian Jewish Christian author of Peter's denial the background for Peter's behavior just after taking an oath, when the cock crowed a second time: "he broke down and wept" (Mark 14:72 – ἐπιβαλὼν ἔκλαιεν).

R. Brown calls the meaning of the verb ἐπιβάλλω here "a famous problem."[48] Strangely, neither Matthew nor Luke takes over the Markan expression. Instead, they agree here exactly with καὶ ἐξελθὼν ἔξω ἔκλαυσεν πικρῶς ("And he went out and wept bitterly": Matt 26:75 and Luke 22:62). I suggest that Mark's ἐπιβαλὼν is a mistranslation of פָּרֵשׁ

---

[40] Jastrow 478, who also refers to *m. Beṣ.* 2:5 (Danby 184). The expression "to warm oneself," as well as other similar imagery, has been transferred here from the (inner) Court of the Priests in the Temple to a private residence of the high priest in Jerusalem. Only there could he have a "maid" (Mark 14:66-69), who in the Temple would only have been allowed to enter the (outer) Court of Women.

[41] Jastrow 733.

[42] Cf. John 18:18, where ἀνθρακία is a charcoal fire, and 25.

[43] Jastrow 1515. The Hebrew is in Albeck 2.224, English ("adjure") in Danby 163.

[44] This was directed against the Boethusian (Sadducean) practice of offering up the incense while still outside the Holy of Holies, and not inside. Cf. *t. Yoma* 1:8 (Lieberman 222-223, Neusner 2.187), and *b. Yoma* 19b (Soncino 83-84).

[45] BAGD 565-566.

[46] Matthew intensifies this motif by having Peter already take an oath (the noun ὅρκος) in 26:72.

[47] For the text, cf. n. 44.

[48] Cf. his *The Death* 609, with his discussion extending to p. 610.

above, which means "to go away, go aside, depart."[49] Oral tradition of the Passion Narrative certainly continued after the appearance of Mark's gospel. Both the Christian communities from which Matthew and Luke derived their materials here had continued to preserve the original reading פּוֹרֵשׁ, correctly translated into Greek here as ἐξελθὼν ἔξω. Peter is pictured as going out of the courtyard of the high priest, and in shame, with no one to see him, weeping bitterly in the forecourt over the denial of his own master.

The enigmatic reading ἐπιβαλών in Mark 14:72 probably results from the Greek-speaking Jewish Christian translator's understanding the non-pointed שרפ as פָּרַשׂ, which in the MT means "to spread out," such as a garment, or something over one's face.[50] He pictured Peter as "spreading" part of his garment over himself in shame and weeping. This is a well-attested reading of ἐπιβάλλω.[51] The translator should have added τὸ ἱμάτιον αὐτοῦ, "his garment," or something similar. Out of respect for the "sacredness" of the text, however, he unfortunately left it at ἐπιβαλών, which ever since has been difficult to understand. Here we must be grateful to the continuing oral tradition, which preserved "and he went out," a correct translation of שרפ.

As noted at the outset of this section, of the four occurrences of "cockcrow" (קְרִיאַת הַגֶּבֶר) in the Mishnah, two are found in *Yoma* 1:8.[52] The second of these is: "And the crowing of the cock had not arrived 'before' (עַד שֶׁ) the Temple Court (עֲזָרָה) was full of Israelites."[53] The expression "before" here corresponds to the same expression, πρίν, in Mark 14:72: "'Before' the cock crows twice, you will deny me three times" (cf. also πρὶν ἤ in v 30). The Palestinian Jewish Christian author of Peter's denial thus continued to borrow here from imagery still found in *m. Yoma* 1 regarding the high priest on the eve of the Day of Atonement.

Peter's denying Jesus "three times" may also be due not to the popular proclivity for the number three, but to an enumeration in *m. Yoma* 1:8. It mentions the removal of the ashes from the Temple altar as usually taking place at or near "cockcrow." On the Day of Atonement,

---

[49] Jastrow 1241.

[50] Cf. BDB 831, and 2 Kgs 8:15. The verb is found in rabbinic Hebrew as פרס (see Jastrow 1232, with 3) – to spread). This seems to indicate that the translator had the Semitic narrative before him in written form. If he had heard the verb with a shin and not a sin or samech, he would have translated as in Matthew and Luke.

[51] Cf. BAGD 289, 1.b: lay on, put on, with ἱμάτιον. See also LSJ 624, IV.1. For the motif of covering one's head in shame, see Jer 14:3-4.

[52] A third in *m. Tam.* 1:2 is connected to "warming oneself at the fire" in 1:1, as remarked above.

[53] Albeck 2.225; cf. Danby 163.

however, this was (already) done at midnight, and on the feasts[54] (even earlier) at the first watch. That is, the order presupposed here is the first watch, midnight and cockcrow. "Cockcrow" is at any rate the last and third in the sequence, which may stand behind Peter's denying Jesus "three times" (τρίς in Mark 14:72 and 30). This sequence make sense in the present Markan order, for directly after v 72 it is stated in 15:1: "And as soon as it was morning...."

Another biblical term for the עזרה, the Temple Court of *m. Yoma* 1:8, is חָצֵר.[55] This was later used for a private courtyard.[56] For this reason both the Hebrew New Testaments of Delitzsch and the United Bible Societies have it for the αὐλή, "courtyard," of the high priest in Mark 14:66 and 54.[57]

*   *   *

The general setting of the high priest, with Jesus pictured as being above and inside, and Peter below and outside; warming oneself at a fire; taking an oath; going away and weeping; cockcrow; "before..."; the number three; and the term "courtyard" itself all appear to have been borrowed by a Palestinian Jewish Christian from what is still found in *m. Yoma* 1 (and the closely related *Tam.* 1:1-2). He masterfully combined these and other elements to create a very vivid scene of Jesus' main disciple Peter denying his master below in the courtyard at the same time as the latter himself acknowledged his true identity as the Christ, the Son of the Blessed, and the Son of man before the high priest, chief priests, elders and scribes assembled above in the high priest's residence. For the author, Jesus was also the true high priest, who was to offer his own life the next afternoon at Golgotha. He therefore considered it appropriate to apply high priest and Day of Atonement imagery not only to Jesus, but also to Peter during Jesus' hearing before the high priest.

Like the present form of the Gethsemane narrative, the account of Peter's denying Jesus as now found in Mark is not historical. Yet since

---

[54] The pilgrimage festivals: Passover, Pentecost and Booths (Tabernacles). Cf. Danby 163, n. 4. There was a dispute already in Tannaitic times as to whether the night had three or four watches. See Mark 13:35 (evening, midnight, cockcrow and morning), and *b. Ber.* 3a (Soncino 5-6). On these times in *m. Yoma* 1:8, see also *b. Yoma* 20b (Soncino 88-89, with n. 1 on the latter page). See also *b. Yoma* 21a (Soncino 91) for waiting to depart on a journey in the morning until the cock has crowed twice or three times.

[55] Cf. BDB 346-347, 3b-c.

[56] Cf. Jastrow 496.

[57] Cf. pp. 93-94 and 136 respectively. The United Bible Societies' version also has "entrance of the חצר" in v 68 (*ibid.*).

"all" the disciples, including Peter, forsook Jesus and fled when he was arrested in Gethsemane (Mark 14:50), and Peter is represented as saying he never would do so (v 29), there may be an historical core to the narrative.[58] My main concern above, however, has been to point out the high priest and Day of Atonement imagery the author employed in his presentation of Peter's denial of Jesus.

4. *The High Priest "Delivers" the Scapegoat to be "Led Away."*

a) After Jesus' so-called "blasphemy" at a hearing before the high priest, and the incident of Peter's threefold denial of Jesus, the chief priests, elders and scribes, with "the whole council" according to the Evangelist Mark held a consultation in the morning.[59] Then they bound Jesus and "led him away and delivered" (ἀπήνεγκαν καὶ παρέδωκαν) him to Pilate (15:1), who "delivered" (παρέδωκεν) Jesus to be crucified (v 15). Thereupon the Roman soldiers "led him away" (ἀπήγαγον) inside the palace (v 16), and after mocking Jesus "led him out" (ἐξάγουσιν) to crucify him (v 20).

I suggest that the above imagery of "delivering" and "leading away" is based here on the fate of the scapegoat on the Day of Atonement.

b) In *m. Yoma* 6:2 the high priest places his hands upon the scapegoat and makes confession, asking God to forgive the iniquities, transgressions and sins of His people. In doing so, he pronounces the ineffable Name of God when quoting Lev 16:30. At this point the priests and others in the Temple Court knelt, bowed down, fell on their faces, and spoke the special blessing already noted above.

Directly after this the Mishnah states: "They 'delivered' it to the person who should 'lead it away'" (6:3; cf. Lev 16:21), and the term "lead

---

[58] On this issue, cf. Brown, *The Death* 614-621, as well as 621-626 on the theology of the Cross, the costs of discipleship, and martyrdom for later Christians.

[59] Cf. *m. Sanh.* 5:5 (Albeck 4.185, Danby 389): If the members of the Sanhedrin find someone guilty of death, "they leave his sentence over until tomorrow." Then "they discussed the matter all night, and early on the morrow they came to the court." See also 4:1 (Albeck 4.180, Danby 387), where a verdict of conviction may not be reached "until the following day." In 11:4 (Albeck 4.208, Danby 400) one condemned to death by the Great Court in Jerusalem was kept under guard there until he was put to death on one of the three pilgrimage festivals, including Passover. This certainly applied to more cases than those listed in 11:1, yet the mention of Yabne raises serious doubts as to its relevance to the period before 70 C.E.

away" is mentioned three more times.[60] "Deliver" here is מסר, and "lead away" is the hiphil of הלך.[61]

Originally the Alexandrians then pulled the hair of the scapegoat and shouted to it: "Bear (our sins) and be gone! Bear (our sins) and be gone!"[62] After it passed the last of the booths set up on the way to the wilderness, the person mentioned above pushed it from behind down a precipice. There it broke into pieces and died.[63] The same person returned to Jerusalem, and if he met the high priest "in his house he would say to him: 'We have fulfilled the request of Him who grants life to all who live.'"[64] This granting of "new life" through the atoning death of the scapegoat was thought to have direct consequences, as *t. Yoma* 4:17 states: "(the death of) the goat makes atonement immediately" (מיד).[65]

The materials found in the above passages from early Judaic tradition regarding the atoning death of the scapegoat, which bears the iniquities, transgressions and sins of all the people, certainly influenced not only the Hellenistic Jewish Christian author of Hebrews, but also the first Palestinian Jewish Christians in describing the death of Jesus. I therefore suggest that the terms "deliver" and "lead away," now found after the "hearing" of Jesus before the high priest and others in Jerusalem, derive from early terminology employed of the scapegoat, still found in *m. Yoma* 6:3.

Another phrase from Jesus' crucifixion also derives from the same complex.

5. *Standing at a Distance and Beholding the Death of the Scapegoat.*

a) At Jesus' death on the Cross, women (stood and) "looked on from afar" (ἦσαν...ἀπὸ μακρόθεν θεωροῦσαι: Mark 15:40). Three of them are enumerated in the same verse.[66] This imagery also has its origin in the scapegoat ritual on the Day of Atonement.

---

[60] Albeck 2.240, Danby 169.

[61] Cf. Jastrow 810 ("Esp. a) to surrender a person to the authorities," and the example from *b. Giṭ.* 7a of bringing someone to judgment through the [Roman] government), and 353, respectively.

[62] Cf. 6:4 in Albeck 2.240, Danby 169. For the "Babylonians" of the text as a derogatory term for Alexandrians, see Danby 509, n. 2. See also *y. Yoma* 6:4, 43d in Neusner 14.178, and *b. Yoma* 66b (Soncino 312, with n. 4).

[63] Cf. 6:6 in Albeck 2.241, Danby 170.

[64] Cf. *b. Yoma* 71a (Soncino 338).

[65] Zuckermandel / Liebermann 192; cf. Neusner 2.210.

[66] While Matthew retains this terminology at 27:55, Luke 23:49 includes males by stating: "all his acquaintances and the women who had followed him from Galilee stood at a distance and saw these things." John 19:25-26 has Jesus' mother,

b) Directly after the Mishnah describes the scapegoat's being "delivered" to one of the high priest's fellow priests to "lead it away" (*Yoma* 6:3), it continues by describing how there were ten booths between the Jerusalem Temple and the precipice in the wilderness. At the end this person pushed the scapegoat from behind down the precipice, and it broke into pieces, dying. This was then reported to the high priest, who in the meantime had concerned himself with the bullock and he-goat which were to be burnt upon the altar (6:4-8).

Some of the eminent Jerusalemites accompanied the scapegoat and its "driver" to the first booth, reached by a causeway. Archaeological remains of this "gangway," leading from the southern section of the eastern wall of the Temple precinct to the wilderness, have been found.[67] At each of the ten booths people offered the "driver" food and water and then accompanied him to the next booth. The only exception was the last one, "for none used to go with him to.the ravine; but 'they stood at a distance and beheld' what he did" (6:5). That is, they watched as he pushed the scapegoat to its death from the precipice.[68] Danby's translation here correctly employs the plural "they" because all those at the last booth are meant. The Hebrew, however, is literally in the singular: עוֹמֵד מֵרָחוֹק וְרוֹאֶה, "he stands from afar and beholds."[69]

I suggest that the Palestinian Jewish Christian who first formulated the scene of women, also coming from Jerusalem, and "(standing and)[70] looking on from afar" at Jesus' death on the Cross, also borrowed imagery here from the Day of Atonement, described above. For him Jesus was the innocent, unblemished scapegoat, who died on the Cross to bear the sins, iniquities and transgressions of all the people.

6. *The Place Golgotha.*

a) The above female followers of Jesus who are represented as standing and looking on from a distance viewed him on his Cross at "the place called Golgotha, which is translated 'the place of the skull'"

---

his aunt and two other women called Mary "standing by the Cross," and the disciple whom Jesus loved "standing near" his mother. John modifies the tradition he received in order to have the beloved disciple take care of his new "mother," Mary. On Mark 15:40-41 par. as unhistorical, see Bultmann, *The History* 274.

[67] Cf. the art. "Temple" in *EJ* (1971) 15.964.

[68] Danby 170. My reasons for employing "precipice" and not "ravine" are found below in section six.

[69] Albeck 2.241.

[70] Luke 23:49 and John 19:25 expressly have "standing," which is simply assumed by Mark and Matthew.

(τὸν Γολγοθᾶν τόπον, ὅ ἐστιν μεθερμηνευόμενον Κρανίου Τόπος: Mark 15:22 par.).[71] It was located outside Jerusalem, as indicated by Mark 15:20 ("they led him out") and 21 (Simon of Cyrene, who was compelled to carry Jesus' Cross, was "coming in from the country").[72]

This site has never been identified.[73] No confirmation of it has ever been found in Judaic sources. I suggest that a Palestinian Jewish Christian firmly believed that Jesus as the scapegoat bore on his Cross all the iniquities, transgressions and sins of the people (Lev 16:21-22), thereby making atonement for them through his blood. This person created a name for the site of the Crucifixion based on terminology employed of the scapegoat and the site of its being killed: גולגולתא.[74]

b) Lev 16:10 states that the scapegoat should be "sent away into the wilderness to Azazel." The high priest on the Day of Atonement sends it away "into the wilderness by the hand of a man who is in readiness" (v 21). There it bears all the people's iniquities "to a solitary land; and he shall let the goat go in the wilderness" (v 22). Originally the scapegoat was thus not killed, nor was a definite site associated with its being "sent off / let go."

The Mishnah, however, describes in the tractate *Yoma* a practice established long before the destruction of the Temple in 70 C.E. As related in 5) above, a causeway or gangway was built, which then led down from the southern section of the eastern wall of the Temple. The scapegoat and its guide went this way, which was lined by ten booths with people in them between Jerusalem and the *ṣoq*. There the guide pushed the goat backwards, and before it got halfway down it was broken in pieces, i.e. it was dead.[75] If it somehow survived this ordeal,

---

[71] Matt 27:33 has Γολγοθᾶ, as does John 19:17; Luke 23:33 only has "the place called the skull."

[72] Cf. John 19:17 ("he went out"), and Heb 13:12 (see Num 15:35).

[73] Many favor the present site of the Holy Sepulchre, now within Jerusalem, and some "Gordon's Tomb" north of the city wall. Cf. the art. "Golgotha" by K. Clark in *IDB* 2.439, as well as J. Jeremias, *Golgotha* (Leipzig: Pfeiffer, 1926 [= Angelos 1]) 33. P. Billerbeck in Str-B 1.1037 correctly states, however: "It is uncertain from where the place got its name...." The name was most likely derived from its shape, and perhaps even from "skulls." See below.

[74] The second lamed was dropped in the Greek through dissimilation. Cf. BDF § 39 (6) on p. 22. This was already true in Syriac. Cf. Levy 1.330 on גולגלתא, and J. Lightfoot, *A Commentary on the New Testament from the Talmud and Hebraica* (original Oxford University Press, 1859; Peabody, MASS: Hendrickson, 1989) 2.366.

[75] Cf. *m. Yoma* 6:4-6 in Albeck 2.240-241, Danby 169-170. The latter phrase is literally "and it turned into limbs, limbs," i.e. pieces. See Jastrow 9 on אבר.

the guide went down after it and killed it, according to *t. Yoma* 3:14.[76]
This was due to the principle: without blood, no atonement (Lev 17:11).[77]

The site at which the scapegoat was pushed down to its death is
called צוק in the Mishnah at *Yoma* 6. From the root "to be narrow," the
term means a "narrow point, peak, precipice," especially applied to "the
mountain from which the scapegoat was precipitated."[78] The word
behind "mountain," הָר, in *m. Yoma* 6:6 can also mean "hill," as Danby
translates.[79]

The Mishnah in *Yoma* 6:8 states that the distance from Jerusalem to
"Beth Haduré" (בֵּית הַדּוּרֵי) was three *mil*. It was the point at which the he-
goat reached the wilderness.[80] M. Jastrow defines it as the "name of a
summit from which the scape-goat was thrown down...."[81] *Targum
Pseudo-Jonathan* explicitly states this on Lev 16:21. The guide "takes him
to the wilderness of *ṣoq*, which is Beth Haduré."[82] The same is true for
this targum on 16:10, which speaks of a rough and hard "place" (אתר =
Hebrew מָקוֹם)[83] in the wilderness of *ṣoq*, which is Beth Haduré.[84]

---

[76] Zuckermandel / Liebermann 188, Neusner 2.203.

[77] It certainly was ironic to the first Palestinian Jewish Christians that the death of
the scapegoat was also thought to atone for the sins of those punished by death at
the hands of an earthly court. For them, the opposite was the case: the scapegoat
Jesus also atoned for the sins of the "court" which helped to have him sentenced
to death. See *m. Šebu.* 1:6 (Albeck 4.248, Danby 410), quoted in *Sifra* Aḥare Mot,
Pereq 5 on Lev 16:22 (Neusner 3.34). Josephus in *Ap.* 2.187 notes that one of the
tasks of the priests, directed by the high priest (185), was "the punishment of
condemned persons."

[78] Jastrow 1270. Danby's translation of "ravine" is misleading because it
emphasizes what is below, not a site much higher than the present level.

[79] Albeck 2.241, Danby 170.

[80] Albeck 2.242, Danby 170. On the spelling, see below. In *Ant.* 3.241 Josephus, a
native of Jerusalem, says the kid is sent alive into the wilderness "beyond the
frontiers."

[81] *A Dictionary* 332-333. Levy in 1.455 has "ein steiniges felsiges Gebirge...."

[82] Rieder 2.170, referring to his n. 5 on p.169.

[83] Jastrow 133.

[84] Rieder 2.169. Cf. the translation of Etheridge 196. Verse 22 also describes a
desolate "place," parallel to the wilderness of *ṣoq*. Here the goat "goes up" (נסק –
Jastrow 918) to the mountains / hills (pl.) of Beth Haduré, where a tempestuous
wind from the Lord carries it away to die (Rieder 2.170). The Targum here may
wish to draw attention away from human responsibility for killing the goat; it is
really all a part of God's plan, as also shown in the words spoken afterwards to
the high priest (*b. Yoma* 71a, Soncino 338). See also the statement in 67b (Soncino
315, with n. 9, and 316): "I have decreed it, and you are not permitted to criticize
it."

After this rite was discontinued in 70 C.E., the name of the no longer used place and its exact distance from Jerusalem were soon forgotten by most of the priests and Sages. This accounts for the later copyists' guessing at the spelling of the name,[85] as well as the rabbinic calculation of the distance from Jerusalem.[86]

The name בית הדורי literally means "place of roundings," the former word from the root הדר. It is already found in Isa 45:2 as הֲדוּרים, swelling places, "hills."[87] Ps 110:3 also probably means הדרי as "in the 'mountains' of holiness" (RSV: "upon the holy mountains").[88] Jastrow defines the term הֲדוּרָא in rabbinic sources as either a spiral road, a hill which can only be tilled by spiral movements, or as a "steep hill."[89] The latter suits the ṣoq, the precipitous site from which the scapegoat was thrown down, very well. The verb הָדַר in rabbinic Hebrew means "to enclose, go around," and the passive participle הָדוּר "rounded."[90] That is, the ṣoq was also labeled a "place of roundings" because of its high, round shape.

A synonym for הָדוּר, "rounded," in rabbinic Hebrew is the passive participle of גִּלְגֵּל, "to roll, turn": מְגוּלְגָּל, rolled or "rounded."[91] For example, *b. B. Bat.* 16b says: "just as the lentil is 'round'..." (מגולגלת).[92] An egg which is rolled or made to go around (= roasted) in *b. Ber.* 44b is in Aramaic: מגולגלתא.[93] The basic meaning of numerous words from the root גלגל is "something round."[94] The same is true of a "skull," in Aramaic גּוּלְגּוּלְתָּא or גּוּלְגָּלְתָּא.[95] An Aramaic-speaking Palestinian Jewish Christian describing the site of Jesus' Crucifixion in terms of the ṣoq, because of its

---

[85] Cf. J. Meinhold, *Joma* 63 on 6:8, with variants on p. 79; MS "M" of *b. Yoma* 68b with הרורי (Goldschmidt 2.950; Soncino 320, n. 5; daleth and resh were often confused); and the Jerusalem Talmud's "Beth Ḥoron."

[86] In *m. Yoma* 6:4 the distance to the ṣoq is given as ninety *ris*, which is defined as 7 1/2 to the *mil*. This would produce twelve *mil*, a distance favored by R. Meir in *t. Yoma* 3:13 (Neusner 2.203; R. Judah and R. Yose maintain ten). Yet *m.* 6:8 says there were three *mil* from Jerusalem to Beth Haduré (Danby 169-170). Exact knowledge of the site was apparently lost at a very early time.

[87] BDB 213.

[88] *Ibid.*, 214.

[89] *A Dictionary* 333.

[90] *Ibid.*, 334.

[91] *Ibid.*, 244.

[92] Soncino 84.

[93] Soncino 271.

[94] Cf. Levy 1.329-330 ("etwas Rundes") many times. See an "eyeball," גולגולתא, in *b. Tam.* 32b (Soncino 29), and a (round) "stone," גלנלתא, in *b. Giṭ.* 47a (Soncino 207).

[95] Levy 1.330, Jastrow 221.

round shape also called "the place of roundings" (Beth Haduré), could thus have easily thought of a synonymous term meaning "something round," גולגולתא, to describe it. He got his major impetus to do so from early Judaic tradition on the scapegoat.

The Mishnah at *Yoma* 6:6 says that the guide commissioned by the high priest pushed the scapegoat backwards over the precipice (*ṣoq*). It then states: "And it rolls (מִתְגַּלְגֵּל), and goes down. And it did not get halfway down the hill / mountain before it broke into pieces."[96] In other words, the scapegoat "rolls" (גלגל) here to its certain death. It could be described in Aramaic as "a goat rolled (down)": צפירא מגולגלתא. Since the rite had certainly already been carried out at this particular site for a long period of time, there were undoubtedly many skulls (and other bones) from countless earlier scapegoats on the side, or at the bottom of the hill / mountain. No pious Jew would have touched or removed them, for the scapegoat had aided in effecting his own atonement.

The *ṣoq*, because of its round shape also called "the place of roundings," is thus a site (אתר) of death, and with its many scapegoat skulls easily recalled another term derived from גלגל: "skull," גולגולתא. It is even possible that the *ṣoq* was also called "the place of skulls" in the vernacular. The Aramaic אתר, related to the *ṣoq* in *Targum Pseudo-Jonathan* on Leviticus 16 and equivalent to the Hebrew מָקוֹם ("place"), is thus possibly also behind the Greek τόπος in Mark 15:22 par.[97]

I therefore propose that the scapegoat's "place of rolling / being rolled" to death became the inspiration for "the place Golgotha," "the place of the skull," in the Passion Narrative. The exact site of Jesus' Crucifixion outside Jerusalem will probably never be known.[98] It may even be found under the present Church of the Holy Sepulchre or at the "Garden Tomb." Its name, however, most probably has nothing to do with the actual site of Jesus' crucifixion. This explains why it is not found in a single Judaic source. The name of Jesus' site of death is not historical, yet it expresses a major religious truth. "Golgotha" was employed by a Palestinian Jewish Christian in order to depict Jesus' atoning work on the Cross, his suffering and dying as the scapegoat for all the sins of the people.

Finally, those Palestinian Jewish Christians who contributed individual accounts to what is now the Passion Narrative may have

---

[96] Albeck 2.241.

[97] Cf. Hatch and Redpath 1364-1367 for מקום as usually behind τόπος. Including variants, בית is found in the MT in six cases.

[98] I had earlier made a different suggestion in regard to Golgotha in *Barabbas and Esther* 44-45; it must now be withdrawn in favor of the above proposal.

made an intentional contrast between the place of Jesus' death, Golgotha, and the place of his Resurrection, the empty tomb, signifying new life.

Mark 15:46 says that Joseph of Arimathea, after having taken Jesus down from the Cross, wrapped him in a linen shroud, laid him in a tomb, and "rolled" (προσκυλίω) a stone against the door of the tomb. According to John 19:41 the tomb was in a garden (next to) where Jesus was crucified.

Like the shepherds who were unable to "roll away" (גָּלַל)[99] the stone from the mouth of the well in Gen 29:8,[100] the three women at Jesus' tomb on Easter Sunday morning ask: "Who will 'roll away' the stone for us from the door of the tomb?" (Mark 16:3). Looking up, however, "they saw that the stone was 'rolled back' – it was very large" (v 4).[101] The verb ἀποκυλίω is employed in both these verses and is only found in this context in the NT (here, in Matt 28:2 and Luke 24:2). The same is true for προσκυλίω in Mark 15:46 (Matt 27:60).[102]

The large stone rolled before the entrance to Jesus' tomb in order to seal it and prevent theft was called a גּוֹלֵל,[103] which derives from the above verb גלל. Aramaic- or Hebrew-speaking Jewish Christians in Palestine knew this. A fine example of such a round stone is still preserved at the grave thought to be for members of Herod's family. It is found behind the King David Hotel in Jerusalem.[104]

The site of Jesus' Crucifixion ("Golgotha," based on the scapegoat's "rolling [נלגל] down" to death from the ṣoq) was thought to be close to his tomb, sealed by a גּוֹלֵל, which was now "rolled away" (נגללה).[105] An association of both places via the root גל(ג)ל was thus probably originally intentional, and not simply by chance. The site of Jesus' death as a scapegoat was described as now superseded by the site of his victory over death through the Resurrection.[106]

---

[99] Cf. BDB 164.

[100] Cf. *Pirq. R. El.* 36 (Friedlander 268), where the "strong hero" Jacob resembles the angel at Jesus' tomb in Matt 28:2.

[101] On rolling "large" stones, in part to cover a well or cave, cf. Gen 29:2; Josh 10:18; and 1 Sam 14:33.

[102] On these two verbs, cf. BAGD 94 and 716 respectively.

[103] Cf. Str-B 1.1051 and the examples cited by Jastrow, 222.

[104] Cf. Vilnay, *Israel Guide* 91-92.

[105] See the Hebrew New Testaments of Delitzsch (p. 97) and the United Bible Societies (p. 140) on Mark 16:4.

[106] Like Bultmann (*The History* 290), I consider the story of the empty tomb to be legendary. The Apostle Paul betrays no knowledge of it, although he could have employed it well. Originally, Jesus was most probably considered to have been raised by God already from the Cross. This was then developed into the narrative

7. *Jesus' Wearing a White Robe, and His Change of Garments.*

a) Having bound Jesus in the morning after a consultation, the Jewish authorities led him away and delivered him to Pilate. After "trying" Jesus (Mark 15:2-5), Pilate then released Barabbas to the crowd,[107] but had Jesus scourged, and delivered him to be crucified (v 15). Before the Galilean prophet was brought to Golgotha, Mark (15:16-20), Matthew (27:27-31) and John (19:2-5) depict him as being mocked by the Roman soldiers. They clothe him in a (royal) purple cloak, put a crown of thorns on his head, salute him with "Hail, King of the Jews!" and kneel down in pretended homage to him. After this mocking of Jesus as the messianic king,[108] the soldiers "stripped him of the purple cloak and put his own clothes on him" (Mark 15:20).

The Evangelist Luke omits this "royal" mockery and inserts a different type of derision within the scene of the "trial" by Pilate. In 23:6-12 he alone describes how Pilate, discovering that Jesus was a Galilean, then sent him to Herod (Antipas), who was also in Jerusalem. When his "subject" refused to speak to him after a lengthy interrogation, the tetrarch with his soldiers treated Jesus with contempt and also mocked him. Dressing him in a "white / bright garment" (ἐσθῆτα λαμπράν),[109] Herod then sent Jesus back to Pilate (23:11).

In contrast to the mocking of Jesus as a king in the other three gospels, this scene depicts his being mocked as the high priest. The noun ἐσθής, meaning "clothing," is only found in the NT in Luke-Acts.[110] In Acts 1:10 two angels appear in "white (λευκαῖς) garments." Philo employs the plural in *Mos.* 2.152 of priests' garments, which in 143 are (white) linen tunics.[111]

The adjective λαμπρός in connection with garments means "esp. white ones, 'bright, shining.'"[112] In Acts 10:30 an angel appears before

---

of Easter Sunday three days later, primarily on the basis of Hos 6:2. See my *Samuel, Saul and Jesus. Three Early Palestinian Jewish Christian Gospel Haggadoth* (SFSHJ 105; Atlanta: Scholars Press, 1994) 173-187, including a discussion of 1 Cor 15:4.

[107] On this incident as unhistorical and derived from Judaic Esther traditions, cf. my essay "The Release of Barabbas (Mark 15:6-15 par.; John 18:39-40), and Judaic traditions on the Book of Esther" in *Barabbas and Esther* 1-27.

[108] Cf. the very frequent Judaic designation "the King, the Messiah / Anointed One" = "the messianic king" in Str-B 1.6-7.

[109] Cf. the German translation in the Luther Bible: "ein weisses Gewand."

[110] Cf. BAGD 312.

[111] Cf. Exod 28:42.

[112] BAGD 495. Cf. LSJ 1028: "2. of white cloths and the like, 'bright.'"

Cornelius and is described by the same expression as in Luke 23:11. This shows that "white" and λαμπρός are basically the same, with the latter emphasizing the "brightness" of the white.

b) The four garments of a priest in the Jerusalem Temple consisted of a tunic, drawers, turban and girdle.[113] They were of (white) wool and linen.[114] The high priest, in contrast, had eight garments: the above four, yet made exclusively of linen (Lev 16:4, 23); as well as four (outer) garments: the breastplate, apron, upper garment and frontlet.[115]

Usually the high priest performed the Temple services in his golden garments. Only on the Day of Atonement did he change a number of times from golden to linen or white garments for the five services.[116] And only on the Day of Atonement, when he entered the Holy of Holies, did the high priest wear only the four linen garments which were white or lustrous.[117]

At each garment change on the Day of Atonement the high priest "stripped off his clothes" (פָּשַׁט).[118] In the scene of Pilate's soldiers' mocking Jesus, they "stripped" (ἐξέδυσαν) him of his purple robe and then "dressed" (ἐνέδυσαν) him with his own garments (Mark 15:20). This recalls the phraseology of *m. Yoma* 7:4, where the high priest "stripped off his clothes. Then they brought him his own raiment, and 'he put it on'" (לְבַשׁ).[119] The verb ἐκδύω in the active, "to strip, take off,"[120] only occurs in the NT in Mark 15:20 and in the Matthean parallel (27:31). The

---

[113] Cf. *m. Yoma* 7:5 in Albeck 2.244, Danby 171.

[114] Cf. *b. Yoma* 12b (Soncino 55, with n. 6, and p. 54, notes 5-6). See also *y. Yoma* 7:3, 44b (Neusner 14.199).

[115] Cf. n. 113.

[116] These services are enumerated in *b. Yoma* 32a (Soncino 149).

[117] Cf. *b. Yoma* 32b (Soncino 150, with n. 2), from the School of R. Ishmael. See also Philo, *Quaes. Exod.* 2.107 on Exod 28:2, where the linen garment for service in the Holy of Holies is made for greater and more perfect honor and glory; *Spec. Leg.* 1.84; and *Ebr.* 86. In *m. Yoma* 3:7 (Albeck 2.230, Danby 165), the extremely expensive Pelusium and Indian linen garments are described. The Tosefta at 3:4 (Zuckermandel and Liebermann 187, Neusner 2.200) has white garments for the high priest's serving inside, golden garments for outside. Sir 50:5-10 also describes the splendor of the appearance of the high priest Simon II, son of Onias, when he came out of the "house of the veil."

[118] Jastrow 1245-1246, 2) to strip; to undress. Cf. *m. Yoma* 3:4, 6 (twice); 7:3, 4 (three times) in Albeck 2.229-230, 243-244; Danby 164-165, 171.

[119] Albeck 2.244, Danby 171.

[120] BAGD 239.

same is true of the active form, ἐκδύω, "to dress, clothe."[121] These Greek verbs correspond exactly to the hiphil of פשט and לבש.[122]

I suggest that the Palestinian Jewish Christian who first formulated the singular tradition now found in Luke 23:6-12 was aware of the high priest terminology of "stripping" and "dressing" as is now found in Mark 15:20. Although he did not himself use the latter,[123] it led him to describe Herod and his soldiers as dressing Jesus in a "white / shining garment," like that of the high priest on the Day of Atonement.[124]

>   8. *Jesus' Tunic Without a Seam, Woven in One Piece from the Top (John 19:23).*

a) Mark 15:24 states that (the Roman soldiers) crucified Jesus, dividing his garments among them by lot to determine what each should take. The number of the garments is not given. Not only those who passed by derided Jesus. The chief priests also mocked him to one another, together with the scribes (vv 31-32).

The Gospel of John differs here in a major way. After the chief priests objected to the title on the Cross (19:21-22), the soldiers, having crucified Jesus, took his garments (ἱμάτια) and made "four parts, a part for each soldier, and above all the tunic (χιτών). Now the tunic was 'seamless, woven in one piece from the top' (NRSV, v 23; ἄραφος, ἐκ τῶν ἄνωθεν ὑφαντὸς δι' ὅλου). Therefore they said to each other: 'Let us not tear it, but cast lots for it to see whose it will be.' This was to fulfill the Scripture: 'They divided my garments among themselves, and for my garment they cast lots' (LXX Ps 21:19 [MT 22:19])" – v 24.

---

[121] BAGD 264.

[122] Cf. Jastrow 691 on לבש hiphil, with an example from *Exodus Rabbah* of "stripping" and "putting on a garment." In his Hebrew New Testament (p. 95), Delitzsch employs the hiphil of the two verbs in Mark 15:20.

[123] In Luke 23:11 he employs περιβάλλω, "to put on," as in the royal mocking in John 19:2 (BAGD 646). Delitzsch on Luke 23:11 (Hebrew New Testament 157) has the piel of לבש.

[124] When Luke incorporated this incident into his gospel, he forgot and left Jesus in the "white / bright garment" until his Crucifixion, when the soldiers divided up his "garments" among them by lot (23:34). If this was intentional, for Luke Jesus as the high priest offered his own blood on the Cross (cf. the Philonic thought noted above). I derive part of the basic idea for this section from S. Ben-Chorin, *Bruder Jesus. Der Nazarener in jüdischer Sicht* (Munich: List, 1967) 203-204, which, however, I greatly expand and modify in numerous ways. Ben-Chorin uncritically combines the Lukan and Markan texts. It is also incomprehensible to me how Jesus' own clothes are supposed to present him as the suffering Messiah (p. 204).

The Hebrew of Ps 22:19 has first "my garments" (בגדי) in the plural, then in typical parallelism to express the same thing "my clothing" (לבושי)[125] in the singular. The latter term thus does not signify a fifth garment. The LXX first employs the plural of ἱμάτιον for "my garments." Then it translates "my clothing" by the singular ὁ ἱματισμός, which is also the generic "clothing, apparel."[126] It is very improbable therefore that the Fourth Evangelist meant a fifth piece of clothing by "the tunic." Rather, the word καί before it is probably meant in the sense of "and above all," as I have translated above.[127] This emphasizes that of the four pieces of clothing Jesus wore, the tunic was especially valuable. Therefore the soldiers cast lots to see who would get the prize piece.

J. Lightfoot in 1859 already called attention to the fact that *Targ.* Ps 22:19b reads: "they cast lots for my פְתָאנָא."[128] This is a piece of cloth, sheet, or "cloak," which in *Targ.* Prov 31:24 translates the Hebrew term סָדִין.[129] The latter is a "linen wrapper."[130] This is also its meaning in *m. 'Ed.* 4:10.[131] In *m. Yoma* 3:4 and 6 it is used of a sheet of linen (בוץ) spread between the high priest and the people before he stripped off his clothes, immersed, dried himself, and put on other garments to be used in the worship service on the Day of Atonement.[132]

The author of the Fourth Gospel, or the tradition he incorporates here, thus probably described Jesus in 19:23 as wearing a linen tunic before he "offered himself" on the Cross. This imagery, including the seamlessness of the tunic and the number four, derives from the high priest's garments on the Day of Atonement.

b) As noted in 7) b) above, a common priest in the Jerusalem Temple had four garments, made of wool and linen: tunic, drawers, turban and girdle. The high priest, in contrast, had eight: breastplate, apron, outer garment and frontlet, all of the color gold, as well as the other four white

---

[125] Cf. BDB 528 on this noun: "garment, clothing, raiment."

[126] LSJ 829.

[127] LSJ 857 on καί, A.2.

[128] *A Commentary* 3.433. The Aramaic is found in Merino, *Targum de Salmos* 92 (פיתגיי), and de Lagarde, *Hagiographa Chaldaice* 12.

[129] Jastrow 957; Aramaic in de Lagarde 144.

[130] BDB 690, specifically a "wrapper or rectangular piece of fine *linen*, worn as outer, or (at night) as sole garment." It is probably the linen cloth worn and lost by a young man when Jesus was taken captive in Gethsemane (Mark 14:51).

[131] Cf. this translation as employed by M. Segal in *b. 'Ed.* (Soncino 27). Danby (430) has "a linen garment." The Hebrew is found in Albeck 4.302.

[132] Albeck 2.229-230, Danby 164-165.

priestly garments. These four, however, were only of linen, as prescribed by Lev 16:4 and 23.

This explains how Jesus' tunic in John 19:23, as proposed above an inner garment[133] made of linen on the basis of *Targ.* Ps 22:19, and his other clothes were distributed among *four* soldiers, a number not mentioned by the Synoptics. I suggest that Jesus is presented here as the high priest, wearing three other garments and the "linen tunic" (LXX Lev 16:4 – χιτῶνα λινοῦν) in which the high priest entered the Holy of Holies on the Day of Atonement to offer the blood of bullock and goat.

John 19:23 also states that Jesus' tunic was "seamless, woven in one piece from the top." This description also derives from the high priest's garment, which only he was allowed to wear. Specifically, it is associated with Moses as high priest. As noted above, the third generation Tanna Joshua b. Qorḥa stated: "Throughout the forty years spent by Israel in the wilderness Moses did not refrain from ministering in the High Priesthood." This is based on Ps 99:6, "Moses and Aaron among His priests."[134] That is, Moses is thought to have been a high priest up to his death, which occurred at the very end of the forty years of wandering in the wilderness. This most probably helps to explain how Jesus can also be described in high priestly terms in Gethsemane, as I pointed out in regard to numerous aspects of the Moses / Jesus typology in section IB above.

Another third generation Tanna, R. Eliezer b. R. Yose,[135] taught: "We have a tradition that Moses, in a white linen garment (חָלוּק לָבָן), served as High Priest in the wilderness."[136] He also taught that on each of the seven days of consecrating Aaron and his sons as priests (Exodus 29 and Leviticus 8), "Moses, wearing 'a white linen garment that had no seam'

---

[133] For the χιτών as a tunic or shirt, "a garment worn next to the skin," cf. BAGD 882 and LSJ 1993.

[134] Cf. *Lev. Rab.* Shemini 11/6 on Lev 9:1 (Margulies 226, Soncino 4.142), with parallels in *Pesiq. R.* 14/11 (Friedmann 63b, Braude 285) and *Pesiq. Rav Kah.* 4/5 (Mandelbaum 1.70, Braude and Kapstein 76). For Moses as high priest in Philo, see *Mos.* 2.3 and 5, and *Praem.* 53.

[135] "The Galilean": Strack and Stemberger, *Introduction* 85. The name is sometimes spelled "Eleazar."

[136] Cf. *Pesiq. R. ibid.* (n. 134, with Braude's n. 71); *Pesiq. Rav Kah. ibid.* (n. 134, where the name R. Eliezer bar Joseph is given in error; no such rabbi is known to exist); and *y. Yoma* 1:1, 38b (Neusner 14.17). For the חָלוּק as an undershirt, see Jastrow 465. In his translations, Braude has correctly added "linen" on the basis of Lev 16:4. See the next note.

(חלוק בד לבן שאין בו אימרא),[137] ministered as high priest."[138] In his monumental work *Talmudische Archäologie,* S. Krauss describes various methods of weaving garments in Palestinian Judaic sources. Referring to the above tradition, he maintains that a special shirt-like garment is that which is "seamless" (ἄρραφος), that is, without an אִימְרָא.[139] Because it was "woven of one piece," it had to have an opening at the neck.[140]

Jesus' (white, linen) tunic without seam, woven in one piece (John 19:23), is thus meant to represent him as the high priest. He is intentionally made to appear like Moses, who as high priest functioned in such a garment, and who remained a high priest up until his death. This means that the blue / purple outer garment of the high priest, mixed with gold, is not meant here, although descriptions of it in Philo and Josephus bear some similarities.[141] Also, Jesus' seamless tunic has nothing to do with being a symbol of unity.[142]

Again, the seamless tunic of Jesus, one of four (high priestly) pieces of clothing for which the Roman soldiers cast lots beneath his Cross, is not historical. It belongs to the great narrative artistry of the Evangelist John, or to the Palestinian Jewish Christian who first formulated this tradition. The author wished to portray Jesus' death on the Cross in terms of the Jewish high priesthood. Jesus' sacrifice of himself, the true high priest, provided atonement for the sins of all the people. His seamless garment of one piece pointed to this.

9. The Tearing of the Temple Curtain / Veil.

At the moment Jesus died on the Cross, "the curtain of the Temple was torn in two, from top to bottom" (Mark 15:38). Elsewhere I have proposed that the background of this motif is God's mourning for His only Son by tearing His purple garment (פֻּרְגּוֹד), which can also mean the

---

[137] For בַּד as "chosen, fine linen," see Jastrow 138.

[138] Cf. *Midr. Pss.* 99/4 (Buber 424; Braude 2.145). This is wrongly attributed to R. Aqiva in *b. 'Abod. Zar.* 34a (Soncino 165); in *b. Ta'an.* 11b (Soncino 52) R. Kahana, a second generation Palestinian Amora (Strack and Stemberger, *Introduction* 95), repeats it.

[139] Cf. Jastrow 51, who calls the seam "fringe, border." On not tearing / rending the neck of such a woven garment, cf. *b. Makk.* 3b (Soncino 12). See also *b. Šabb.* 48a (Soncino 218-219, and n. 1).

[140] In 1.152, with n. 315 on p. 568, Krauss notes John 19:23. P. Billerbeck in Str-B 2.573 also calls attention to the works of Lightfoot and Krauss.

[141] Cf. Exod 28:31-32 and 39:22-23; Philo, *Mos.* 2.118-121 and *Quaes. Exod.* 2.118; and Josephus, *Ant.* 3.159, 161.

[142] Cf. Brown, *The Death* 957-958, who believes there is more evidence for this interpretation than for that of the high priest.

curtain / veil separating God on His heavenly throne from the angels and the souls of the righteous. The Herodian or Second Temple in Jerusalem was considered to be His earthly dwelling, exactly opposite the heavenly one. As God rent in mourning the heavenly curtain / veil, so He did with the earthly one. The larger, outer curtain of the Temple was probably meant.[143]

Yet the Evangelist Mark, unaware of this Palestinian Jewish Christian interpretation, may himself have thought instead of the rending of the inner curtain or veil before the Holy of Holies. A favorite interpretation in this respect is that at Jesus' death the Temple and its cult have lost their significance for Christians.[144] Jesus, the true high priest, through his death on the Cross has made offerings such as those brought by the high priest in the Temple on the annual Day of Atonement superfluous.

*   *   *

The above nine allusions to Jesus as the high priest or to Day of Atonement imagery in other incidents of the Passion Narrative show that the Palestinian Jewish Christian author of the Gethsemane account was not the only one to make such comparisons. Others definitely did so before and after him, and the earlier descriptions may have encouraged him to do likewise. I now turn to an analysis of his own presentation of Jesus as the high priest in Gethsemane, on the night before he offered himself on the Cross at Golgotha.

2.   High Priest and Day of Atonement Imagery in Gethsemane.

Before analyzing such imagery in the Markan account of Gethsemane, I would like to call attention to an independent trace of this in Luke's parallel narrative (22:39-46).

a) The textual tradition of vv 43-44 does not allow an easy answer in regard to whether they stood in the original of Luke's gospel. The earliest definite attestation for them derives from the middle of the second century C.E.[1] Whether or not they are original, however, they point to Palestinian Jewish Christian influence on the Gethsemane narrative, outside the traditions found in the Markan account, in regard to high priestly and Day of Atonement imagery.

---

[143] Cf. my volume *Samuel, Saul and Jesus* 147-157.

[144] Cf. a sketch of this line of interpretation given by Gnilka in *Das Evangelium nach Markus* (Mk 8, 27 – 16, 20) 323-324.

[1] Cf. the evidence as summarized by R. Brown in *The Death* 180-181.

Luke 22:43 states that an angel from heaven appeared to Jesus, "strengthening" (ἐνισχύω) him. This is the only occurrence of the verb in the active form in the NT.[2] I suggest that it is due to Jesus' being "weak," like the high priest on the Day of Atonement.

Secondly, in anguish Jesus prayed more earnestly, and his sweat became like "drops of blood" (θρόμβοι αἵματος) falling down upon the ground (v 44).[3] The noun θρόμβος, "drop," is very rare, occurring only here in the LXX, NT, Philo and Josephus.[4] It too derives from an activity of the high priest on the Day of Atonement.

b) For an analysis of the high priest as "weak," and thus in need of strengthening precisely on the Day of Atonement, see below, section 1) F., on the "weakness" of the flesh in Mark 14:38.

"Drops of blood" play a major role in the activity of the high priest on the Day of Atonement. Lev 16:3 prescribes that the high priest enter "the holy place" (the Holy of Holies within the veil – v 2) with a young bull for a sin offering. It is to atone for the sins of him and his house (vv 6 and 11). He then takes some of the blood of the bull and "sprinkles" (hiphil of נזה)[5] it with his finger seven times on the front of, or before the mercy seat (v 14). After killing the goat of the sin offering for the people, he also brings its blood within the veil and repeats the above procedure (v 15). With some of the blood of the bull and the goat he then cleanses and hallows the altar because of the people's uncleanness, also sprinkling it with his fingers seven times (vv 18-19).

The exact procedures for implementing the above are given in the Mishnah, Tosefta and the two Talmuds in the tractate *Yoma*, the "Day" of Atonement, and in *Sifra*, the Tannaitic commentary on Leviticus. At *m. Yoma* 4:3 it is stated that the high priest slaughtered (the young bull) and received it in a "bowl" (מְזְרָק).[6] The same is true for the ram or he-goat in 5:4.[7] Normal parlance for this vessel was "cup" (כּוֹס), as noted by the Talmuds.[8] Since these texts repeatedly speak of the blood in the cups as "poured out" (שָׁפַךְ), Palestinian Jewish Christians easily associated this

---

[2] Cf. BAGD 267. The only occurrence in the intransitive form is found in Acts 9:19.

[3] There is no justification for the addition in the RSV and NRSV of "great" to "drops of blood."

[4] Cf. BAGD 383 and LSJ 807.

[5] BDB 633 and Jastrow 890-891.

[6] Albeck 2.233; Danby 166, who has "basin." On the term, see Jastrow 756.

[7] Albeck 2.237, Danby 168.

[8] Cf. *y. Yoma* 5:4, 42d (Neusner 14.147-149), and *b. Yoma* 57b (Soncino 268-269).

imagery with the "Lord's Supper." On that occasion, immediately before Gethsemane, Jesus spoke of the Passover wine in a "cup" from which all the disciples drank as "my blood of the (new) covenant, which is 'poured out' for many" (Mark 14:24).[9] This imagery thus also derives in part from the activity of the high priest in the Holy of Holies on the Day of Atonement.

The Holy of Holies behind the veil at the time of the Second Temple was completely empty.[10] In separate acts the high priest entered it and sprinkled the blood of the young bull and the he-goat "once upwards and seven times downwards," following the prescription in Lev 16:14-15. Either inadvertently or intentionally, some of this sprinkled blood got onto the curtain / veil.[11] It is in this context that the rare phrase "drops of blood" appears.

Josephus relates that at the Roman conquest of Jerusalem in 70 C.E., some time after Titus and his generals entered and beheld the content of the Holy of Holies, without touching anything, a priest voluntarily handed over to him the curtains.[12] Josephus also describes Vespasian's and Titus' triumphal procession in Rome. He expressly mentions "the purple hangings of the sanctuary" which were afterwards not placed with the other booty in the Temple of Peace, but in the palace.[13]

On a visit to Rome in order to get anti-Jewish legislation revoked, R. Simeon b. Yoḥai and R. Eliezer b. Yose (the Galilean), two third

---

[9] In this respect, cf. again the action of the high priest Simon II, son of Onias, on the Day of Atonement: "he reached out his hand to *the cup* and *poured* (out) a libation of *the blood* of the grape" at the foot of the altar in the Jerusalem Temple (Sir 50:15). See also the dashing or pouring out of the blood of the Passover lamb at the base of the altar, which effected atonement (*y. Pesaḥ.* 9:7, 37a in Neusner / Schiffman 13.464, and p. 237), and 1 Cor 5:7, "Christ, our paschal lamb, has been sacrificed."

[10] Cf. *m. Yoma* 5:2 and *Šeq.* 6:1-2 (Danby 158 and 167), as well as Josephus, *Bell.* 5.219.

[11] For the latter, which seems more probable, cf. the opinion of R. Judah (bar Ilai), a third generation Tanna (Strack and Stemberger, *Introduction* 84-85), in *m. Yoma* 5:4 (Albeck 2.237, Danby 168).

[12] Cf. *Bell.* 6.260 and 389-390. In *Syr Bar* 6:7 the veil of the Holy of Holies is also preserved at the destruction of Jerusalem by Nebuchadnezzar (*OTP* 1.623). Actually, the destruction of 70 C.E. is meant (1.615). The writing appears to have been originally in Hebrew, from Palestine, in "the first or second decade of the second century" C.E. (1.617).

[13] Cf. *Bell.* 7.162. They were certainly carried in the procession and are most probably included in the tapestries "of the rarest purple" in 134. I had earlier described this in *Samuel, Saul and Jesus* 152.

generation Tannaim,[14] entered the "treasure house" there and were allowed to tear up the bill of negative legislation.[15] It is tempting to associate this "treasure house" with the "palace" mentioned above by Josephus. This is because R. Eliezer b. Yose relates in regard to the same visit in Rome and the curtain / veil (פָּרֹכֶת)[16] of the Holy of Holies: "I myself saw it in Rome, and there were many 'drops of blood' (טיפי דמים) on it. And he[17] told me: These are from the blood of the Day of Atonement."[18] In the *b. Yoma* 57a version of this, the "many drops of blood" are said to be "both of the bullock and the he-goat."

The noun טִיפָה / טִפָּה does not occur in the Hebrew Bible.[19] The Mishnah mentions a drop (of milk) "falling" upon a piece of meat, which recalls the Greek καταβαίνοντες of drops of blood "descending / falling" to the ground in Luke 22:44.[20] Only once is a "drop of blood" spoken of in the Mishnah, and then in regard to the pierced ear of a firstling.[21] The expression "drops of blood" in Judaic sources thus appears to be primarily related to the activities of the high priest on the Day of Atonement, especially in regard to the sprinkling of the atoning blood of the bullock and he-goat and the curtain / veil of the Holy of Holies.[22]

One other early association of the expression "drop(s) of blood" may have influenced the Palestinian Jewish Christian author of Luke 22:43-44. In *t. Ohol.* 4:11, R. Judah (bar Ilai), a third generation Tanna,[23] deals with

---

[14] Strack and Stemberger, *Introduction* 84-85.

[15] Cf. b. *Me'il.* 17b (Soncino 64).

[16] Jastrow 1220.

[17] Either their local Jewish "guide," or perhaps R. Simeon b. Yohai.

[18] Cf. *b. Me'il.* 17b (Soncino 64); *t. Yoma* 2:16 (Lieberman, *The Tosefta.* Mo'ed 239, where the כמה of MS Erfurt should be preferred; Neusner 2.199); *y. Yoma* 5:4, 42d (Neusner 14.145, where in the following discussion he makes "they" explicit with "the drops of blood"); and *b. Yoma* 57a (Soncino 266). On the expression "many drops of blood," see also *b. Keth.* 10a (Soncino 50), as well as *b. Nid.* 58b and 59a (Soncino 411 and 413). For knowledge of the curtain as bespattered with blood, see also the legendary account in *Lev. Rab.* Ahare Mot 20/5, where Titus in the interior of the Holy of Holies "cut into the curtain, and his sword came out 'full of blood'" (Margulies 458, Soncino 4.257).

[19] Cf. BDB 643, where the related term נֵטֶף, "drop," only occurs in Job 36:27.

[20] Cf. *Ḥul.* 8:3; see also *t. 'Abod. Zar.* 7:4, 6; and *Makš.* 1:7.

[21] Cf. *Bek.* 6:1 in Albeck 5.173, Danby 536.

[22] For "not seven drops (of blood)" in regard to the sprinkling of the altar by the high priest, cf. *Sifra* Ahare Mot 4 on Lev 16:19 (and *m. Yoma* 5:5) in Neusner 3.27, Winter 460. The "drops of blood" of a menstruant woman in the Tosefta and elsewhere are irrelevant here.

[23] Cf. n. 11.

a slain person whose blood dripped from the bier into a hole. He maintains this blood is unclean "because the drop of (blood of) death is mixed (up in the remainder)." Sages, however, declare it clean. Then R. Simeon (b. Yoḥai), the same third generation Tanna as above, mentions a crucified person (צלוב) whose blood gushed forth. If a quarter (-*log*) of blood is found under him, he is clean. This, however, is not true for a corpse whose blood drips forth. R. Judah then disagrees, declaring this blood clean, "For I say that the final drop of (blood of) death remained on the wood."[24]

If the expression "the final drop of (blood of) death" in regard to a crucified person was already a fixed topos before this third generation Tanna mentions it, it too may have caused the author of Luke 22:44 to describe Jesus' sweat as being like "drops of blood" falling down to the ground in Gethsemane. On the next afternoon he too would be "crucified."

The Palestinian Jewish Christian author behind the special Gethsemane tradition in Luke 22:43-44[25] probably consciously described Jesus in terms of traditions well-known to him: the high priest as weak especially on this occasion, "drops of blood" from the offerings brought by the high priest in the Holy of Holies on the Day of Atonement, and possibly the last drop(s) of blood of a crucified person. These traditions he applied to Jesus, who for him and many other Jewish Christians had become by his atoning death on the Cross their high priest par excellence.

*   *   *

After describing high priest and Day of Atonement imagery in Luke's Gethsemane account, I now turn to the same type of imagery as found in the Markan narrative.

1.   *The Seclusion of the High Priest Before the Day of Atonement.*

Up to now sufficient attention has not been called to the fact that Jesus was forced to stay awake the entire first night of Passover before he was crucified at Golgotha the next afternoon. This too represented him to the first Palestinian Jewish Christians as their high priest, who offered himself the next day. The high priest also had to spend a sleepless night before performing the services of atonement the next day in the Temple.

---

[24] Zuckermandel / Liebermann 601, Neusner 6.90. On the liquid measure *log*, comparable to the quantity of six eggs, cf. Jastrow 694.

[25] It was certainly modified by the Evangelist Luke when he took it over, or perhaps when it was later incorporated into the Gospel.

Numerous expressions and motifs from this night are also found in the Markan Gethsemane narrative.

A) A SECLUDED PLACE, GETHSEMANE.

a) Mark 14:32 par. has Jesus take his eleven disciples to the place called Gethsemane; it was located somewhere on the Mount of Olives (v 26). The Evangelist John says Jesus and his disciples went across the Kidron Valley to reach it, a garden known also to Judas because Jesus and the disciples often met there (18:1-2; cf. Luke 22:39, "as was his custom").

The gospels are unanimous in representing Gethsemane as a place to which Jesus retreated to be alone with his closest followers. This motif of a place of "seclusion" most probably also derives from the site of the high priest where he stayed the night before his bringing offerings of atonement the next day.

b) The high priest was only allowed to function in a state of absolute purity. If he had intercourse with his wife and her menstrual period began, for example, this rendered him impure for seven days (Lev 15:24). Therefore the high priest was "separated" (פרש)[26] from his own house (= his wife) seven days before the Day of Atonement. Nothing should "befall" (ארע)[27] him (*m. Yoma* 1:1).[28] Uncleanness due to marital life was considered to happen "often" (שְׁכִיחָא),[29] and a seminal emission was thought to be "commonplace" (מָצוּי).[30] A man who had a nocturnal pollution was called a בעל קרי.[31] One of the ten miracles attributed to the Temple was supposed to be the fact that the high priest never suffered a pollution during (the night of) the Day of Atonement.[32] Yet this in fact did occur.[33]

---

[26] Jastrow 1242, hiphil.

[27] Jastrow 124.

[28] Albeck 2.223, Danby 162.

[29] Cf. *b. Yoma* 6b (Soncino 26) and 13a (Soncino 57), and for the term, Jastrow 1573.

[30] For the expression, see Jastrow 825. Cf. *y. Yoma* 1:1, 38d (Neusner 14.31). See also Philo, *Spec. Leg.* 1.119 – πολλάκις, and "ordinarily" in *Sifre* Deut. Ki Tiṣa 255 on Deut 23:11 (Finkelstein 280; Hammer 256).

[31] Cf. Jastrow 1419.

[32] Cf. *m. 'Avot* 5:5 (Danby 456), with many parallels.

[33] Cf. for example Joseph b. Elim of Sepphoris, who "served in the place of the high priest for one hour" on the Day of Atonement because of such an invalidation of the high priest, in *t. Yoma* 1:4 (Neusner 2.186); *b. Meg.* 9b (Soncino 52); *Hor.* 12b (Soncino 89); Josephus, *Ant.* 17. 165-166 (more correctly, "for one

To prevent such an "accident," the high priest was separated from his wife by being taken seven days before the Day of Atonement to the "Councillors' Chamber" (לִשְׁכַּת פַּלְהֶדְרִין) within the Temple.[34] The term "councillors" here is a corruption of פרהדרין, from πάρεδροι, assessors or "councillors."[35] The gemara in *b. Yoma* 8b states that the chamber was earlier called that of the "senators," בּוּלְבוּטֵי, from βουλευταί.[36] Yet in *t. Yoma* 1:3 Abba Saul, a third generation Tanna,[37] used to call it "the Chamber of the Storeroom of Oil" (לשכת בֵּית שְׁמַנְיָא).[38] The Jerusalem Talmud in *Yoma* 1:1, 38c comments upon Abba Saul's statement as follows: "In the beginning they used to call it the chamber of oil, but now they call it the councillors' chamber. 'The chamber of oil' is a nickname."[39]

I suggest that the Palestinian Jewish Christian author of the Gethsemane narrative modeled the name of the site for Jesus' seclusion the night before he offered himself on the Cross, "Gethsemane," on the place where the high priest was secluded the night before he entered the Holy of Holies on the Day of Atonement and encountered death there (see below). He simply changed the בֵּית to the construct form גִּית or גַּת, from גַּת, which here does not mean a "vat" for wine pressing, but a "marked off space," a "place."[40] The "place of oil," גִּית שמניא or גַת שמניא,

---

day," the day of the "fast" [= Day of Atonement; see below], due to a nocturnal emission); and *y. Yoma* 1:1, 38d (Neusner 14.27).

[34] Cf. *m. Yoma* 1:1 in Albeck 2.223, Danby 162.

[35] Jastrow 1216-1217, who has the similar "counsellor," as does Danby. Jeremias in *Jerusalem* 153, n. 22, interprets the room rather as that of the "court presidents," the πρόεδροι. In this understanding, the presiding high priest was the court president (head of the Sanhedrin, which met in the nearby Chamber of Hewn Stone – cf. n. 39 of the previous section). On the Greek term πρόεδρος, see LSJ 1476.

[36] Soncino 35, with n. 5; Jastrow 146; LSJ 324: "councillor, senator." The gemara explains how the designation "councillors" came to be applied to the chamber or cell. Cf. Joseph of Arimathea in Mark 15:43 par. as a respected member of the "council."

[37] Cf. p. 116, n. 39.

[38] Lieberman 2.220 (MS "ל" has שמנייה); Zuckermandel / Liebermann 180; Neusner 2.185, without "storeroom of." Cf. *b. Yoma* 16a (Soncino 71), and *m. Midd.* 2:5 (Albeck 5.322, with שמניה; Danby 592). On בית as "storeroom," see Jastrow 168, 7).

[39] Neusner 14.24. I do not find this in my edition of Yerushalmi, yet Neusner's translation is certainly correct because it was also checked against the Leiden MS and the *editio princeps* (14.x).

[40] Jastrow 274. He points out that this is a contraction of גַּנַּת, which means "garden" (p. 240, with the construct of גינתא as גִּנַּת). This may explain John's

very appropriate to the setting on the Mount of "Olives," was then later transliterated into Greek as the "place" (χωρίον) Γεθσημανι.[41]

If this proposal is basically correct, it explains why the place or garden of "Gethsemane," like "Golgotha," is not found in a single Judaic source. It was an attempt by a Palestinian Jewish Christian to describe Jesus as the high priest during the night before his offering himself on the Cross as also staying in a secluded place. The Jewish high priest did exactly the same in the "Storeroom of Oil."

B) SLEEP.

a) In Gethsemane Jesus returns from praying and finds Peter, James and John "sleeping." He then asks Peter: "Simon, are you 'sleeping'?" (Mark 14:37) After praying and returning, Jesus again found the three "sleeping" (v 40). Finally he returned a third time and asked: "Are you still 'sleeping' and resting?" (v 41). This fourfold emphasis on "sleeping" (καθεύδω) shows how much importance the Palestinian Jewish Christian author of vv 32-42 attached to this motif. It too derives from the high priest in seclusion during the night of the Day of Atonement.

b) While the high priest was allowed to eat and drink as much as he wanted during the week of seclusion, on the evening of the Day of Atonement toward nightfall he was not allowed to eat much "because food brings about 'sleep' (שֵׁנָה)," as *m. Yoma* 1:4 states.[42] The gemara in *b. Yoma* 18a-b and *y. Yoma* 1:4, 39a state Tannaitic traditions regarding which foods and beverages the high priest may not now eat and drink. By avoiding them, he would not fall asleep, have a pollution, and invalidate himself.[43]

It was seldom the case that the high priest was a Sage. Therefore the disciples (see below) of the Sages would read before him on the eve of the Day of Atonement from Job, Ezra and Chronicles (*m. Yoma* 1:6).[44] Leo

---

reference to a "garden" (κῆπος) in 18:1, without mentioning "Gethsemane" explicitly.

[41] J. Klausner in *Jesus von Nazareth* (Jerusalem: The Jewish Publishing House, Ltd, 1952[3]) 455, n. 109 calls the name Gethsemane "very strange," noting that גת is almost never used in Judaic sources for oil (שמן), only for grapes. He also calls attention to Abba Saul's statement, and considers this as a second possible origin of the name Gethsemane. On χωρίον in Mark 14:32 par. as "place," cf. BAGD 890. The Greek term was necessary because ג(י)א as "place" was no longer recognizable in the Semitic, transliterated as Γεθσημανι.

[42] Albeck 2.224, Danby 163.

[43] Cf. Soncino 78 (with notes 5 and 7), 79, and Neusner 14.39 respectively.

[44] Albeck 2.225, Danby 163.

Jung, the English translator of the Soncino edition of *Yoma* in the Babylonian Talmud, appropriately remarks on the latter: "These books, less known, might arouse his interest and keep him awake. Sleep was to be prevented, because of the risk of pollution."[45] The Mishnah continues by having Zechariah b. Qebutal state: "Many times I read before him out of Daniel."[46] The Jerusalem Talmud also cites a Tannaitic tradition here: "They read Proverbs and Psalms, because their message disturbs one's 'sleep' (שינה)."[47]

The Mishnah continues by stating that if the high priest sought to "slumber / drowse off" (נום, hithpalpel),[48] young priests would snap their middle fingers before him and say to him: "Get up and drive off (sleep by walking) for a change on the (cold) pavement!" This is how they would divert him until the time of slaughter arrived (and he himself became active).[49] The Tosefta at *Yoma* 1:9 says regarding this: "They did not 'sleep' all night."[50] And the Babylonian Talmud notes here: "Some of the worthiest of Jerusalem did not 'go to sleep' all the night in order that the high priest might hear the reverberating noise, so that 'sleep' should not overcome him suddenly."[51]

All the above references show how important it was during the night of the Day of Atonement for the high priest not to drowse off or even to fall asleep. This could lead to his having a pollution, causing him to become disqualified to perform the services of atonement. The great efforts made by others to prevent him from falling asleep are to be contrasted to the behavior of Jesus' disciples, who themselves fall asleep. I shall comment more extensively on their failure in section E. below.

C) KEEPING WATCH / WAKING.

a) In Gethsemane Jesus told Peter, James and John: "Remain here and 'watch'" (γρηγορέω: Mark 14:35). Having returned from praying, he asked Peter if he was sleeping. "Could you not 'watch' one hour?" (v 37). Then he addressed the three again with the words: "'Watch' and pray that you may not enter into temptation" (v 38). The latter verses also employ γρηγορέω.

---

[45] Soncino 81, n. 1.

[46] Cf. n. 44. Str-B 6.249 notes that he was a first century Tanna.

[47] Cf. *y. Yoma* 1:6, 39b in Neusner 14.44.

[48] Jastrow 887.

[49] Cf. *m. Yoma* 1:7 in Albeck 2.225, Danby 163.

[50] Lieberman, Mo'ed 223; Neusner 2.188.

[51] Cf. *b. Yoma* 19b in Soncino 86.

The threefold emphasis on "watching" here also shows the importance of this motif for the Palestinian Jewish Christian author of the Gethsemane account. It too derives from imagery traditionally associated with the high priest in the night of the Day of Atonement.

b) The Tosefta at *Yoma* 1:9 states that the young priests "kept" the high priest "engaged" (עסק, hiphil),[52] that is, they kept him awake through speech, not with a wind or stringed instrument. They used to cite Ps 127:1, "A song of Ascents. Of Solomon. Unless the Lord builds the house, those who build it labor in vain. Unless the Lord 'watches over' (יִשְׁמָר) the city, the 'watchman' (שׁוֹמֵר)[53] 'stays awake' (שָׁקַד) in vain." The (young priests) did not sleep all night, but "kept watch" (שׁקד)[54] by the high priest to keep him engaged through noise.[55] As noted in section B) above, some of the worthiest people in Jerusalem did not go to sleep all this night so that the high priest would also hear (their) noise, and not fall asleep.

Of the five occurrences of the verb γρηγορέω in the LXX with a Hebrew equivalent, four translate שׁקד, the verb found above.[56] Since שׁקד means both "to watch" and "to be awake," as does γρηγορέω,[57] the RSV is correct in having "watch" in the Markan passages cited above in a), but also "keep awake" in a footnote.

The Evangelist Matthew recognized this imagery as deriving from those who watched over the high priest in the night of the Day of Atonement. Only he adds in 26:38 and 40 to "watch / stay awake": "with me." Jesus, depicted as the high priest who offers himself the next afternoon at Golgotha, here admonishes the three disciples and then Peter to watch "with me."

---

[52] Jastrow 1098. On this motif, cf. also n. 10 on p. 67.

[53] The Palestinian Jewish Christian author of the Gethsemane narrative may have combined the "watching" on the Day of Atonement with that of the first night of Passover, known as the "night of watching" (ליל שמרים). Cf. Exod 12:42, as well as *Mek. R. Ish.* Pisḥa 14 on this verse (Lauterbach 1.115-116) for the future redemption also to occur in this night according to R. Joshua (b. Ḥananyah), an older second generation Tanna (see p. 78, n. 53). A parallel is found in *b. Roš Haš.* 11b (Soncino 42).

[54] Jastrow 1621: "to watch"; BDB 1052: watch, wake; be wakeful.

[55] Lieberman, Mo'ed 223; Neusner 2.187-188. Ps 127:1 is also cited in *b. Yoma* 19b at this point (Soncino 86); see also *y. Yoma* 1:4, 39a (Neusner 14.39).

[56] Cf. Hatch and Redpath 1.278.

[57] Cf. n. 54, and BAGD 167.

D) SITTING.

a) When Jesus went to the place called Gethsemane, he said to his disciples: "'Sit' (καθίζω) here, while I pray" (Mark 14:32). At the very end of the episode he told them to "rise" (v 42), implying that they had been sitting the entire time.

The motif of "sitting" may also derive from imagery associated with those keeping watch over the high priest in the night of the Day of Atonement.

b) If the high priest in the night of the Day of Atonement sought to slumber, young priests would snap their middle fingers before him and tell him: "'Rise' (עֲמֹד), drive away..." (as above in section B: *m. Yoma* 1:7). That is, he (and they) were sitting together, they engaging him through talk and noise so that he would not fall asleep, have a pollution and become impure. This may have inspired the Palestinian Jewish Christian author of the Gethsemane account to have the disciples "sit," and finally to "rise."

E) DISCIPLES.

a) In Mark 14:32 Jesus tells his "disciples" (μαθηταί) to sit down while he prays. While he is then concerned with only Peter, James and John, especially with Peter, at the end of the episode all the (eleven) disciples are meant again when Jesus tells them to rise (v 42).

Disciples also play an important role in watching over the high priest in the night of the Day of Atonement.

b) As noted above, very few high priests were Sages. Therefore *m. Yoma* 1:6 says that the "disciples" (תַּלְמִידִים) of the Sages interpreted (the Scriptures) before the high priest, and they read to him from less known biblical books (to keep him awake).[58]

No instance is recorded in Judaic sources of these disciples' lack of success.[59] They kept such good watch of the high priest that he remained awake and eligible to begin his work at the services of atonement the next morning.

The opposite is the case with Jesus' disciples. He had asked them to watch / keep awake. Yet he returned three times from praying to find them sleeping. Instead of watching over him, who the next afternoon

---

[58] Albeck 2.224, Danby 163. Cf. also *b. Yoma* 4a (Soncino 12), where in the future two "disciples" of the Sages will train the high priest for seven days in the services of the Day of Atonement.

[59] One possible exception is the incident mentioned in n. 33. However, it too may not have been their fault.

would offer his atoning blood at Golgotha, they failed miserably.[60] This adumbrates the fact that at Jesus' arrest in Gethsemane shortly afterwards, all the eleven forsook him and fled (Mark 14:50 par.). They were also conspicuously absent at Jesus' Crucifixion (15:40-41 par.).[61]

Another intentional sign of the main disciple Peter's failure to remain awake / watch over Jesus is the latter's calling him "Simon" in Mark 14:37. This name only occurs here in the Markan Passion Narrative. The Semitic שִׁמְעוֹן means "one who hears, listens, obeys."[62] Because he too fell asleep, Simon could not "listen" to the prayer of Jesus. He could not "obey" his request to remain awake / watch for one hour. His specific failure, emphasized here, adumbrates his threefold denial of Jesus in the courtyard of the high priest shortly afterwards (14:66-72).

F) WEAK.

a) In Mark 14:38 Jesus, after speaking to Peter alone, tells him, James and John: "Watch and pray that you may not enter into temptation; the spirit is willing, but the flesh is 'weak' (ἀσθενής)." At least the latter phrase, "the flesh is weak," derives from imagery associated with the high priest on the Day of Atonement.

b) The high priest was considered weak on the Day of Atonement because of two factors. First, he was not allowed to fall asleep as of the beginning of the previous evening so that he would not become unclean and thus unable to perform the prescribed services, as indicated above. That is, he missed a whole night's sleep.

Secondly, Lev 16:29 and 31 as well as Num 29:7 state that "you shall afflict your souls" on the Day of Atonement. Judaic tradition interpreted this "affliction" to mean: "On the Day of Atonement eating, drinking, washing, anointing, putting on sandals, and marital intercourse are forbidden" (*m. Yoma* 8:1).[63] Having had only a light supper before the beginning of the Day of Atonement so that there would be less danger of his falling asleep, like all other Jews the high priest was now obligated to

---

[60] Cf. also 1 Samuel 26, where those with Saul are accused of not having kept watch over their lord, the Lord's anointed (v 16). They had all fallen asleep (v 12).

[61] Luke adds "all his (Jesus' male) acquaintances" in 23:49, but these certainly excluded the disciples. John inserts the disciple whom Jesus loved at the Cross in 19:25-27 to show Jesus' concern for his own mother even at the point of death (and of course to emphasize the role of the beloved disciple).

[62] Jastrow 1598, and the name on p. 1600. Cf. the wordplay with this name in *Gen. Rab.* Vayetze 71/3 on Gen 29:32 (Soncino 2.654).

[63] Albeck 2.245, Danby 171.

renounce eating and drinking for one whole day. That is, he was to "fast."

Philo in *Spec. Leg.* 1.186 calls the Day of Atonement "the fast" (ἡ νηστεία; cf. *Mos.* 2.23; the same term is employed in Acts 27:9). In *Ant.* 3.240 Josephus states that on the tenth of (Tishri) they "fast" (διανηστεύοντες) until evening. According to *b. Meg.* 31a, the haftarah or reading from the prophets for the (morning of the) Day of Atonement was Isa 57:15 (ff.).[64] This included 58:3-6, which deal with fasting.[65] In rabbinic sources the Day of Atonement is sometimes called the "Great Fast."[66]

Due to lack of sleep, fasting, and the extreme pressure of correctly performing all the five services required of him on the Day of Atonement, the most important day of the year, the high priest was frequently described as "weak." In *b. Yoma* 20b, for example, it is stated that the ashes are usually removed from the altar in the Temple at cockcrow (*m.* 1:8). "On the Day of Atonement, when the high priest is 'weak' (חֻלְשָׁא),[67] we do it (already) about midnight...."[68]

The Mishnah even employs the loanword אסטניס, ἀσθενής,[69] of the high priest in *Yoma* 3:5. If he were old or "weak," hot water was prepared and poured into the cold water (used for his frequently necessary immersions).[70]

---

[64] Soncino 188. The reading from the Pentateuch was Leviticus 16.

[65] For the haftarah as extending from Isa 57:15(14) to 58:14, cf. M. Herr, art. "Day of Atonement" in *EJ* (1971) 5.1379. In the Mishnah tractate on fasting, *Ta'anit*, the Day of Atonement is mentioned in 4:8 (Danby 200). Fasting is also found in the targums on Leviticus 16. See *Pseudo-Jonathan* on v 29; *Fragment Targum* on v 30; and *Neofiti 1*, MS "M" on v 29, and MS "I" on v 31. See also *Pirq. R. El.* 46 (Friedlander 362).

[66] Cf. for example *y. Yoma* 8:1, 44d (Neusner 14.209), with a parallel in *y. Ta'an.* 1:6, 64c (Neusner 18.167). See also the Qumran "festival of fasting" in 4Q Festival Prayers[b] (4Q508) in Martínez 412.

[67] Jastrow 434; cf. the verb and adjective on p. 474.

[68] Soncino 89. Cf. also p. 90, with n. 3; 36a, twice (Soncino 166, with n. 10); 44b (Soncino 212, with n. 3); 56b, three times (Soncino 264-265); and 70b (Soncino 335).

[69] Cf. Jastrow 58 under איסתנים, and Krauss, *Lehnwörter* 2.98-99. The only other occurrence of the expression in the Mishnah is in *Ber.* 2:6 (Albeck 1.18, Danby 4).

[70] Albeck 2.230, Danby 165. On this, cf. *b. Yoma* 34b (Soncino 160); *y. Yoma* 3:6, 40c (Neusner 14.84); and *t. Yoma* 1:20 (Neusner 2.191). On the Day of Atonement R. Joshua b. Levi, a first generation Palestinian Amora (Strack and Stemberger, *Introduction* 72-73), later appropriated the term "weak / frail" from the high priest of the Mishnah for himself. See the first sources in n. 66.

Only after having performed all the required services, when the Day of Atonement was over, did the high priest remove his "weakness" by arranging a festival (including eating and drinking) for his friends. The Mishnah says this was primarily because he had emerged safely from the Sanctuary.[71]

The Palestinian Jewish Christian who had Jesus state Mark 14:38b to the three disciples thus most probably borrowed from imagery closely connected with the status of the high priest during the entire Day of Atonement. His spirit was willing, but his flesh / body was indeed "weak" on this occasion.[72]

*   *   *

Sections 1) A-F above describe various aspects of the high priest during his seclusion on the (evening and) Day of Atonement. Two other motifs in the Gethsemane narrative, however, also go back to the high priest and the Day of Atonement. To these I now turn.

2.   *Other High Priest and Day of Atonement Motifs.*

A)   FEAR OF DEATH WHEN ENTERING THE HOLY OF HOLIES.

a) In Gethsemane, on the evening before Jesus died on the Cross, he began to be "greatly distressed and troubled," saying to Peter, James and John: "My soul is very sorrowful, even to death." He also asked God to remove the cup (of death) from him (Mark 14:33-34, 36).

This trepidation in regard to possible imminent death is also found with the high priest on the Day of Atonement.

b) After having performed all the required services on the Day of Atonement, the high priest used to make a festival for his friends "because he had come out of the Sanctuary 'safely' (בְּשָׁלֹום)": *m. Yoma* 7:4.[73] Earlier, after having emerged from the Holy of Holies, he prayed a short prayer in the Sanctuary. Yet "he did not extend his prayer so as not to frighten Israel" (*m. Yoma* 5:1).[74] The people, who could not see him, were very worried that something terrible would happen to him inside. Judaic tradition helps to explain why.

God was believed to dwell in His heavenly Temple, where He sits upon His throne. Yet He was also thought to dwell within the earthly

---

[71] Cf. *m. Yoma* 7:4 (Albeck 2.244, Danby 171).

[72] The motif of "watching" also derived from the Day of Atonement, as shown above. "Praying" was also a major motif, as will be shown below.

[73] Albeck 2.244, Danby 171.

[74] Albeck 2.236, Danby 167. Cf. the hiphil of בעת in Jastrow 183.

Temple directly below, specifically, within the Holy of Holies.[75] His holiness, however, could be deadly. This is shown by God's remark to Moses in Exod 33:20, "you cannot see My face; for man shall not see Me and live."

The best negative example of this was the incident of Aaron's sons, Nadab and Abihu, who offered "unholy fire" (incense)[76] before the Lord. The result was that "fire came forth from the presence of the Lord and devoured them, and they died before the Lord." This showed the Lord's holiness (Lev 10:1-3).[77]

This narrative is continued at the beginning of Leviticus 16, which deals with the rites of the Day of Atonement.[78] After the death of the two sons of Aaron, when they drew near before the Lord and died, the Lord had Moses tell his brother Aaron (in Judaic thought the high priest) not to come "at all times" into the holy place within the veil, before the mercy seat which is upon the ark, "lest he die." This is because God Himself will appear in a cloud upon the mercy seat (vv 1-2). Then instructions are given as to the specific times on the Day of Atonement when (the high priest) may and definitely should enter the Holy of Holies. This includes the bringing of incense within the veil in the proper manner, "lest he die" (v 13). *Targum Pseudo-Jonathan*, certainly reflecting popular belief here, adds to the latter: "by the flaming fire before the Lord."[79]

This explains the narrative now found in *t. Yoma* 1:8, commenting on why an oath had to be imposed on the high priest on the Day of Atonement (*m. Yoma* 1:5). It was to prevent the recurrence of the behavior

---

[75] Cf. Jesus' words in Matt 23:21-22; *Mek. R. Ish.* Shirata 10 on Exod 15:17 (Lauterbach 2.78), with Ps 11:4 and 1 Kgs 8:13; *'Avot R. Nat.* A 34 (Goldin 140-141) with Ezek 44:2; and the consolation given to a mourner on the Temple Mount: "May He who dwells in this House comfort you" (*Semaḥot* 6:11 in Soncino, *The Minor Tractates* 1.353).

[76] Cf. Exod 30:34-38 on the incense, part of which is to be put "before the testimony in the tent of meeting where I shall meet with you; it shall be for you most holy" (v 36).

[77] Cf. *Targ. Pseud.-Jon.* Lev 10:3, "if they be not heedful in the service of the oblations, I will burn them with flaming fire from before Me, that in the sight of all the people I may be glorified" (Rieder 2.158, Etheridge 173).

[78] In *b. Giṭ.* 60a (Soncino 283), R. Levi, a third generation Palestinian Amora (see p. 76, n. 41), says that Leviticus 16 was one of eight sections separately dictated to Moses before he wrote down the whole Torah. This was on the day on which the Tabernacle was erected, according to Braude and Kapstein in *Pesiqta de Rav Kahana* 401, n. 38, the New Moon of Nisan, the day of the death of Nadab and Abihu.

[79] Rieder 2.169, Etheridge 196. Cf. also n. 77.

of a certain Boethusian (Sadducee),[80] "who offered up the incense while he was still outside (the Holy of Holies), and the cloud of incense went forth and frightened the entire house." He had not inserted a smoke raiser into the incense, which made him liable to the death penalty. The latter was corroborated by his death within three days.[81] One opinion was that the man "was thrown on the dung heap, and worms came forth from his nose." Another view was that he "was smitten as he came out (of the Holy of Holies)." A third was that "an angel had come and struck him down on his face (to the ground), and his brethren the priests came in, and they found the trace as of a calf's foot on his shoulder," fulfilling the description of an angel in Ezek 1:7.[82]

The latter belief in angels present within the Holy of Holies seems to have been widespread. R. Abbahu, a third generation Palestinian Amora,[83] maintained for example in *y. Yoma* 1:5, 39a that although no "man" should be in the tent of meeting when the high priest entered to make atonement in the holy place (Lev 16:17), this applied only if he entered in the proper manner. Otherwise Ezek 1:10 applies regarding the angels supporting God's throne chariot, who are described with the face of a "man." This is used to connect them to Lev 16:17.[84] That is, the angels within the Holy of Holies cause the death of a high priest who does not do everything in the service properly. These two texts, Lev 16:17 and Ezek 1:10, are applied in *Pesiq. R.* 47/3 (on Lev 16:1) to the ministering angels, who pay honor to the high priest when he enters the Holy of Holies (in a proper manner) by fleeing from his presence.[85] Section 47/4 notes that without Israel's meritorious deeds, Aaron would not have been able to bear the ministering angels for one moment in the Holy of Holies. Also, when he entered on the Day of Atonement, (the angel) Satan came to accuse (Israel). Yet when Satan saw Aaron, he would flee from him because of the many meritorious deeds which entered with him.[86]

---

[80] Cf. Jastrow 168 on ביתוסי and ביתוס.

[81] Lieberman, Mo'ed 222-223; Neusner 2.187. Cf. *Sifra* Aḥare Mot, Pereq 3 (Neusner 3.19-20); and *y. Yoma* 1:5, 39a (Neusner 14.40-41).

[82] Cf. *b. Yoma* 19b (Soncino 84-85, with the relevant notes); see also 53a (Soncino 247).

[83] Strack and Stemberger, *Introduction* 98.

[84] Neusner 14.42. Contrast *y. Yoma* 5:2, 42c (Neusner 14.139), where Abbahu is said to think of God, not an angel. Or is this the opinion of the high priest Simeon the Righteous, the narrative having been taken up again?

[85] Friedmann 190a, Braude 803-804.

[86] Friedmann 191a, Braude 806. Cf. *Lev. Rab.* Aḥare Mot 21/4 on Lev 16:3 in Soncino 4.267-268, which has the princes or guardian angels of the nations of the

All of the above explains the great fear of the high priest on the Day of Atonement, when he alone entered the Holy of Holies. If he performed the rites of the services inadequately, he too might be killed by the ministering angels, as had already happened to the sons of Aaron and others. This in turn also helps to explain why Jesus in Gethsemane was greatly distressed and troubled, with a great sorrow "even to death." He asked the heavenly Father to remove the cup (of death) from him. Yet at Golgotha the next afternoon he as the high priest, unblemished, made atonement for all by offering his own blood on the Cross. He then drank the cup of death given him by the Father.

B)   HIGH PRIESTLY PRAYER.

a) Having arrived in Gethsemane, Jesus told his disciples: "Sit here while I pray" (Mark 14:32). Then he alone went off a ways to pray, which occurred three times (vv 35-41). While he told Peter, James and John to watch / keep awake and pray so as not to enter into temptation (v 38), there is no record of their praying. Only Jesus does so. This is also true of the high priest.

b) Philo of Alexandria notes that in the diaspora the Day of Atonement "is entirely devoted to prayers and supplications, and men from morn to eve employ their leisure in nothing else but offering petitions of humble entreaty..." (*Spec. Leg.* 2.196). The appropriateness of this praying is emphasized in 2.203.

In Palestine it was above all the prayer of the high priest in the Sanctuary, directly after his offering incense and leaving the Holy of Holies (see above on *m. Yoma* 5:1), to which great importance was attached. Like Jesus' threefold prayer in Gethsemane, it was heard by no one else.[87] Yet nothing spoke against the high priests' relating the contents of their prayer to other priests and the Sages. The prayer appears to have had a number of standard petitions, all concerned with the welfare of Israel in the coming year: no exile, no decree of want, enough food and rain, no dominion over one another.

---

world, and Satan and Sammael. Section 6 (Soncino 269-270) names the different types of merit the high priest had with him when he entered the Holy of Holies.

[87] All attempts to rescue the historicity of Jesus' exact words by maintaining the three disciples were to be sure very sleepy, but close enough to hear the prayer, spoken out loud, are in vain. See for example R. Gundry, *Mark* 864 (6). Rather, the Palestinian Jewish Christian author of the Gethsemane account formulated the prayer himself. I intentionally leave out a discussion of the so-called "high-priestly prayer" in John 17. On the designation, cf. R. Brown, *The Gospel According to John* (AB 29A; Garden City, New York: Doubleday, 1970) 747.

The version now found in *y. Yoma* 5:2, 42c relates that this was "the prayer of the high priest on the Day of Atonement when he left the holy place whole and in one piece."[88] Four petitions begin: "May it be Your will (יהי רצון מלפניך), Lord, our God, and God of our fathers, that...." Since the Palestinian Jewish Christian author of the Gethsemane account thought of Jesus as the high priest who atoned for all the sins of the people the next day at Golgotha, this standard phrase from the prayer of the high priest may also have influenced his choice of the words: "But not what I will, but what You (will)" in Mark 14:36.

Finally, the end of the version of the high priest's prayer known to R. Judah (b. Ilai), a third generation Tanna,[89] was as follows in Aramaic: "May a ruler (שׁוּלְטָן) not cease from the house of Judah...."[90] This is a clear allusion to Mic 5:1 (Eng. 2): "But you, O Bethlehem Ephrathah, who are little to be among the clans of 'Judah,' from you shall come forth for Me one who is to be 'ruler' (מוֹשֵׁל) in Israel...." *Targum Jonathan* on this verse reads in part: "from you shall come forth before Me the Anointed One / Messiah, to exercise dominion (שׁולטן) over Israel...."[91] In other rabbinic sources the Messiah is also the "ruler" of Mic 5:1, and he is to be born in Bethlehem.[92]

If it was widely known that the high priest's special prayer on the Day of Atonement, after leaving the Holy of Holies, also included a petition in regard to the Messiah, this was one more reason for the Palestinian Jewish Christian author of the Gethsemane narrative to describe Jesus, for him the long-awaited Messiah, who had finally come, in terms of the activities of the high priest on the Day of Atonement.

*   *   *

Again, the above eight similarities in sections 1) A-F and 2) A-B in terminology and motifs between the Gethsemane narrative and the activities of the high priest on the Day of Atonement may be questioned

---

[88] Neusner 14.138. Cf. partial parallels in *b. Yoma* 53b (Soncino 251); *b. Ta'an.* 24b (Soncino 128); *Lev. Rab.* Aḥare Mot 20/4 on Lev 16:1 (Soncino 4.256); *Pesiq. Rav Kah.* 26/4 (Mandelbaum 391, Braude and Kapstein 400); *Pesiq. R.* 47/3 (Friedmann 190b, Braude 805); *Tanḥ.* Aḥare Mot 3 (Eshkol 571); *Tanḥ.* B Aḥare Mot 4 (Buber 2.59, Bietenhard 2.90-91); and *Midr. Haggadol,* Leviticus, ed. Steinsalz, 481.

[89] Cf. p. 136, n. 11.

[90] Cf. *b. Yoma* 53b (Soncino 251) and *b. Ta'an.* 24b (Soncino 128). See Jastrow 1534 on "ruler."

[91] Cf. also the English translation of Cathcart and Gordon in *The Targum of the Minor Prophets* 122; Aramaic in Sperber, *The Bible in Aramaic* 3.446.

[92] Cf. Str-B 1.83, and my *Weihnachtsgeschichte* 22-23.

individually. Some similarities are greater than others. Cumulatively, however, they make a strong argument for the Palestinian Jewish Christian author of Mark 14:32-42 as appropriating not only Judaic materials concerning Psalm 116 and the time of the imminent death of Israel's first redeemer, Moses. He also employed traditions from the most important annual event in Judaism, the Day of Atonement. For him, Jesus as the Christians' high priest atoned for the sins of all the people the next afternoon at Golgotha.

III
The Original Language.

In sections I and II above I have argued extensively for a Palestinian Jewish Christian as the author of the Gethsemane narrative. He cast the scene in terms of expressions and motifs he was personally acquainted with: Psalm 116, part of the Passover Hallel; Moses' struggle with the Angel of Death at the very end of his life; and the activities of the high priest on the eve and Day of Atonement. Again and again I have called attention to the Semitic background of particular expressions, such as ἀπέχει. Such a puzzling term makes good sense if it is seen as an insufficient Greek translation of a Semitic original, in this case from Moses' extensive prayer to remain alive just before his imminent death.

Almost all the sources I have cited are now found in Hebrew, with only a very few in Aramaic (the targums, for example). In addition, almost all the rabbinic traditions I quote are Palestinian, even if they are now found in the Babylonian Talmud. That is, it is very probable that the author of the Gethsemane account himself was a Palestinian. He may even have been a priest, well acquainted with Judaic traditions on Moses as a high priest up until his death, the Day of Atonement rites in the Temple, and the geography of the Jerusalem area, including the Kidron Brook,[93] the Mount of Olives and the place of the scapegoat's death. This does not necessarily mean, however, that he was from Jerusalem or the surrounding area. He could just as well have been a priest from Galilee, who served twice a year in the Jerusalem Temple when his "course" came round.

It is possible that the Gethsemane narrative was originally composed in Hebrew, like the present form of the sources on which it is for the most part dependent. If so, it was then certainly translated into Aramaic at a very early stage so that it would also be available to those members of

---

[93] Cf. its mention in the ritual of the Day of Atonement in *m. Yoma* 5:6 (Danby 168), as well as *Me'il.* 3:3 (Danby 577), and *Midd.* 3:2 (Danby 594). Its connection to the eve of Passover in the Temple Court is found in *b. Pesaḥ.* 65b (Soncino 330, n. 11).

the Aramaic-speaking Christian congregations who could not understand spoken Hebrew. Or the account was from the outset formulated in Aramaic. For my thesis that the original account was Semitic, no final decision must be made in this matter.

Only after the Gethsemane narrative circulated for some time in Aramaic was it then translated into Greek by a Hellenistic Jewish Christian (perhaps even in Jerusalem – see the Introduction to section II above). In this form it became available in writing to Mark, who incorporated it into his gospel.[94]

IV
The Extent of the Original Narrative.

Next to the "trial" before Caiaphas in Mark 14:53-65, the Gethsemane narrative in vv 32-42 is the longest account in the Markan Passion Narrative. It is a complete unit as it now stands. J. Gnilka has conveniently summarized the three major theories in regard to the history of its tradition. One group of scholars, such as E. Lohmeyer, regard it as an undivided, complete unit. Another group, including people like K. Kuhn, see two independent traditions woven together in the narrative. A third, begun by R. Bultmann, proceed from a basic core, which was then added to later on.[95]

Gnilka himself concedes that it is "extremely difficult" to decompose the pericope, as the most varying results show.[96] W. Schmithals notes that one also cannot get at the narrative via literary or form criticism.[97] I suggest that these difficulties are for the most part resolved if one does not propose two different sources, which were later combined. Rather, from the very outset the same narrator intentionally interwove imagery and expressions from two different complexes: Judaic interpretation of Psalm 116, including the struggle of Israel's first redeemer, Moses, at the very end of his life with the Angel of Death; and the high priest during

---

[94] It is not my task here to ascertain whether or not it was already in a larger complex by the time it reached Mark. However, I consider this quite probable because it makes sense only between the "Lord's Supper" and the scene of the arrest. I also avoid addressing the question of whether or not the *original* narrative was already written down. Feldmeier (*Die Krisis* 125), for example, argues strongly for its non-literary origin in oral tradition. For my purposes this is immaterial. It probably achieved written form at the latest, however, when it was translated into Greek.

[95] Cf. Gnilka's *Das Evangelium nach Markus* (*Mk 8, 27 – 16, 20*) 256.

[96] *Ibid.* Cf. Feldmeier, *Die Krisis* 111-112: the narrative cannot be divided into various sources.

[97] See his *Das Evangelium nach Markus, Kapitel 9, 2 – 16,* p. 634.

the eve and Day of Atonement, when he entered the Holy of Holies and sent off the scapegoat to its death. Even the structure of the entire narrative, Jesus' going off with his main disciple (and successor) Peter and two brothers, James and John, and then by himself, derives from a similar action on the part of Moses, his successor Joshua, and the two brothers Eleazar and Ithamar just before his death. Jesus' threefold prayer in Gethsemane was also based on Moses' praying three times that his imminent death be removed from him and he be allowed to enter the promised Land. The result for both the first redeemer of Israel and for the final redeemer, Jesus the Messiah, was negative.

As I have pointed out extensively in my analysis of the Judaic Moses and high priest materials above, there is hardly a single expression or motif in Gethsemane which does not derive from them. Even the most difficult term, ἀπέχει in Mark 14:41, stems from the scene of Moses' imminent death. It thus seems very improbable that the earliest evangelist, Mark, changed the pericope in a major way from the form in which he received it.[98] Because of 9:6 (Peter "did not know what to say"), some scholars have considered 14:40c to be from the hand of Mark.[99] Yet it was the evening of Passover, when after the meal of the Passover lamb and cups of wine there was a strong tendency to "drowse off." Commenting on the latter expression in *m. Pesah.* 10:8, the gemara in *b. Pesah.* 120b has R. Ashi, perhaps a sixth generation Babylonian Amora,[100] say this state is "a sleep which is not sleep, a wakefulness which is not wakefulness. E.g., if he answers when called, cannot make a reasoned statement...."[101] Although R. Ashi's statement is very late, it most probably accurately describes the state of the disciples at the late hour in Gethsemane: "and they did not know what to answer him (Jesus)." Thus great caution is appropriate here in ascribing this clause to Mark on the basis of 9:6. It was more probably already in the original narrative.

John 14:31 ("Rise, let us go hence") logically ends one section of Jesus' farewell discourse (then continued to 17:26), held after the Lord's Supper, before he and the eleven disciples proceeded across the Kidron Valley to the garden (of Gethsemane: 18:1). This phrase shows that Mark 14:42a ("Rise, let us be going") is a piece of early material appropriated by the author of the Gethsemane narrative from the tradition available to him. Before he very masterfully created the account of Jesus' final

---

[98] Feldmeier (*Die Krisis* 111-112) and Holleran (*The Synoptic Gethsemane* 206) agree that it was not decisively formed or redacted by Mark.

[99] Cf. for example W. Grundmann, *Das Evangelium nach Markus* 399.

[100] Strack and Stemberger, *Introduction* 107, who state that he died in 427 C.E.

[101] Soncino 620.

struggle with death in Gethsemane, the Passion Narrative only had Jesus and the eleven disciples go from the Lord's Supper to the Mount of Olives, where Jesus was then arrested. The Evangelist John may have known of the Markan Gethsemane scene, or of an earlier, oral form of it.[102] Yet he correctly omitted it, not only in order to insert his extensive "high-priestly prayer," but also more probably because he knew the account did not belong to the earliest Passion Narrative.[103]

It is thus improbable that the Evangelist Mark himself composed 14:42.[104] While in part repetitious of the end of v 41, it rather stems from the original narrator, who intended his account from the very outset to connect the departure from the Lord's Supper and the scene of Jesus' arrest, both known to him from tradition. He filled up the gap of time he sensed existed in "Gethsemane" before Jesus' arrest.

In contrast to most scholars, I thus see no major signs of Markan redaction in 14:32-42. The earliest evangelist basically included it just as he received it from the Christian community in which he lived.

V
The Historicity and Purpose of the Original Narrative.

There is no reason to doubt that after the "Lord's Supper," Jesus proceeded to a site beyond the Kidron Brook on the western side of the Mount of Olives. There he was later arrested, at which point all the eleven disciples fled for their lives. It is even possible that Jesus prayed with (some of) them there. This was in contrast to the great majority of his fellow Jews' celebrating the joyous Passover feast of redemption, who after the main (Seder) meal joined in some kind of revelry.[105] That, however, is the most one can presume to be historical.[106]

---

[102] Cf. Jesus' words in 18:11, "shall I not drink the cup which the Father has given me?" and Mark 14:36.

[103] Cf. on this also D. Lührmann, *Das Markusevangelium* (HNT 3; Tübingen: Mohr, 1987) 241.

[104] Against, for example, Holleran, *The Synoptic Gethsemane* 108. I also doubt whether Mark was responsible for adding ὁ πατήρ to αββα in 14:36. Even Paul probably found this Aramaic-Greek expression already in the tradition (Rom 8:15 and Gal 4:6).

[105] Cf. *m. Pesaḥ.* 10:8 (Albeck 2.179; Danby 151, with n. 9). Constrast *t. Pesaḥ.* 10:11 (Zuckermandel / Liebermann 173, Neusner 2.166): "A man is obligated to busy himself in the study of the laws of the Passover all night...even between himself and his disciple." An example is then given in 10:12 of doing so "until the cock crowed." While the destruction of the Temple in 70 C.E. may have encouraged this practice, it most probably already prevailed in Jesus' time in regard to a teacher and his disciples. The reading "dessert" for "revelry" came about at an early time when the original meaning of the Greek expression ἐπὶ κῶμον was

Elsewhere in regard to the death of John the Baptist in Mark 6:17-29 and the release of Barabbas in 15:6-15, I have called attention to the strong trend in Judaic haggadic writings to "fill in gaps."[107] Here too the Palestinian Jewish Christian who composed the original, oral narrative of Gethsemane typically filled in the almost empty scene between the Lord's Supper and Jesus' arrest known to him from the earliest Christian tradition. He did so in order to explain what happened there during the time before Jesus' arrest and, more importantly, in order to express definite religious truths (described below).[108]

To do so, he borrowed a structural pattern[109] from the struggle of Israel's first redeemer, Moses, with the Angel of Death at the very end of his life, as well as many expressions and motifs from Judaic lore on this complex, including the well-known Hallel Psalm 116. His second major source was Judaic haggadic material on the high priest during the evening and Day of Atonement. These he blended to make an impressive narrative which even today is deeply moving for believing Christians, as the many paintings of Jesus praying in Gethsemane show, done throughout the centuries.

---

forgotten. See LSJ 1018 on κῶμος as "revel, carousal, merry-making" and the phrase, as well as Jastrow 104 on אפיקומן. See also "Kinds of music [characteristically played at after-dinner revelries]" in *y. Pesaḥ.* 10:7-8A, 37d (Neusner / Bokser 13.503).

[106] Gundry in *Mark* 863-864 lists six reasons why he considers the pericope historical. V. Taylor in *The Gospel According to St Mark* 551 states that "in the narrative we stand near the bedrock of primitive tradition"; he thinks it goes back to Peter. Regarding Mark 14:33, C. Mann in *Mark* 589 notes that "the very force of the words guarantees that we are here dealing with the primitive tradition." Both Feldmeier (*Die Krisis* 137) and Holleran (*The Synoptic Gethsemane* 221) believe that Jesus' prayer and the sleep of the disciples are historical, Holleran adding the distress of Jesus. Bultmann (*The History* 267), in contrast, states that the Gethsemane narrative "is originally an individual story of a thorough-going legendary character...."

[107] Cf. my *Water into Wine and the Beheading of John the Baptist* 39-74, and *Barabbas and Esther* 1-27, respectively. See also J. Goldin's statement in *The Song at the Sea* 27 that "imaginative dramatization" is one of the "familiar devices of haggadic Midrash...."

[108] Cf. the statement by M. Herr in the art. "Aggadah" in *EJ* (1971) 2.355: "the *aggadah* does contain truth which is greater than that of historical and philological reality, and more important than that of the natural sciences."

[109] While R. Pesch, *Das Markusevangelium*, II. Teil, 388 maintains there is no genre pattern for the whole narrative, I agree with Feldmeier (*Die Krisis* 126, 130) in labeling its form a "narrative report" ("berichtende Erzählung"). This simple designation is the best that can be offered.

The original narrator knew that all the disciples fled at Jesus' arrest (Mark 14:50, 27), and *perhaps* that Peter later denied Jesus (14:72, 30 – see the discussion in II.1.3 above). He then amplified this motif by emphasizing the failure of even the core group, Peter, James and John, to watch with Jesus shortly before his arrest. Jesus' successor Peter could not even do so for one hour, in spite of his earlier bragging. Here the original Palestinian Jewish Christian hearers of the narrative automatically contrasted the negative behavior of Jesus' disciples with that of the disciples who did their very best to keep the high priest awake the entire night before he made the offering of incense in the Holy of Holies, prayed, and conducted other parts of the ritual of the Day of Atonement such as sending off the scapegoat to its certain death, bearing the sins of all the people.

By emphasizing the failure of Jesus' disciples at this point, the narrator simultaneously offered comfort and encouragement to those Christians who occasionally failed in their own loyalty to the Messiah Jesus. If the disciples themselves, including Peter, utterly failed their master in his darkest hour, yet were later forgiven by Jesus through his appearing to them,[110] they too could hope for forgiveness for their own shortcomings.

Instead of portraying Jesus as the suffering Servant of the Lord, who like a lamb about to be slaughtered did not open its mouth (Isa 53:7), the narrator of the Gethsemane account presents him like Moses, as actively struggling with his impending death. He asks in prayer three times that the hour pass from him, that the cup (of death) be removed from him. Yet Jesus finally submits to the will of the heavenly Father.[111] Through this very "human" portrayal of Jesus' struggle with his impending death, the narrator brought him back from any early Christian tendencies to make Jesus more than human before God resurrected him from the dead. He also made Jesus more attractive to those Christians who suffered from various causes, physical or mental / spiritual,[112] including impending death. Like Jesus, they could ask God in prayer to remove their source of affliction. Yet like him too, they could ask that the will of the heavenly Father be done even if He appeared to be "silent" at the moment, as at the Crucifixion the next afternoon. Jesus in Gethsemane is

---

[110] Cf. Mark 14:27-31; 15:66-72; 16:7; John 21; as well as 1 Cor 15:5-9, where Jesus appears not only to Cephas and the twelve, but also to Paul, who had earlier persecuted him.

[111] Cf. again Heb 5:7-8.

[112] Here persecution of the early Jewish Christian communities is not meant primarily, although it certainly happened on occasion (cf. Rom 15:31; Gal 1:13, 22; Acts 8:1-3; 9:21; 22:4; and Mark 13:9-13).

represented not as the object of Christian faith, but as a positive role model for praying in distress.

In addition, Mark 14:38 exhorts the Jewish Christians of the Palestinian narrator's community to watch and pray that they not enter into temptation. They are encouraged to avoid from the very outset situations in which they could be tempted to compromise their loyalty to Jesus. This is the paranetic highpoint of the narrative.

Finally, as noted above, the first Palestinian Jewish Christians who heard this description of Jesus and the disciples in Gethsemane were strongly reminded of the scene of the impending death of Moses, Israel's first redeemer. They would have appreciated the narrator's great skill in depicting Jesus, their Messiah, the last or great redeemer of Israel, in similar terms. Like Moses, Jesus struggled with (the Angel of) Death, yet as God's obedient Son, he finally subjected himself to the Father's will. The first hearers were also reminded here of Jesus as the high priest, whom disciples kept awake so that he could properly function on the Day of Atonement. These disciples greatly contrasted to Jesus' followers, who repeatedly fell asleep. In addition, the high priest, like Jesus, was much afraid of death when he made his incense offering in the Holy of Holies. Through his vicarious death on the Cross the next afternoon, Jesus effected atonement for the sins of all the people. He was considered to be the scapegoat, sent to his death for the benefit of all. If the Hellenistic Jewish emphasis still found in Philo was also known in Jerusalem and thus in Palestinian Jewish Christianity, Jesus as the high priest may also have been thought of as offering "himself" at Golgotha.[113]

Unfortunately, because Palestinian Jewish Christianity became either almost insignificant or heretical at a very early date, and because very few NT scholars deal extensively with Judaic materials in Hebrew and Aramaic, the origin of the Gethsemane narrator's expressions and imagery – Judaic lore on Psalm 116, Moses' impending death, and the activities of the high priest on the eve and Day of Atonement – were forgotten at a very early time, like the exact site of the scapegoat's death. Yet they contribute in a very significant way to the richness of the narrator's masterful presentation of Jesus' struggle with his impending death. Even today Christians should be grateful for the important religious truths expressed in the gifted narrator's portrait, and for the

---

[113] The standard volumes on NT christologies have only a meagre section on Jesus as the high priest. They should now be supplemented by Jesus as high priest in Gethsemane, and the other passages in the Passion Narrative I have analyzed above in 1.1)-9).

vivid, moving colors from Palestinian Judaic haggadah with which he painted it.

Appendix One

Paul's Calling and Re-Commissioning in 2 Cor 12:1-10 and Moses' Calling and Death Scene

A. 2 Cor 12:1-10.

In Second Corinthians Paul defends his apostleship over against the "superlative apostles" (11:5; 12:11) of Jewish background (11:22), who preach another Jesus and have a different spirit and gospel from that which the Corinthians accepted from him (11:4). Paul's opponents commend themselves (10:12), boasting of their mission (11:12) and of worldly things (v 18); they put on airs (v 20).

Pushed into a corner by such "false apostles, deceitful workmen" (11:13), Paul defends his ministry first by boasting of his own Jewish ancestry (v 22), then of the great physical and mental hardships he has endured, including an experience in Damascus (vv 23-29 and 30-33). These incidences show Paul's weakness (vv 29-30; cf. the irony in v 21).

In 12:1-10 the Apostle to the Gentiles feels himself forced to continue boasting. He speaks of "visions and revelations of the Lord (Jesus)" (ὀπτασίας καὶ ἀποκαλύψεις κυρίου – v 1), which he experienced fourteen years ago when he was caught up to the third heaven, which is Paradise (τὸν παράδεισον – vv 3-4). There Paul heard "things which cannot be told (ἄρρητα ῥήματα), which man may not utter" (οὐκ ἐξὸν ἀνθρώπῳ λαλῆσαι – v 4). To keep him from being too elated by the abundance of "revelations" (τῶν ἀποκαλύψεων), Paul states that "a thorn was given me in the flesh" (ἐδόθη μοι σκόλοψ τῇ σαρκί), an angel / messenger of Satan. This "harasses" him (v 7). Therefore the apostle besought (παρεκάλεσα) the Lord three times (τρίς) that it keep away from him (v 8).

Yet He told Paul: "My grace is sufficient for you (ἀρκεῖ σοι ἡ χάρις μου), for My power (ἡ γὰρ δύναμις) is made perfect in weakness (ἐν ἀσθενείᾳ)." Therefore Paul all the more gladly boasts of his "weaknesses" (ἀσθενείαις) so that "the power" (ἡ δύναμις) of Christ may "dwell" (ἐπισκηνώσῃ) upon him (v 9). In the final verse of the thought unit, the apostle again speaks of "weaknesses" (ἀσθενείαις), and enumerates his sufferings: insults, hardships, persecutions and calamities. Then he concludes by stating that when he is "weak" (ἀσθενῶ), then he is "strong" (δυνατός – v 10).[1]

Much of the vocabulary in this unit occurs in Paul only here. This is true of ὀπτασία, παράδεισος, ἄρρητος, σκόλοψ, ἀρκέω and ἐπισκηνόω. In addition, "revelations," "weaknesses / being weak," and "power" are emphasized. I suggest that Paul derived this imagery, including the Lord (Jesus') "grace" (χάρις) as being sufficient for him (v 9), primarily from Judaic interpretation of the call of Moses in the thornbush (Exod 3:1 – 4:17). This incident was also connected in Judaic tradition to Moses' death scene. After the great lawgiver requests three times to be allowed to continue to live and to enter the Land of Israel, God tells him that what he has already received is sufficient. The following analysis supports this proposal.

B. Moses' Call in the Thornbush, and His Death Scene.

The appearance of the Lord to Moses in a thornbush (סְנֶה,[2] LXX βάτος), which burned but was not consumed (Exod 3:1 – 4:17), is one of the most colorful incidents in the Hebrew Bible. Jesus himself quoted 3:6 to prove the resurrection of the dead in Mark 12:26 par. ("in the book of Moses, in the passage about the bush"). The popular narrative of Moses' calling soon became the object of haggadic interpretation, as numerous

---

[1] On secondary literature on this pericope, cf. the commentaries of C. Wolff, *Der zweite Brief des Paulus an die Korinther* 239 and the notes on pp. 239-250; R. Martin, *2 Corinthians* (Word Biblical Commentary 40; Waco, Texas: Word Books, 1986) 387-388; and V. Furnish, *II Corinthians* (AB 32A; Garden City, New York: Doubleday, 1984) passim (523-532, 542-552).

[2] BDB 702: "a thorny bush, perh. blackberry bush." It only occurs in Exod 3:2-4 and Deut 33:16. In rabbinic Hebrew, the term means not only thornbush, but also "prick, thorn" (Jastrow 1005 – important for Paul's "thorn" in the flesh, as will be shown below). Another designation of Mount Horeb in Exod 3:1 is Mount "Sinai," סִינַי (BDB 693), which led to numerous word plays in Judaic sources.

Judaic sources attest.[3] I will concentrate in the following on Ezekiel the Tragedian, Philo of Alexandria, Josephus and the rabbis.

1. Ezekiel the Tragedian.

Writing in Greek, perhaps at the beginning of the second century B.C.E. in Alexandria, this Jewish dramatist described the exodus from Egypt in his "Exagōgē" or "Leading Out."[4]

Of greatest relevance to Paul's "vision" in 2 Cor 12:1-10 is the section regarding the dream Moses had at the time of his calling from the thornbush of Exod 3:1 – 4:17. Moses states: "On Sinai's peak[5] I saw what seemed a throne so great in size it touched the clouds of heaven." On it sat God, who beckoned Moses to mount the throne and gave him His scepter and crown. There Moses saw things under the earth and high above heaven. At the end of the dream / vision, Moses' father-in-law interprets it of his ruling over and governing men.

Ezekiel continues by describing Moses' encounter with God in the thornbush. The burning bush is a "sign" (σημεῖον), a "great wonder" (τεράστιον μέγιστον). From it God's word shines forth to him, and God tells him: "Take courage, son (ὦ παῖ), and listen to My words; as mortal man you cannot see My face, although it is allowed for you (δ' ἔξεστί σοι) to hear My words...." Moses objects that he is "not by nature eloquent" (Οὐκ εὔλογος πέφυκα), he being "difficult of tongue" (δύσφραστος), with a speech impediment (ἰσχνόφωνος), [6] unable to speak before the king (Pharaoh). God then assures Moses that He will give the (proper) words to him, and he will give them to Aaron, who will speak to the king. When Moses casts the rod down and sees a fearful serpent, he exclaims: "Be gracious, Lord" (δέσποθ', ἵλεως γενοῦ).[7]

Here Moses "sees" God in heaven, including what is below the earth (probably Gehenna, Hades) and above heaven (probably Paradise). Yet this is corrected by the dramatist's having God tell His "son" he may not see His face (cf. Exod 33:20). However, he has permission to hear His words. Moses objects to his being sent / commissioned to Egypt because

---

[3] Cf. Ginzberg, *Legends* 2.302-326, and the relevant notes in 5.414-422, as well as E. Levine, *The Burning Bush*. Jewish Symbolism and Mysticism (New York: Sepher-Hermon, 1981).

[4] Cf. R. Robertson in *OTP* 2.803-804. See also the special study by P. van der Horst, "Moses' Throne Vision in Ezekiel the Dramatist" in *JJS* 34 (1983) 21-29.

[5] Cf. Exod 3:1, "Horeb, the mountain of God," elsewhere called Sinai.

[6] Cf. LXX Exod 3:10 on this last expression, which Robertson translates as "I stammer" (*OTP* 2.813).

[7] *OTP* 2.811-813, where I slightly modify Robertson's translation. The Greek is found in *Eusebius Werke*, 8: Die Praeparatio Evangelica, I, as 9:29 on pp. 529-531.

of his speech problems – from nature, i.e. probably from birth on. I shall propose below that within the vision Paul describes in 2 Cor 12:1-10, his "thorn in the flesh" is his lack of eloquence, perhaps a speech impediment. This dream or vision of Moses at his calling from the thornbush in Ezekiel the Tragedian is the earliest such account. It shows, however, that the later rabbinic narratives noted below stand in a very old line of tradition.

2.   Philo.

The Alexandrian philosopher, born ca. 20 B.C.E. and probably active during much of Paul's ministry,[8] retells the narrative of Exod 3:1 – 4:17 in *Mos.* 1.63-84 (12-14) and refers to it numerous times elsewhere. For him, the burning bush was "thorny" (ἀκανθῶδες) and of the "weakest" (ἀσθενέστατον) kind – 65. He repeats the latter in 68, adding that it is not "without thorns" (ἄκεντρον), easily wounding one. In regard to the afflictions of the Israelites in Egypt (Exod 3:7, 9, 17), Philo says that the voice from the thornbush tells the sufferers: "Do not lose heart; 'your (pl.) weakness is (your) strength'" (τὸ ἀσθενὲς ὑμῶν δύναμίς ἐστιν). It can "prick" (κεντεῖ), and the Egyptians will greatly suffer from it – 69.[9] They should not exult in their own "strength" (ἀλκαῖς) or their apparently "invincible might" (ἀμάχους ῥώμας – 70). Elsewhere, Philo also emphasizes God's power in this context.[10] His concern for the afflicted Israelites shows that He is "kind" (ἤπιος) and "gracious" (ἵλεως – 72), and of great "grace" (χάρις).[11]

Philo's interpretation of the Lord's revelation to Moses in the thornbush shows that Alexandrian Judaism emphasized the motifs of sufferings,[12] weakness, strength / power, and grace in this narrative. Paul lists his sufferings in 2 Cor 12:10 (insults, hardships, persecutions and calamities). He employs weakness(es) five times in vv 5 and 9-10; power in vv 9 (twice) and 10; and grace in v 9. "For when I am weak,

---

[8] Cf. LCL 1.ix-x.

[9] Cf. also 76 on the Israelites' weakness. U. Heckel in *Kraft in Schwachheit.* Untersuchungen zu 2 Kor. 10-13 (WUNT 2.56; Tübingen: Mohr, 1993) 116, n. 305, denies the relevance of *Mos.* 1.69 here, as he does that of Judaic (rabbinic) tradition on Deut 3:26 (p. 89) in regard to 2 Cor 12:9. Because Paul Billerbeck cites no Judaic passages here, however, does not mean that there are none which are pertinent! J. Wettstein had already called attention to *Mos.* 1.69 in 1752. See his *Novum Testamentum Graecum* 2.212.

[10] Cf. *Leg. All.* 3.214 and *Fug.* 141.

[11] *Leg. All.* 3.215; *Fug.* 141, 162; and *Her.* 25.

[12] In addition to the passages cited above, cf. especially *Mos.* 1.67, 69 and 72.

then I am strong" in v 10 is very similar to the above statement by Philo: "Your weakness is your strength."

In addition, Philo states in regard to Moses' assertion that the Israelites will want to know God's name: "I am the Existent One" (Exod 3:14) is "equivalent to 'My nature is to be, not to be spoken'" (οὐ λέγεσθαι – *Mut.* 11). Precisely in this context the Alexandrian states that God did not reveal to Moses His proper name, only a substitute. The Existent One is "impossible to name" (ἄρρητον – 14), or "unnamable" (15 – twice). It is this very term (lacking in the LXX, and only occurring once in Josephus and thirteen times in Philo) which Paul employs in 2 Cor 12:4. He heard in the third heaven, Paradise, words which may not be uttered (ἄρρητα), which it is not permitted for man to speak. I suggest that Paul borrowed this Greek term from the Hellenistic Jewish interpretation of God's not revealing His real name (the LORD) to Moses in the thornbush, as shown in Philo.[13]

In the above narrative, it is also stated that Moses should not ask to know God's name. "'It is enough for you,' He says, 'to profit through My benediction...'" (ἀπόχρη γάρ σοι, φησίν, ὠφελεῖσθαι κατὰ τὰς ἐμὰς εὐφημίας...: *Mut.* 14).[14] This phraseology, coupled with God's not allowing Moses something, strongly recalls 2 Cor 12:9, where the Lord refuses Paul's request by stating: "My grace is sufficient for you" (ἀρκεῖ σοι ἡ χάρις μου).

Finally, in *Det.* 160 Philo speaks of the "tent" (σκηνή) of the Existent One in regard to Exod 3:14. In 2 Cor 12:9, Paul, after the above sentence, states that he will all the more gladly boast of his weaknesses so that the power of Christ may "tent (ἐπισκηνώσῃ) upon him. I suggest that this image of the Lord's "tenting" / dwelling with Paul is derived from the context of the Lord's revealing Himself to Moses in the thornbush. Rabbinic sources in section 4. below especially emphasize this.

---

[13] In his art. "'Merkabah' Visions and the Visions of Paul" in *JSS* 16 (1971) 168, n. 1, J. Bowker maintains that Paul in 2 Cor 12:4 possibly alludes to hearing the divine name pronounced, yet he does not refer to these Philo passages. In *Things Unutterable. Paul's Ascent to Paradise in its Greco-Roman, Judaic, and Early Christian Contexts* (Studies in Judaism; Lanham, Maryland: University Press of America, 1986) 122, J. Tabor notes *Det.* 175 in Philo, where "unutterable words" are parallel to secrets. Without analyzing the other occurrences of ἄρρητος in Philo, he wrongly states regarding 2 Cor 12:4: "It is a word drawn from the vocabulary of the mystery cults and reflects the common belief of secrecy found in most Hellenistic religions."

[14] Cf. LSJ 227 on ἀποχράω: suffice, be sufficient, be enough.

3. *Josephus.*

This Aramaic-speaking native of Jerusalem, born in 37-38 C.E.,[15] retold with many haggadic additions the narrative of God's revelation of Himself to Moses in the thornbush in *Ant.* 2.264-276 (12.1-4).[16] Like Ezekiel the Tragedian, Josephus changed "Horeb, the mountain of God," in Exod 3:1 to "the mount called Sinai" (264). He must have understood סנה in the Hebrew text primarily as "thorn," for he felt compelled to add "bush" (θαμνός) to the term βάτος found at this point in the LXX (266).

In 2.267 Josephus relates that the voice from the fire told Moses to depart as far as possible from the flame (cf. Exod 3:5) and , as a virtuous person who derived from great men, "'to be content' with the things he had seen..., and to inquire no further" (ἀρκεῖσθαι μὲν οἷς ἑώρακεν... πολυπραγμονεῖν δὲ μηδέν). It is precisely this Greek term, ἀρκέω,[17] which is found in 2 Cor 12:9 – "My grace 'is sufficient' (ἀρκεῖ) for you."

The Jewish historian also betrays (Palestinian) Judaic emphasis on sufferings, weakness and strength / power here. The Israelites endured outrage in Egypt (268), they suffered evil in servitude (274). Moses acknowledged the Lord's "power" (δύναμις – 270), yet also that he himself does not abound in "strength" (ἰσχύς – 271). Then God encouraged him by promising to provide him with "strength" (272). Moses thereupon prayed for this "power" in Egypt (275). These motifs of suffering, weakness and power are also emphasized in 2 Cor 12:1-10, as pointed out in section A and Philo above.

A special aspect of Moses' lack of strength for Josephus is that the shepherd maintains he is an "unskilled man" (ἰδιώτης ἀνήρ), not knowing how he should find "words" to persuade the Israelites to leave Egypt, or Pharaoh to allow them to do so (271). Josephus alludes here to Moses' not being a "man of words," but rather "heavy of mouth and heavy of tongue" in Exod 4:10.

It is precisely this term, ἰδιώτης,[18] which Paul employs of himself in 2 Cor 11:6 – "Even if I am 'unskilled in speaking' (ἰδιώτης τῷ λόγῳ), I am not in knowledge...." The apostle's lack of impressive oratorical ability was used against him by the superlative apostles in Corinth. They maintained there: "His letters are weighty and strong, but his bodily

---

[15] LCL 1.vii.

[16] These certainly did not derive from Josephus, but from Palestinian Judaic tradition available to him. Cf. for example Sinai as the best mountain for pasturage (265), and the thornbush with "fruit-laden branches," not consumed although the flame was "great and exceedingly fierce" (266).

[17] BAGD 107, LSJ 242.

[18] LSJ 819, III: "opp. to a professed orator," 2. "unpracticed, unskilled in a thing."

presence is weak, and 'his speech of no account' (ὁ λόγος ἐξουθενημένος – 10:10).[19] As I will argue below, this lack of eloquence, (perhaps with a physical cause), like Moses', was probably Paul's "thorn in the flesh."

Finally, Josephus notes that at the scene of the thornbush God "revealed" (σημαίνει) to Moses His name, up to then not having been given to men, "concerning which I am not permitted (θεμιτός) to speak" (276). This recalls 2 Cor 12:4, where Paul in Paradise heard unutterable words, "which it is not permitted (ἐξόν) for man to speak." Below I will also suggest that one of the unutterable words Paul heard in his heavenly vision, part of his call to be an apostle, was "LORD," just as Moses also heard the divine name for the first time at his call from the thornbush.

4. Rabbinic Traditions.

Palestinian traditions now found in rabbinic writings corroborate the close connections between the Lord's calling Moses from the thornbush, including the revelation of His name, and 2 Cor 12:1-10, as already ascertained in Philo and Josephus, and in part in Ezekiel the Tragedian. In addition, they provide other important points of comparison.

1) VISIONS AND REVELATIONS.

Just after mentioning as a concrete example of his "weakness" how he barely escaped from the governor of Damascus (2 Cor 11:32-33), Paul states that he must boast, now proceeding to "visions" (ὀπτασίας) and "revelations" (ἀποκαλύψεις) of the Lord (12:1). He has had an "abundance" of the latter (v 7).[20]

It is significant that of the other three occurrences of ὀπτασία in the NT, one is found in Acts 26:19.[21] There Paul is described by Luke as relating to King Herod Agrippa II in Caesarea the "heavenly vision" he had of the Lord (Jesus) on the road to Damascus. In v 13 it is stated that the light of this vision came "from heaven." In LXX Dan 10:1 and Theod

---

[19] Cf. 10:1, "I who am humble when face to face with you," which certainly also includes Paul's limited rhetorical abilities. He partly defends his plain speaking style by maintaining that the Corinthians at least can read and understand what he writes them (1:13). In addition, the apostle openly acknowledges that another brother is famous among all the churches for his preaching of the gospel (8:18). In *Ap.* 223 Josephus notes that Plato is admired by the Greeks "as one who in oratorical power and persuasive eloquence 'outmatched' all other philosophers." The verb ὑπεραίρω here is employed twice by Paul in the passive in 2 Cor 12:7.

[20] Cf. for example Gal 2:2, where Paul went up to Jerusalem "by revelation," and Acts 22:17-21.

[21] The others are Luke 1:22 and 24:23.

9:23, ὀπτασία translates מַרְאֶה, the same Hebrew term employed in Exod 3:3 of Moses' seeing "this great 'sight,'" the burning thornbush.[22]

This is the third account in Acts of Jesus' calling Paul on the road shortly before Damascus in a vision to be his apostle. The accounts also share four other major motifs derived from the Lord's appearance to Moses in the thornbush, His call to Moses to be His messenger.[23]

I suggest that Paul describes in 2 Cor 12:2-4 one particular example of the "visions" and revelations of the Lord he mentions in v 1. It took place when he was caught up to "heaven" (v 2) at his calling before Damascus. Because of the catchword "Damascus" mentioned twice in 11:32, Paul decided to relate his "Damascus experience," a heavenly vision, at this point.[24] It was something of which the "superlative apostles" could not boast, not having been called in such a way.

Paul could also describe his calling as a "revelation." In Gal 1:12 he states that he did not receive the gospel from man, nor was he taught it, "but it came through a 'revelation' (ἀποκάλυψις) of Jesus Christ." God had set him apart before he was born and had called him through His grace, pleased to "reveal" (ἀποκαλύπτω) His Son to him so that Paul could preach him among the Gentiles (1:16). After going off to Arabia, the

---

[22] The very similar Hebrew term מַרְאָה lies behind four of the other five occurrences. In his Hebrew New Testament, Delitzsch has מַרְאוֹת for the "visions" of 2 Cor 12:1 (p. 343).

[23] Cf. the following:
a)   A light from heaven, brighter than the sun, shining round Saul and those with him in Acts 9:3; 22:6, 9, 11; and 26:16. See Philo, *Mos.* 1.66 for the divine image in the thornbush as "refulgent with a light brighter than the light of fire," and its gaining "additional brightness" in 68.
b)   Jesus' calling Saul with the words "Saul, Saul" in Acts 9:4; 22:7; and 26:14. See Exod 3:4 for "Moses, Moses." In *Exod. Rab.* Shemoth 2/6 on this verse R. Simeon b. Yoḥai, a third generation Tanna (Strack and Stemberger, *Introduction* 84), says this is "an expression of love and exhortation" (Soncino 3.56; Mirqin 5.64).
c)   In Acts 22:9, those with Saul saw the light but did not hear the voice of the Lord, Jesus, speaking with him; in 9:7 it is related that they heard the voice but saw no one. See especially in regard to the latter, *Exod. Rab.* Shemoth 2/5 on Exod 3:2 (Mirqin 5.61; Soncino 3.53), where the angel of the Lord appears "to him." The commentator asks: "Why 'to him'? To teach you that others were with him, yet Moses alone saw; as it is written of Daniel: 'And I Daniel alone saw the vision' (Dan 10:7; מראה, LXX ὀπτασία).
d)   In Acts 26:14 the Lord (Jesus) tells Saul: "It hurts you to kick against the 'goads' (from κέντρον, which also means "prick"). This imagery ultimately derived from a different translation of סנה (or קוץ) into Greek than σκόλοψ, found in 2 Cor 12:7. See 2) below.

[24] I shall comment below in section C. on the chronology of "fourteen years ago" in v 2, relating this to the re-commissioning event of Acts 13:2-3.

apostle "again returned to Damascus" (v 17). This strongly suggests that he had received his original calling / revelation (near) there, as described in the Acts passages cited above.

Paul's choice of the term "revelations" in 2 Cor 12:1 may have been influenced by Palestinian Judaic tradition on the calling of Moses in the thornbush. R. Eliezer (b. Hyrcanus), an older second generation Tanna,[25] asks for example in *Mek. R. Šim. b. Yoḥ.* on Exod 3:1-2, "Why did the Holy One, blessed be He, 'reveal Himself' (נגלה) from heaven on high and speak with (Moses) from the thornbush?"[26] All three targums (Onqelos, Pseudo-Jonathan and Neofiti 1) also speak of the glory of the Lord being "revealed" (איתגלי) at Mount Horeb in Exod 3:1, and of an angel of the Lord as being "revealed" (איתגלי) to Moses in a flame of fire from the thornbush in v 2.[27]

2) THORNBUSH AND THORN.

R. Eliezer answers the question he posed above by saying: "Only because the thornbush is the lowliest (שָׁפָל מ')[28] of all the trees in the world."[29] *Exod. Rab.* Shemoth 2/5 on Exod 3:2 first quotes regarding the situation of the Israelites in Egypt Isa 63:9, "in all their affliction He was afflicted." Then God says to Moses: "Do you not realize that I live in trouble, just as Israel live in trouble? Know from the place from which I speak to you – from the midst of thorns (קוֹצִים) – that I am, as it were, a partner in their trouble."[30]

I suggest that Paul's emphasis on his weaknesses in 2 Cor 12:5, 9 and 10 derives from his comparing his own situation, including "insults, hardships, persecutions and calamities" (v 10), with the situation of the greatly afflicted Israelites in Egypt, described in the narrative of Moses' calling (Exod 3:7, 9 and 17). Not only Philo and Josephus, but also early rabbinic tradition compare this situation of affliction / weakness / lowliness with סנה, the thornbush of Exodus 3. As noted at the outset, this term in rabbinic Hebrew also means simply "thorn."

---

[25] Strack and Stemberger, *Introduction* 77.

[26] Epstein and Melamed 1.

[27] Cf. Drazin 53-54; Rieder 1.84 and Maher 167; and Díez Macho 2.13 and 411, respectively.

[28] Jastrow 1617; the term also means humble.

[29] Cf. n. 26. In *Exod. Rab.* Shemoth 2/5 (Mirqin 5.62; Soncino 3.53) he compares the Israelites in Egypt, who are also lowly and humble, to the thornbush.

[30] Mirqin 5.61; Soncino 3.53, which I slightly modify. *Pirq. R. Èl.* 40 (Eshkol 151, Friedlander 312) gives a more extensive version of this narrative. On קוֹץ, "thorn," see Jastrow 1339-1340.

In connection with a description of his original calling, one example of the visions and revelations of the Lord he has had, Paul states that a "thorn" (σκόλοψ)[31] in the flesh was given him (by God: the divine passive – 2 Cor 12:7). That is, it is a physical impediment or ailment. Paul borrowed this term from the context of Moses' being called by the Lord out of the סנה, "thorn(bush)," full of קוֹצִים, "thorns."

3) *MOSES' SPEECH IMPEDIMENT, AND PAUL'S SPEECH IMPEDIMENT.*

When God tells Moses at his calling that He will send (שׁלח) him to Pharaoh to bring forth the Israelites, the prophet answers modestly: "Who am I that I should go to Pharaoh, and bring the sons of Israel out of Egypt?" (Exod 3:11). After objecting that the Israelites will not believe him or listen to his voice, Moses tells the Lord: "Oh, my Lord, 'I am not a man of words' (לֹא אִישׁ דְּבָרִים), either heretofore or since You have spoken to Your servant, for 'I am heavy of mouth and heavy of tongue' (כְבַד~פֶּה וּכְבַד לָשׁוֹן אָנֹכִי) – 4:10)."[32] Therefore Moses asks the Lord to "send" someone else (v 13). Angered at Moses, the Lord calls his attention to his eloquent brother Aaron, who shall be his mouth, and He will be with Moses' and Aaron's mouths.

LXX Exod 4:10 has Moses say: "I am not 'sufficient' (ἱκανός)." Rather, "I am weak-voiced / have an impediment in my speech, and slow of tongue" (ἰσχνόφωνος καὶ βραδύγλωσσος).[33] In v 13 Moses asks the Lord to send another, who is "strong" (δυνάμενον).[34] *Targ. Onq.* 4:10 has "heavy / slow in speaking and of faint / indistinct tongue."[35] *Targum Pseudo-Jonathan* and the *Fragment Targum* have Moses say here: "I am halting / hesitant of mouth and difficult of speech."[36] *Neofiti 1* reads first: "I am

---

[31] LSJ 1613,2: thorn. He did not employ κέντρον, a "prick" or sharp point, goad (LSJ 939). This was the Greek translation for סנה (or קוֹץ), however, in the account of Paul's calling on the road before Damascus in Acts 26:14, where the Lord (Jesus) tells him: "It hurts you to kick against the 'goads.'"

[32] The NRSV has here: "I have never been eloquent" and "I am slow of speech and slow of tongue." Cf. also 6:12 and 30, where Moses says he is "of uncircumcised lips." The NRSV has: "poor speaker that I am."

[33] Cf. LSJ 843 and 327 respectively on these adjectives.

[34] This interprets the Hebrew בְּיַד, "by the hand of." For יַד as "strength, power," see BDB 390,2.

[35] Cf. Drazin 66, who translates: "I have heavy speech and indistinct articulation."

[36] Cf. on *Pseudo-Jonathan* Rieder 1.86 and Maher 171, who translates: "I am tongue-tied and I speak with difficulty"; as well as Klein 1.164 and 2.124 on the *Fragment Targum*, MS Vatican.

not a man (who is) a master of speech." Then it has: "I am halting / hesitant of mouth, halting / hesitant of speech."[37]

Pirq. R. El. 40 has Moses respond to the Lord's request to send him to Pharaoh in Exod 3:10 in the following way: "'Sovereign of all worlds! Have I not spoken thus to You three or four times that I have no power (כֹּחַ), for I have a speech impediment.'[38] As it is written, 'And Moses said unto the Lord: O Lord, I am not eloquent' (4:10). Not only this, but moreover You are sending me into the power (יד) of my enemy, who seeks my hurt."[39] Here, as elsewhere, Moses' lack of eloquence and his speech impediment are his lack of power / strength, his great weakness.

All of the above, coupled with Josephus' remarks in *Ant.* 2.270-271 regarding Moses' assertion that he is an "unskilled" person with no strength to persuade with words, and Philo's description of Moses' protest in *Mos.* 1.83, caused the great Jewish exegete Rashi (d. 1105 C.E.) to maintain that Moses was a "stutterer."[40] He is definitely described both in the Bible and in Judaic tradition as being ineloquent and as having some sort of speech impediment.

I suggest that Paul, in describing his calling on the road to Damascus in terms of the calling of Moses in the thorn(bush), also described his own lack of eloquence as his "thorn" in the flesh (2 Cor 12:7). He too may have been a stutterer, or simply "of slow tongue" or of weak voice, unable to impress his hearers with great rhetorical skills.[41] This fits Paul's own statement very well in 11:6, where he admits he is "unskilled in

---

[37] Díez Macho 2.21 and 414. Interestingly, *Exod. Rab.* Shemoth 1/26 on Exod 2:10 (Soncino 3.34) notes that Moses as a child in Pharaoh's palace burnt his tongue on a hot coal, thereby becoming "slow of speech and of tongue."

[38] Cf. Jastrow 1134 on פגם, niphal: to be impaired, defective.

[39] I slightly modify Friedlander (315) here, who translates the A. Epstein MS (xiv). Cf. the Higger edition, p. 217. Eshkol 153 omits "three or four times." A parallel is found in *Pirqe hay-Yeridot* 2, found in Tanna debe Eliyyahu (Braude and Kapstein 535, S54).

[40] Cf. Drazin 67, n. 11. On the text, see *Pentateuch with Targum Onkelos, Haphtaroth and Rashi's Commentary*. Hebrew and English by M. Rosenbaum and A. Silbermann (Jerusalem: The Silbermann Family, 1973) 16.

[41] The divine passive of "was given me in the flesh" may imply that Paul's "thorn" did not first arise at the time of his calling (see Philo, *Her.* 4 on Moses, with Exod 4:10, for this), but that the apostle was born this way. Stuttering has been suggested for different reasons before, e.g. by W. Clarke, "Was Paul a Stammerer?" in *New Testament Problems*: Essays – Reviews – Interpretations (New York: Macmillan, 1929) 136-140, and by C. Barrett, *The Second Epistle to the Corinthians* (London: Black, 1973) 315. For a recent overview of the various interpretations of "thorn in the flesh," see Wolff, *Der zweite Brief an die Korinther* 246-247.

speaking," as well as the superlative apostles' assertion in 10:10 that Paul's "speech is of no account."[42]

4) *MOSES' THREEFOLD REQUEST, AND PAUL'S THREEFOLD REQUEST.*

Moses' encounter with God at the thornbush, especially his reactions in Exod 4:10 and 13, were to have a direct affect upon the length of his life, especially when at its very end he intensely prayed three times to remain alive and to enter the Land of Israel. The Lord responded, however, that His grace was sufficient for him, and he would have to come to terms with his situation as it was. This imagery Paul appropriated in the narrative of his own calling in 2 Cor 12:8-9, as I will show below.

In *Tanḥ.* B Shemoth on Exod 3:1, "He led the flock beyond the wilderness," R. Joshua b. Qorḥa, a third generation Tanna, said regarding Moses: "This announces that his flock (Israel) would cease existing in the wilderness, and he would be taken away (by death – נאסף)[43] with it. 'He led the flock': This hinted to him that he would lead Israel forty years, and afterwards he would be taken away (by death)."[44]

Exod. Rab. Shemoth 2/5 on Exod 3:2, "out of the midst of 'the thornbush,'" also states that "God hinted to (Moses) that he would live 120 years – the numerical value of the letters comprising the word" (הסנה).[45]

The official Judaic chronology found in *Seder 'Olam* 5 states that for seven days God spoke to Moses from the thornbush, as the Hebrew of Exod 4:10 is interpreted, ending with Moses' objecting that he is "heavy of speech and heavy of tongue." The chronology notes that this last day was the day before Passover, just before the fifteenth of Nisan. "At the same time in the next year, on the fifteenth of Nisan, Israel went out of Egypt."[46]

Another early Judaic tradition maintains that God tried to persuade Moses to go on his mission to Egypt all seven days of the thornbush

---

[42] The verb ἐξουθενέω here also implies contempt or scorn (BAGD 277, LSJ 598). Cf. again 2 Cor 1:13 (in writing); 8:18; as well as 1 Cor 2:1 on Paul's rhetorical abilities.

[43] Jastrow 95: niphal, to be taken away (by death).

[44] Buber 2.7; Bietenhard 1.301. Cf. also *Tanḥ.* Shemoth 13 (Eshkol 219).

[45] Mirqin 5.63; Soncino 3.55, with n. 2. Deut 34:7 maintains that Moses was 120 years old when he died (after wandering through the wilderness with Israel for forty years), and Exod 7:7 notes that he was eighty years old when he first spoke to Pharaoh.

[46] Milikowsky 241-242 and 462.

event. R. Samuel b. Naḥman, a third generation Palestinian Amora,[47] stated that six of these days are indicated in Exod 4:10. On the seventh day Moses said: "Oh, my Lord, send, I pray, some other person" (v 13). (This kindled the Lord's anger against Moses – v 14), and He said to him: "'As you live, I will tie this in your skirts.' When did He repay him?" ... R. Levi[48] answered: "The (first) seven days of Adar Moses was offering prayer and supplication that he might enter the Land of Israel, and on the seventh, (on which rabbinic tradition maintains that Moses died,[49]) God said to him: 'You shall not go over this Jordan' (Deut 3:27)."[50]

Moses' calling in the thornbush was thus connected with the scene of his death at an early time in rabbinic sources, particularly in regard to Deut 3:23-27. In the latter Moses' threefold prayer is emphasized, and God's rejecting its contents. On this Paul based his phraseology in 2 Cor 12:8-9.

In section I.3.B)4) above (pp. 78-79) on "Jesus' Threefold Prayer" in Gethsemane, I cited *Pseudo-Philo* 19:6; *Mek. R. Ish.* Amalek 2; *Deut. Rab.* Vezot ha-Berakhah 11/5 and 11/10 in regard to Moses' praying three times at the very end of his life that he may continue to live and to enter the Land of Israel. I showed that this was Judaic interpretation of Deut 3:23, "'And I besought' the Lord...."

I also pointed out in I.3.B)8) (pp. 85-88) that the Lord's answer to Moses' threefold prayer is based on Judaic interpretation of Deut 3:26 – "Let it suffice you (רב לך); speak no more to Me of this matter." In Tannaitic comment on this Hebrew expression, דייך is often employed. For example, *Mek. R. Ish.* Amalek 2 in regard to Deut 3:23 says of Moses in a parable: "It is enough for you to have come this far" (דייך עד כאן). The same is repeated on 3:26.[51]

---

[47] Strack and Stemberger, *Introduction* 97.

[48] Also a third generation Palestinian Amora: *ibid.* 98.

[49] Cf. Ginzberg, *Legends* 3.317, 436-437, 439 and the sources cited in the relevant notes.

[50] *Lev. Rab.* Shemini 11/6 (Margulies 227-228, with many parallels in n. 5 on p. 227; Soncino 4.142, with notes 4-6). One parallel is *Tanḥ.* Wa'ethanan 5 on Deut 3:23 (Eshkol 854). This tradition is of Tannaitic origin, as shown in *Mek. R. Šim. b. Yoḥ.* (Epstein and Melamed 2, with a fine parable of the king [God] and his servant [Moses], and Exod 4:13 as indicating that God swore Moses would not enter the Land of Israel; on the latter, see also p. 3). Another Tannaitic connection between Exod 3:3 and Deut 3:23 is found in *Sifre Num.* Pinḥas 134, which deals with Deut 3:23-29 (Kuhn 553). Notice also the quotation of, and allusion to, Exod 3:1-6 at the scene of Moses' death in the first-century C.E. Palestinian *Pseudo-Philo* 19:9 (*OTP* 2.327).

[51] Lauterbach 2.150-151. G. Kittel in *Rabbinica. Paulus im Talmud* (Leipzig: Hinrichs, 1920) 46, as well as in his art. ἀρκέω in *TDNT* (German 1933) 1.465-466,

Philo in *Mut.* 14 (God in the thornbush tells Moses: "It is enough for you...to profit through My benediction..."), and Josephus in *Ant.* 2.267 (the Lord tells Moses to "be content with [ἀρκεῖσθαι] the things he had seen...and to inquire no further") attest other first-century C.E. application of Deut 3:26 to Moses at the scene of his calling in the thornbush.

I suggest that Paul, continuing the description of his own original call in 2 Cor 12:1-10 in terms of that of Moses in the thornbush, formulated vv 8-9 on the basis of Judaic traditions regarding Deut 3:23 ("three times" – τρίς – he called upon the Lord [in prayer] to remove the thorn in the flesh from him – 12:8) and 3:26 ("Let it suffice you" – 12:9). The same verb Paul employs in his phrase in v 9, ἀρκεῖ (σοι), is also found in Josephus.

"My grace" (ἡ χάρις μου) in 2 Cor 12:9 was not simply due to the great importance the Apostle to the Gentiles attached to this theological term.[52] Rather, like others, Paul derived it here from the opening Hebrew word of Deut 3:23, וָאֶתְחַנַּן,[53] behind his threefold "request" in 2 Cor 12:8. The Hebrew form here is the hithpael of חָנַן, "to be gracious." It contains within it the term חֵן, "grace,"[54] which stands behind χάρις in sixty of seventy-one occurrences in the LXX with a Hebrew background. Paul cites this as a dominical saying, which must originally have been in Aramaic or Hebrew, as in Acts 26:14. Yet he certainly felt free to formulate the contents of this vision in terms well-known to him from another calling, that of Moses in the thornbush.[55]

5) *THE UNUTTERABLE IN HEAVEN.*

In 2 Cor 12:2 Paul says that fourteen years ago he was caught up in a vision to the third heaven, which he equates with Paradise in v 3. He

---

had already called attention to rabbinic exegesis of Deut 3:26, but not to its connection to Moses' calling in the thornbush, nor to Philo and Josephus on this.

[52] Cf. the art. "χάρις D.2 Paul" by H. Conzelmann in *TDNT* 9.393-396. Nor does it derive here from the typical language of a pagan healing miracle. Against H. D. Betz, "Eine Christus-Aretalogie bei Paulus (2 Kor 12, 7-10)" in *ZThK* 66 (1969) 300. Certainly some overlapping of terminology occurs, also in regard to "power." Yet Paul is dependent here on Judaic traditions.

[53] Cf. *Deut. Rab.* Wa'etḥanan 2/1 on Deut 3:23 for Moses' praying only with the term *taḥanunim.* In regard to 3:26, he asks God to grant his prayer as an "act of grace" (Mirqin 11.29-30; Soncino 7.30, with n. 9).

[54] Cf. BDB 335-336 on these.

[55] Cf. Paul's assertion that he "received from the Lord" the sequence and exact words of the Lord's Supper in 1 Cor 11:23-26. It is much more probable that he learned of them in a Christian community; but ultimately, of course, they were "from the Lord."

then relates that he heard there "'unutterable words' (ἄρρητα ῥήματα), which it is not permitted to speak to man" (v 4). In BAGD on this adjective, the phrase is translated "words too sacred to tell," in regard to the meaning "someth. that must not be expressed, since it is holy...."[56]

I suggest that Paul is referring here primarily to his own calling on the road to Damascus, where in a heavenly "vision" he encountered the "Lord," Jesus.[57] In 1 Cor 15:8 the apostle relates that Christ appeared last of all to him. This is the basis of his apostleship, as shown in 9:1 – "Am I not an apostle? Have I not seen Jesus our 'Lord'?" In the early Christian hymn which Paul appropriated and inserted into Philippians 2, he also relates that God has highly exalted Christ Jesus and bestowed on him "the name which is above every name," which is the "Lord" (vv 9-11).

While in Greek Paul had no qualms about calling Jesus "Lord," κύριος,[58] as a typical Jew he would never have even thought of openly pronouncing the divine name LORD in Hebrew (יהוה). Therefore he circumscribed it, including the rest of the vision or revelation, with the phrase "unutterable words" (pl.) in 2 Cor 12:4. This too was due to his comparing his own calling with that of Moses, where the LORD also revealed His divine name to him in the thornbush.

As I pointed out above, *t. Yoma* 2:2 relates that the high priest in the Jerusalem Temple expressed the divine name ten times on the Day of Atonement.[59] The Jerusalem Talmud in *Yoma* 3:7, 40d comments on this by stating that "Those who were nearby would fall on their faces, and those who stood at a distance would say, 'Blessed be the Name of His glorious kingdom for ever and ever.'" This was out of deep reverence for the otherwise unutterable name. R. Tarfon, a second generation Tanna,[60] relates in this section how he himself as a priest experienced the high priest pronounce the divine name in the Temple, swallowing it up in the singing of the priests. Most importantly, the Talmud relates here that after God revealed His divine name, YHWH, to Moses in the thornbush

---

[56] P. 109.

[57] Cf. the three similar accounts in Acts 9:5; 22:8 and 10; and 26:15.

[58] He even appears to identify the Lord (Jesus) and the (divine) Spirit in 2 Cor 3:17-18. In Acts 26:15, Paul is described as asking in Hebrew (probably Aramaic) at the vision of his calling: "Who are you, Lord (κύριε)? And the Lord (κύριος) said...." (See also 9:5 and 22:8, 10.) Is (א)רמ (Jastrow 834) meant for at least the first (see 1 Cor 16:22)? On Paul's application of OT God language to Jesus, especially in strongly eschatological contexts, cf. the references to the Pauline Corpus in my 1971 Yale dissertation, *Comfort in Judgment: The Use of Day of the Lord and Theophany Traditions in Second Thessalonians I* (pp. 274-276 and 370-371).

[59] Lieberman 230; Neusner 2.192.

[60] Strack and Stemberger, *Introduction* 80.

(Exod 3:14), He said in v 15: "this is My name 'for ever' (לְעֹלָם)." However, this phrase is rather to be read: "This is My name, which is 'to be concealed' (לְעַלֵם)."[61]

Exod 3:15, within the call of Moses, was the major text adduced in Judaic sources for not expressing the divine name, but rather substituting "Adonai" for it.[62] This corroborates Philo's use of ἄρρητον precisely in connection with the revelation of the divine name at the call of Moses in the thornbush, and God's stating "My nature is to be, not to be spoken" (see section 2. above), as well as Josephus' statement regarding God's revealing to Moses His name, "concerning which I am not permitted to speak" (see section 3. above).

Palestinian Judaic tradition maintains that Moses had a vision of heaven, or stayed there, at three points in his life. The last was at the time the Lord showed him all the Land of Israel in Deut 34:1-4 just before his death.[63] The second was when Moses ascended from Mount Sinai to heaven for forty days to receive the Ten Commandments.[64] The first vision of heaven, including Moses' visiting Paradise, occurred when Moses saw the "great sight" of the thornbush.[65]

Unfortunately, the Palestinian sources on Moses' vision of heaven / Paradise in regard to Exodus 3 are Amoraic and later. They probably

---

[61] Neusner 14.96, which I slightly modify. Cf. BDB 761 on עָלַם as "conceal."

[62] Cf. *b. Pesaḥ.* 5a (Soncino 241); *Qid.* 71a (Soncino 361); and *Exod. Rab.* Shemoth 3/7 on the verse (Mirqin 5.74; Soncino 3.66, with notes 4-6).

[63] Cf. the Garden of Eden (Paradise) in *Sifre Deut.* Vezot ha-Berakhah 357 on Deut 34:3 (Finkelstein 427, Hammer 380), as well as Paradise in *Pseudo-Philo* 19:10 (*OTP* 2.328).

[64] Cf. Ginzberg, *Legends* 3.109-119, and the relevant notes, including 2 (Syriac) Baruch 4:6 and 59:8 on Paradise (*OTP* 1.622 and 642).

[65] Cf. *Legends* 2.304-316, and the relevant notes. In *Yalquṭ Makiri* on the Psalms (Buber 144), R. Ḥelbo, a fourth generation Palestinian Amora (Strack and Stemberger, *Introduction* 102), says in regard to Est 3:5 that the sight of the eyes of the righteous raises them to the Garden of Eden. This includes Moses, for whom Exod 3:2 is cited. A parallel in *Est. Rab.* 7/9 on Est 3:5 (Lewin-Epstein 19a-b; Soncino 9.84 – references from Levine, *The Burning Bush* 21, n. 28) has instead: it "gives them enlightenment, because it raises them to the loftiest height." The midrash "Gedulath Mosheh," also known as "Like Apples in the Trees of the Woods," also has Gabriel show Paradise to Moses in section 20. See *Batei Midrashot*, ed. S. Wertheimer, second edition enlarged and emended by A. Wertheimer (Jerusalem: Cook, 1954) 1.284. M. Kasher in *Encyclopedia of Biblical Interpretation* 7.130-131 on Exod 4:13 cites *Othioth de R. Aqiva*, letter nun, and *Midrash ha-Gadol* on this verse for Moses' being in God's inner sanctum (after having been translated into heaven at the thornbush). Interestingly, in a midrash anthology on Exod 4:12, (God reminded Moses of the dumb, deaf and blind) "lest he grow conceited" (Kasher 7.127). This recalls 2 Cor 12:7, "to keep me from

derive from earlier traditions, however, such as that still found in Ezekiel the Tragedian described above in section 1. I thus suggest that the heavenly vision of Moses at this calling also influenced the terminology of Paul's being caught up to the third heaven, Paradise, where he heard "words too sacred to tell" in the description of his original calling in 2 Cor 12:1-10.

6) *THE SHECHINAH.*

In 2 Cor 12:9 Paul says he will all the more gladly boast of his weaknesses so that the power of Christ may "dwell" upon him. As noted above, the verb ἐπισκηνόω occurs in the NT only here.[66] It is not found in the LXX. I suggest that the apostle chose this term here because, in its Hebrew form, it was very frequently associated with the Lord's "dwelling" (שכן)[67] in the thornbush.

The only other occurrence of סנה, thornbush, outside of Exodus 3 is in Deut 33:16, which speaks of "the favor of 'Him that dwelt' (שֹׁכְנִי) in the thornbush." This certainly influenced Palestinian Judaic interpretation of the thornbush narrative in Exodus 3. Several examples are the following.

In *Mek. R. Šim. b. Yoḥ.* on Exod 3:1-2, R. Joshua (b. Ḥananyah), a second generation Tanna,[68] says God revealed Himself from heaven on high and spoke to Moses from the thornbush "because when Israel went down to Egypt, the *Shechinah* went down with them."[69] In *Exod. Rab.* Shemoth 2/5 on "out of the midst of the thornbush" in Exod 3:2, R. Joshua b. Qorḥa, a third generation Tanna, said that God chose a thornbush from which to speak to Moses "to teach you that no place is devoid of God's *Shechinah,* not even a thornbush."[70] *'Avot R. Nat.* A 34 states that the fourth of the ten divine descents the *Shechinah* made to the

---

becoming too elated." P. Schäfer in "New Testament and Hekhalot Literature: The Journey into Heaven in Paul and in Merkavah Mysticism" in *JJS* 35 (1989) 19-35 shows merkavah mysticism's lack of relevance to 2 Cor 12:1-10.

[66] The related noun σκῆνος, tent or lodging, occurs only in 2 Cor 5:1 and 4 of the human body. The noun σκηνή does not occur in Paul, but the LXX very frequently uses it to translate the Hebrew מִשְׁכָּן (Hatch and Redpath 1271-1273). The simple verb, σκηνόω, translates the Hebrew שכן in four of its five occurrences in the LXX (Hatch and Redpath 1273). LXX Exod 3:22 has συσκῆνος for the Hebrew שָׁכֵן, neighbor, inhabitant.

[67] On this verb, cf. BDB 1014-1015, and Jastrow 1575: to dwell, rest.

[68] Strack and Stemberger, *Introduction* 77-78.

[69] Epstein and Melamed 1. On the שְׁכִינָה, see Jastrow 1573.

[70] Mirqin 5.61; Soncino 3.53. Cf. the similar terminology found in *b. Soṭa* 5a, with "abiding" (Soncino 19), and *Šabb.* 67a (Soncino 319).

world was that indicated in Exod 3:8.[71] In commenting on this descent, *Pirq. R. El.* 40 says that God "dwelt" (שכן) in the thornbush. This is then repeated, with the addition that because God saw Israel in great grief, which the thornbush stands for, "He also 'dwelt' (שכן) with them."[72]

These examples suffice to buttress my proposal that Paul chose the rare term ἐπισκηνόω in 2 Cor 12:9 because of the very strong emphasis in Judaic sources on God's "Shechinah," His indwelling presence, and His "dwelling" (שכן) in the thornbush at the call of Moses in Exodus 3.

7) *APOSTLESHIP AND SIGNS.*

Paul derives his apostleship from having seen the risen Lord at his calling (1 Cor 15:8; 9:1). This is also the source of his "authority" (ἐξουσία – 2 Cor 10:8 and 13:10). He also maintains to the Corinthians that the signs of a true apostle (himself) were performed among them: "signs and wonders and mighty works" (σημείοις τε καὶ τέρασιν καὶ δυνάμεσιν – 2 Cor 12:12).

I suggest that at least one major influence on Paul's concept of being an ἀπόστολος, one sent or commissioned, derived from his comparing his vision and calling on the road to Damascus, (which I see reflected in 2 Cor 12:1-10), to Moses' vision in the thornbush and his being called or "sent" there.

Nowhere else in the Hebrew Bible is God's sending or commissioning (שלח) a person so emphasized, together with miracles, as in the calling of Moses in the thornbush. Judaic tradition also included Moses' receiving God's authority there.

God's "sending" or commissioning Moses to be His authorized messenger is emphasized six times at the episode of the thornbush (Exod 3:10, 12, 13, 14, 15; 4:13). For שלח the LXX has here everywhere ἀποστέλλω, with the exception of ἐξαποστέλλω in 3:12. *Exod. Rab.* Shemoth 3/4 on Exod 3:12, "And this shall be the sign (אות, LXX σημεῖον) for you, that I have 'sent' you'..."), states in this regard: "by this you will be acknowledged as 'My messenger' (שְׁלוּחִי), that I will be with you and will do all you desire."[73] Another example is 3/14 on Exod 4:10, where Moses says to God: "You are Lord of the Universe, and You want me to be Your 'messenger' (שָׁלִיחַ)?"[74] Moses' divine "commission" (שְׁלִיחוּת)[75] is mentioned

---

[71] Schechter 102, Goldin 140.

[72] Eshkol 151, Friedlander 312.

[73] Mirqin 5.71; cf. Soncino 3.63. See Jastrow 912 on נכר, niphal part.: recognized, acknowledged.

[74] Cf. Mirqin 5.80, and Soncino 3.73. Moses is also a שָׁלִיחַ in *b. B. Meṣ.* 86b (Soncino 498, in regard to Exod 17:6; reference from Str-B 3.3). On this term as also

in *Mek. R. Šim. b. Yoḥ.* in regard to Exod 4:13-14, which also speaks of God's giving him the "authority" (רָשׁוּת)[76] to speak.[77] This corresponds exactly to the ἐξουσία, the "authority," which the Apostle Paul received from the Lord at his own calling.

At the time the Lord appears to Moses in the thornbush and tells him to inform the Israelites that He has sent him to them, He also conveys to Moses that He will stretch out His hand and smite Egypt with "wonders" (נִפְלָאֹת[78]; LXX θαυμάσια – 3:20). When Moses objects that the Israelites will not believe the Lord has appeared to him, He gives him three "signs" (אֹתוֹת[79]; LXX σημεῖα – 4:8-9, 17), which are called "miracles" (מֹפְתִים[80]; LXX τέρατα) in 4:21. These are to indicate that God has sent Moses as His authorized messenger. The emphasis on wonders, signs and miracles as an authentication of Moses' calling is striking here.[81]

It is precisely this threefold combination which Paul also employs in 2 Cor 12:12 – σημεῖα, τέρατα and δυνάμεις. The LXX translates the נִפְלָאֹת, "wondrous works," of Job 37:14 for example as δύναμις. This latter term (here in the plural) was especially important to Paul for his argumentation. Like Moses, he may be apparently weak and ineloquent, or even have a speech impediment. Yet at the vision of Paul's calling, the Lord told him His "power" (δύναμις) was made perfect in the apostle's weakness. Paul then boasts the more gladly of his weakness so that the "power" of Christ may dwell upon him. When he is weak, then he is "powerful" (2 Cor 12:9-10). In contrast to the so-called superlative apostles, Paul's ministry as an apostle in Corinth was accompanied by

---

employed for both Moses and Aaron before Pharaoh, see *Exod. Rab.* Shemoth 5/14 on Exod 5:1 (Mirqin 5.97; Soncino 3.94).

[75] Jastrow 1583.

[76] *Ibid.,* 1499.

[77] Epstein and Melamed 3. The implication is that if God gives Moses the authority (here also meant as permission) to speak before Him, he can also speak so before others like Pharaoh, to whom he is reluctant to go.

[78] BDB 810,4: wonderful acts of the Lord. The ten plagues are primarily meant.

[79] BDB 16. Cf. *Exod. Rab.* Shemoth 3/12 on Exod 4:5 (Mirqin 5.79; Soncino 3.71): "Go and perform before them this miracle (אוֹת) that they should believe that I appeared unto thee."

[80] BDB 68. It is combined with אֹתוֹת in Deut 4:34 and elsewhere.

[81] In his art. ἀποστέλλω etc. in *TDNT* 1.433, K. H. Rengstorf also calls attention to the Exodus 3 narrative and states: "Moses is the typical divine messenger endorsed by signs...." He mentions 2 Cor 12:1ff. and v 12 on p. 440. S. Hafemann in *Paul, Moses and the History of Israel.* The Letter / Spirit Contrast and the Argument from Scripture in 2 Corinthians 3 (WUNT 81; Tübingen: Mohr, 1995) deals with the latter chapter in light of Moses' call, but not with 12:1-10.

concrete signs of his being called by the risen Lord, as at Moses' call in the thornbush.

*   *   *

The above seven comparisons between Moses' vision and calling in the thornbush, and Paul's description in vision form of his first calling in 2 Cor 12:1-10, may also be questioned individually. Here some arguments are clearly stronger than others. Yet the cumulative effect is hopefully persuasive. Paul, *the* ἀπόστολos of the Lord Jesus, stood in the footsteps of the greatest of all Israelites, Moses, *the* שָׁלִיחַ of the LORD.[82]

C. *Pauline Chronology.*

One major problem remains, that of the Pauline chronology. The apostle states in 2 Cor 12:2 that he was caught up to the third heaven "fourteen years ago." After referring to his (Damascus) call in Gal 1:15-16, Paul in 2:1 also mentions "fourteen years" for the time after which he went up again to Jerusalem. It is unclear whether or not he includes the three years he had already spoken of in 1:18. This exact time span of fourteen years may thus be purely accidental.

In a major study of Pauline chronology, R. Jewett maintains that Paul's conversion took place in 34 C.E. and the writing of the last of the Corinthian letters in 56 C.E., that is, twenty-two years later.[83] G. Lüdemann places the conversion of Paul in 30 C.E., and the writing of 2 Corinthians 10-13 in the summer of 50 C.E., that is, twenty years later.[84] Both studies thus maintain that Paul's reference to "fourteen years ago" in 2 Cor 12:2 cannot mean his conversion on the road to Damascus.

I have argued above that 2 Cor 12:1-10 indeed refer to Paul's Damascus experience, and that the verses were "triggered" by the catchword Damascus, mentioned twice in 11:32. Aside from the very remote possibility that Paul's memory may have failed him at this point, or that a scribe later somehow mistakenly changed an originally larger number to fourteen, there is a feasible explanation for this number.

---

[82] I leave the larger task of considering whether Paul in part thought of himself as the "prophet like Moses" (Deut 18:15, 18) to someone else. Then 2 Corinthians 3 *and* 12 should be discussed. My analysis of 2 Cor 12:1-10 was done primarily in light of the relevance of vv 8-9 to the Gethsemane pericope, treated in Chapter Two.

[83] Cf. his *Dating Paul's Life* (London: SCM, 1979), "Graph of Dates and Time-spans" at the end.

[84] Cf. his *Paulus, der Heidenapostel*. Band I: Studien zur Chronologie (Göttingen: Vandenhoeck & Ruprecht, 1980) 273. Alternate dates for him are 33 and 53.

After the Lord appeared to Moses and called him from the thornbush in Exod 3:1 – 4:17, some time elapsed, including accounts of the circumcision of the son of Moses, and of his meeting Aaron at the mountain of God (Sinai), before Moses actually spoke to Pharaoh in 5:1. That is, the first real activity of Moses due to his call did not take place directly after it, but only after a certain period of time. Yet the two were intimately connected.

The same appears to have been true for Paul. According to Acts 9:29, after his conversion Saul preached and disputed among the Hellenists in Jerusalem, then fled for his life to his home town of Tarsus. From there Barnabas brought him to Antioch, where they both taught for a year (11:25-26). The two then brought famine relief funds to the Judean Christians and returned to Antioch (11:30; 12:25). Then prophets and teachers of the church, while worshiping the Lord and fasting, received instructions from the Holy Spirit: "Set apart for me Barnabas and Saul for the work to which I have called them" (13:2). Then they fasted, prayed, laid their hands on the two and sent them off.[85] Verse 4 emphasizes that they were "sent out" (ἐκπεμφθέντες) by the Holy Spirit. This was the beginning of Paul's first great missionary journey.

Paul appears to equate the Holy Spirit with the Lord (Jesus) in 2 Cor 3:17-18. The Spirit, perhaps the Lord Jesus, here in Acts instructs the leaders of the church in Antioch to "set aside" (ἀφορίζω) Barnabas and Saul for the work to which he has "called" (προσκαλέω) them, just as God had "set apart" Paul and "called" (καλέω) him, revealing His Son to him (at his conversion on the Damascus road – Gal 1:15). Saul, although already having performed several tasks for the church, is here divinely re-commissioned and begins his first major missionary enterprise. It is probably significant that from now on he is only called "Paul" (13:9). I suggest that Paul himself combines this "re-commissioning" and second "calling" in Antioch with the vision of his first call on the road to Damascus. He then refers to *both* when he expressly mentions "fourteen years ago" in 2 Cor 12:2.[86] The re-commissioning in Antioch, a confirmation of Paul's first calling, will have taken place at about that time, although the pinpointing of an exact year is difficult.

---

[85] For "send off," "dismiss" them (ἀπολύω), Delitzsch in his Hebrew New Testament (240) has וַיְשַׁלְּחוּם. If the original account now found in Acts was Semitic, this verb signifies a real commissioning, not just an informal "travel blessing." In v 4 Delitzsch also has for αὐτοὶ... ἐκπεμφθέντες: הַמְשֻׁלָּחִים (p. 240).

[86] On this, cf. also the authors cited by Martin in *2 Corinthians* 399; Furnish, *II Corinthians* 524; and N. Taylor, *Paul, Antioch and Jerusalem. A Study in Relationships and Authority in Earliest Christianity* (JSNTSup 66; Sheffield: Sheffield Academic Press, 1992) 90-92. None of them, however, refers to Exodus 3.

*   *   *

Regardless of whether or not the above proposal in respect to Pauline chronology is accepted, it is very probable that Paul's mention of his beseeching the Lord three times to remove his thorn in the flesh, and the Lord's answer that "My grace is sufficient for you" in 2 Cor 12:8-9, derive from the same Judaic complex as Jesus' threefold prayer in Gethsemane: the scene of Moses' impending death, based on early interpretation of Deut 3:23-26.

Appendix Two

The Contrast of God's Taking Away Moses' Soul Through a Kiss, and Judas' Handing Jesus Over to Certain Death Through a Kiss

Directly after the Gethsemane narrative, while Jesus was still speaking to his disciples, Judas entered the site with an armed crowd sent by the chief priests, scribes and elders.[1] The "betrayer" had given this group a sign by which they could recognize Jesus: "The one I shall 'kiss' (φιλήσω) is the man. Seize him and lead him off securely" (Mark 14:44). Then Judas proceeded to Jesus and addressed him as "Master!" "And he 'kissed' (κατεφίλησεν) him" (v 45). Recognizing the agreed upon sign, the armed crowd "laid hands on him and seized him" (v 46).

Matthew follows Mark closely at this point in regard to the kissing motif (26:48-49). Luke, in contrast, omits the agreed upon sign and has Judas approach Jesus "in order to kiss" (φιλῆσαι) him. This does not come about, however, for Jesus then asks him: "'By a kiss' (φιλήματι) you would deliver / hand over the Son of man (= me)?" (22:47-48). The kiss is emphasized here by its position at the beginning of the question. In John 18:2-12 there is no kissing incident at all. Instead, when those who had

---

[1] It is known that the chief priests sent their servants, armed with clubs or staves as in Gethsemane, to forcibly collect their share of the tithes. See *b. Pesaḥ.* 57a (Soncino 285), as well as other references cited by Jeremias, *Jerusalem* 180-181. The "crowd" of Mark 14:43 would have been primarily made up of such people. Verse 47 expressly mentions a slave of the high priest. Josephus in *Bell.* 4.293 notes that at least some of the Temple guards were armed; perhaps they too were employed for police duties by the high priests.

come to arrest Jesus arrived, he went forth to meet them and identified himself (vv 4-8). He is here represented as himself determining the course of action.[2]

Various suggestions have been made as to a possible background to Judas' kiss, including Prov 27:6 ("profuse are the kisses of an enemy") and 2 Sam 20:9 ("And Joab took Amasa by the beard with his right hand to kiss him." Then Joab struck his sword into Amasa's body, killing him – v 10). Rabbinic tradition on Esau's actually wanting to bite his brother Jacob instead of kissing him (Gen 33:4) is of no relevance here, nor are any of the other three or four types of kisses approved by the rabbis.[3]

For these reasons I would like to make a new proposal here as to the Judaic background of Judas' kissing Jesus, which led to his death the same day.[4] It is intimately connected to the portrayal of Jesus' praying three times in Gethsemane that God will remove the cup (of death) from him. As shown above in Chapter II, section I.3.B)4), a Palestinian Jewish Christian described Jesus here in part with exact expressions and motifs from Judaic lore regarding Moses' threefold prayer that the Angel of Death would spare him at the very end of his life, even though his hour had now come. The climax of Judaic haggadic tradition on this scene portrays God Himself as taking away Moses' soul with a kiss. The contrast would have been striking to Palestinian Jewish Christians acquainted with these traditions, and it is most probably intended.

In the last chapter of Deuteronomy (34), Moses ascends Mount Nebo, opposite Jericho. Then the Lord shows him all the land the Israelites are to inherit. Moses may view it, but may not go over there. Verse five then states: "So Moses the servant of the Lord died there in the land of Moab, 'according to the word of the Lord.'" Afterwards the Lord buried him in an unknown place.

The Hebrew for "according to the word of the Lord" is literally "'by the mouth' (עַל פִּי) of the Lord." The construct פִּי is from פֶּה,"mouth." While the Septuagint, Targum Onqelos and the Fragment Targum (MS "V") on Deut 34:5 simply have "the word of the Lord" here, Targum

---

[2] Cf. Brown, *The Death* 1.259. Pages 252-262 are the most recent treatment of this pericope, and Brown carefully summarizes other relevant secondary literature. Recent and older bibliography is found on pp. 237-238. I agree with Brown that there is no increase in emotion between φιλέω and καταφιλέω (p. 253). The Hebrew, for example, is the same for both (נשק; Jastrow 941-942), as shown in Delitzsch's Hebrew New Testament (p. 93).

[3] Cf. Str-B 1.995-996.

[4] According to Judaic time reckoning, the day extended from sunset to sunset. Thus Jesus' Crucifixion the next afternoon was part of the same day.

Pseudo-Jonathan reads: "by the kiss (עַל נְשִׁיקַת) of the word of the Lord."[5] The Lord's mouth is represented here as "kissing" Moses, who earlier had spoken "mouth to mouth" to God (Num 12:8).

Judaic haggadah concerned itself with the Lord's "mouth" here at an early time. *Pseudo-Philo* 19:16, for example, paraphrases Deut 34:5-6 regarding Moses in the following way: "and he died in glory (*in gloria*) according to the word of the Lord, and He buried him...."[6] Here "in glory" has been added by the Palestinian author, writing in Hebrew at about the time of Jesus.[7] He may have thought that God's kissing Moses was a "glorious" way to die, although he does not explicitly state this.

In *'Avot R. Nat.* A 12 God tells the Angel of Death to go and bring Him the soul of Moses. This he attempts to do, but in anger Moses drives him off. This occurs several times until God Himself addresses Moses: "Moses, you have had enough (דַיָּיךְ)[8] of this world. Behold, the world to come is awaiting you." Then God "took the soul of Moses and stored it under the Throne of Glory. And when He took it, He took it only 'by a kiss' (בנשיקה), as Scripture states: 'By the mouth of the Lord' (Deut 34:5)." The narrative continues by noting that the souls of all the righteous are preserved under the Throne of Glory.[9]

A variant of this narrative is found in *Deut. Rab.* Vezot ha-Berakhah 11/10, where God informs Moses' soul: "Your end has come; depart, do not delay." To the soul's objections God replies: "Go forth, do not delay, and I will elevate you to the highest heavens, and I will place you under the Throne of My Glory with the cherubim, seraphim, and troops (of angels)." Moses' soul then maintains that Moses was purer than two angels. "'I implore You, let me remain in the body of Moses.' In that hour God 'kissed him' (נְשָׁקוֹ – Moses) and took away his soul 'by a kiss of the mouth' (בִּנְשִׁיקַת פֶּה)."[10]

---

[5] Rieder 2.308; English in Etheridge 683. I have not had access to the study of M. Fishbane, *The Kiss of God: Spiritual and Mystical Death in Judaism* (Seattle: University of Washington Press, 1994).

[6] *OTP* 2.328; Latin in *Les Antiquités Bibliques* 1.164.

[7] Cf. D. Harrington in *OTP* 2.298-300.

[8] Cf. Chapter II, section I.3.B)8) above on the relevance of this term for ἀπέχει in Mark 14:41.

[9] Schechter 50; cf. also Goldin 65. The dative φιλήματι in Luke 22:48, "by a kiss," corresponds exactly to the Hebrew phrase. In *b. Ber.* 8a (Soncino 40), a Tannaitic tradition notes that the divine kiss is the easiest of the 903 forms of death in the world.

[10] Mirqin 11.159-160; cf. Soncino 7.186-187. See also *Midr. Departure / Death of Moses* A (Jellinek 1.129) and B (Jellinek 6.77).

Another variant, showing the great popularity of this tradition, is found in *Tanḥ.* B Wa'ethanan 6. The Israelites went to Moses and informed him that he had only another half moment to live. Moses then "placed both his arms on his heart and said to the Israelites: 'See the future of flesh and blood! These two hands, which received the Torah from the mouth of the Almighty, are falling into the grave!' In this moment his soul departed 'by a kiss' (בְּנֵשִׁיקָה)," as is written in Deut 34:5.[11]

In *b. B. Bat.* 17a "our rabbis taught" that there were six persons over whom the Angel of Death had no dominion (since they died by a kiss of God). They are the Patriarchs, as well as Moses, Aaron and Miriam. "By the mouth of the Lord" (in Deut 34:5 and Num 33:38) applies to Moses and Aaron. R. Eleazar then adds that Miriam also died "by a kiss," deriving this from the occurrence of "there" both in Num 20:1 and Deut 34:5.[12]

Finally, Judaic tradition considered the Song of Songs to be a dialogue between God and Israel.[13] *Cant. Rab.* 1:2 § 5 on "Let Him kiss me with the kisses of His mouth," states for example: "The Rabbis say: The souls of these (viz. the righteous) will be taken away with a kiss." R. 'Azariah, a fifth generation Palestinian Amora,[14] then explains this in regard to Aaron (Num 33:38), Moses (Deut 34:5), and Miriam (Num 20:1 and Deut 34:5). Cant 1:2 is cited to show that this also applies to *all* righteous persons (כל הצדיקים).[15]

The latter is already implied in *'Avot R. Nat.* A 12. After stating that God took the soul of Moses by a kiss (Deut 34:5), the midrash says He stored it under the Throne of Glory, where the souls of all the righteous are preserved (see above).

Jesus was considered by early Palestinian Jewish Christians to be not only the Righteous One (ὁ δίκαιος in Acts 3:14; 7:52; 22:14), and thus also deserving of having God take his soul from him by a kiss. As the Messiah, he was also thought to be the final or great redeemer, the successor of Israel's first redeemer, Moses.[16]

---

[11] Buber 2.13; Bietenhard 2.456. A parallel is found in *Tanḥ.* Wa'ethanan 6 (Eshkol 2.860).

[12] Soncino 86. The text continues by stating that "our rabbis taught" that there are seven others over whom the worms had no dominion. "By the mouth of the Lord" here also applies to Moses, Aaron and Miriam. A parallel to the first tradition is found in *b. Mo'ed Qaṭ.* 28a (Soncino 181).

[13] Cf. S. Donsqi's remarks in his edition of *Midrash Rabbah. Shir ha-Shirim* 29-30.

[14] Strack and Stemberger, *Introduction* 104.

[15] Cf. Donsqi 16, and Soncino 9.28.

[16] Cf. p. 73, n. 25.

I therefore propose that, as in the Gospel of John, historically there was no kiss by Judas in Gethsemane as a sign of recognition.[17] The enigmatic figure of Judas was quickly developed in an haggadic style by early Palestinian Jewish Christians.[18] Jesus was portrayed in Gethsemane with expressions and motifs derived from Judaic tradition on the hour of Moses' death. Palestinian Jewish Christians also knew how Moses died. The Angel of Death had no authority over him, therefore God Himself took his soul "with a kiss." They therefore described Jesus, the "new" Moses (final redeemer), in the same terms: Judas' kiss of Jesus in Gethsemane meant his death the next afternoon on a cross at Golgotha. A great contrast was intentionally made: God Himself gave Moses the kiss of death. This He did not do with His Son Jesus. Instead, acting as the agent of wicked Sammael, the Angel of Death and the chief Satan, it was Judas who gave Jesus the kiss of death. Paradoxically, however, the narratives of the empty tomb and the Resurrection on Easter Sunday show that God had indeed taken Jesus to Himself at the time of his death.

This Palestinian Jewish Christian haggadic development of Judas' giving Jesus the "kiss of death" must have taken place at an early date, for it is already found in the Gethsemane scene of Jesus' arrest in the earliest gospel, Mark.

---

[17] Many elements in John's presentation are, however, patently late.

[18] For an overview of the relevant passages in the NT, cf. E. Blair, art. "Judas," 7, in *IDB* 2.1006-1008.

Sources and Reference Works

I. *The Bible.*

Kittel, *Biblia Hebraica,* ed. R. Kittel et al. (Stuttgart: Privilegierte Württembergische Bibelanstalt, 1951[7]).

Rahlfs, *Septuaginta,* ed. A. Rahlfs (Stuttgart: Württembergische Bibelanstalt, 1962[7]).

Hatch and Redpath, *A Concordance to the Septuagint,* ed. E. Hatch and H. Redpath (Oxford: Clarendon, 1897; reprint Grand Rapids, Michigan: Baker Book House, 1983).

Nestle / Aland, *Novum Testamentum Graece,* ed. E. Nestle, K. Aland, et al. (Stuttgart: Deutsche Bibelgesellschaft, 1990[26]).

The Greek New Testament, ed. K. Aland, M. Black, B. Metzger and A. Wikgren (London: United Bible Societies, 1966).

Hebrew New Testament, by F. Delitzsch (Berlin: Trowitzsch and Son, 1885).

Hebrew New Testament (Jerusalem: The United Bible Societies, 1979).

II. *The Targums.*

Sperber, *The Bible in Aramaic,* ed. A. Sperber (Leiden: Brill, 1959), 4 volumes.

Drazin, *Targum Onkelos to Exodus,* ed. and trans. I. Drazin (New York: Ktav; Denver: Center for Judaic Studies, University of Denver, 1990).

Grossfeld, *The Targum Onqelos to Exodus,* trans. B. Grossfeld (The Aramaic Bible, 7; Edinburgh: Clark, 1988).

Díez Macho, *Neophyti 1, Tomo II, Éxodo,* Targum Palestinense MS de la Biblioteca Vaticana, ed. and trans. A. Díez Macho (Madrid: Consejo Superior de Investigaciones Científicas, 1970). Tomo V, Deuteronomy: 1978.

McNamara / Maher, *Targum Neofiti 1: Exodus, Targum Pseudo-Jonathan: Exodus,* trans. M. McNamara and M. Maher (The Aramaic Bible, 2; Edinburgh: Clark, 1994).

Rieder, *Targum Jonathan ben Uziel on the Pentateuch,* ed. with a Hebrew translation by D. Rieder (Jerusalem, 1984), 2 volumes.

Klein, *The Fragment-Targums of the Pentateuch,* ed. and trans. M. Klein (AnBib 76; Rome: Biblical Institute, 1980), 2 volumes.

Etheridge, *The Targums of Onkelos and Jonathan Ben Uzziel on the Pentateuch with the Fragments of the Jerusalem Targum,* trans. J. Etheridge (New York: KTAV, 1968; original 1862).

Stenning, *The Targum of Isaiah,* ed. and trans. J. Stenning (Oxford: Clarendon, 1949).

Chilton, *The Isaiah Targum,* trans. B. Chilton (The Aramaic Bible, 11; Edinburgh: Clark, 1987).

Cathcart and Gordon, *The Targum of the Minor Prophets,* trans. K. Cathcart and R. Gordon (The Aramaic Bible, 14; Edinburgh: Clark, 1989).

Lagarde, *Hagiographa Chaldaice,* ed. P. de Lagarde (Leipzig: Teubner, 1873; reprint Osnabrück: Zeller, 1967).

Merino, *Targum de Salmos.* Edición Príncipe del Ms. Villa-Amil n.5 de Alfonso de Zamora, ed. L. Merino (Madrid: Consejo Superior de Investigaciones Científicas, 1982).

III. *The Mishnah and Tosefta.*

Albeck, *Shisha Sidre Mishna,* ed. Ch. Albeck (Jerusalem and Tel Aviv: Bialik Institute and Dvir, 1975), 6 volumes.

Danby, *The Mishnah,* trans. H. Danby (London: Oxford University, 1933).

Neusner, *The Mishnah,* trans. J. Neusner (New Haven: Yale University, 1988).

Meinhold, *Die Mischna,* II.5. *Joma,* ed. with a German translation by J. Meinhold (Giessen: Töpelmann, 1913).

Zuckermandel, *Tosephta,* ed. M. Zuckermandel, with a supplement by S. Liebermann (Jerusalem: Wahrmann, 1970).

Lieberman, *The Tosefta.* Seder Mo'ed, ed. S. Lieberman (New York: The Jewish Theological Seminary of America, 1962).

Neusner, *The Tosefta,* trans. J. Neusner et al. (Hoboken, New Jersey: KTAV, 1977-1986), 6 volumes.

IV. *The Talmuds.*

Soncino, *The Babylonian Talmud,* ed. I. Epstein, various translators (London: Soncino, 1952), 18 volumes and index.

Soncino, *The Minor Tractates of the Talmud,* ed. A. Cohen, various translators (London: Soncino, 1965), 2 volumes.

Goldschmidt, *Der Babylonische Talmud,* ed. with a German translation by L. Goldschmidt (Haag: Nijoff, 1933), 9 volumes.

Krotoshin, *Talmud Yerushalmi,* Krotoshin edition (Jerusalem: Shilah, 1969).

Neusner, *The Talmud of the Land of Israel,* trans. J. Neusner et al. (Chicago: University of Chicago, 1982-1995), 34 volumes.

V. *Halakhic Midrashim.*

Lauterbach, *Mekilta de-Rabbi Ishmael,* ed. and trans. J. Lauterbach (Philadelphia: The Jewish Publication Society of America, 1976), 3 volumes.

Epstein / Melamed, *Mekhilta d'Rabbi Šim'on b. Jochai,* ed. J. Epstein and E. Melamed (Jerusalem: Hillel Press, 1955; reprint 1979).

Neusner, *Sifra.* An Analytical Translation, trans. by J. Neusner (BJS 138-140; Atlanta: Scholars Press, 1988), 3 volumes.

Winter, *Sifra.* Halachischer Midrasch zu Leviticus, German by J. Winter (Breslau: Münz, 1938).

Horowitz, *Siphre ad Numeros adjecto Siphre zutta,* ed. H. Horowitz (Jerusalem: Wahrmann, 1976).

Neusner, *Sifre to Numbers,* trans. J. Neusner (BJS 118-119; Atlanta: Scholars Press, 1986), 2 volumes.

Kuhn, *Der tannaitische Midrasch Sifre zu Numeri,* German by K. Kuhn (Stuttgart: Kohlhammer, 1959).

Finkelstein, *Sifre on Deuteronomy,* ed. L. Finkelstein (New York: The Jewish Theological Seminary of America, 1969).

Hammer, *Sifre.* A Tannaitic Commentary on the Book of Deuteronomy, trans. R. Hammer (YJS 24; New Haven: Yale University, 1986).

Neusner, *Sifre to Deuteronomy.* An Analytical Translation, trans. J. Neusner (BJS 98 and 101; Atlanta: Scholars Press, 1987), 2 volumes.

VI. *Haggadic Midrashim.*

Soncino, *Midrash Rabbah*, ed. H. Freedman and M. Simon (London: Soncino, 1939), 9 volumes and index.

Midrash Rabbah (Vilna: Romm, 1887).

Mirqin, *Midrash Rabbah*, Pentateuch. Ed. and vocalized by M. Mirqin (Tel Aviv: Yavneh, 1981), 11 volumes.

Margulies, *Leviticus Rabbah:* Midrash Wayyikra Rabbah, ed. M. Margulies (Jerusalem: Ministry of Education and Culture of Israel, American Academy for Jewish Research, 1953-1960).

Neusner, *Judaism and Scripture.* The Evidence of Leviticus Rabbah, trans. J. Neusner (Chicago Studies in the History of Judaism; Chicago: University of Chicago, 1986).

Liebermann, *Midrash Debarim Rabbah*, ed. S. Liebermann (Jerusalem: Wahrmann, 1964²).

Buber, *Midrasch Ekha Rabbati*, ed. S. Buber (Vilna: Romm, 1899).

Donsqi, *Midrash Rabbah. Shir ha-Shirim*, ed. S. Donsqi (Jerusalem: Dvir, 1980).

Midrash Tanḥuma, Eshkol edition (Jerusalem: Eshkol, no date).

Buber, *Midrasch Tanḥuma:* Ein agadischer Commentar zum Pentateuch, ed. S. Buber (Vilna: Romm, 1885).

Bietenhard, *Midrasch Tanḥuma B,* German by H. Bietenhard (Judaica et Christiana 5-6; Bern: Peter Lang, 1980-1982), 2 volumes.

Midrash Haggadol on the Pentateuch, ed. M. Margulies. Leviticus, ed. A. Steinsalz (Jerusalem: Kook, 1976).

Schechter, *Aboth de Rabbi Nathan* (A and B), ed. S. Schechter (Vienna, 1887; reprinted New York: Feldheim, 1945).

Goldin, *The Fathers According to Rabbi Nathan* (A), trans. J. Goldin (YJS 10; New Haven: Yale University, 1955).

Neusner, *The Fathers According to Rabbi Nathan.* An Analytical Translation and Explanation, trans. J. Neusner (BJS 114; Atlanta: Scholars Press, 1986).

Saldarini, *The Fathers According to Rabbi Nathan* (B), trans. A. Saldarini (SJLA 11; Leiden: Brill, 1975).

Mandelbaum, *Pesikta de Rav Kahana*, ed. B. Mandelbaum (New York: The Jewish Theological Seminary of America, 1962), 2 volumes.

Braude and Kapstein, *Pesikta de-Rab Kahana*, trans. W. Braude and I. Kapstein (Philadelphia: The Jewish Publication Society of America, 1975).

Neusner, *Pesiqta de Rab Kahana. An Analytical Translation*, trans. J. Neusner (BJS 122-123; Atlanta: Scholars Press, 1987).

Friedmann, *Pesikta Rabbati*, ed. M. Friedmann (Vienna, 1880; reprint Tel Aviv, 1962-1963).

Braude, *Pesikta Rabbati*, trans. W. Braude (YJS 18; New Haven: Yale University, 1968), 2 volumes.

Friedmann, *Seder Eliahu rabba und Seder Eliahu zuta*, ed. M. Friedmann (Vienna, 1902-1904; reprint Jerusalem, 1969).

Braude and Kapstein, *Tanna debe Eliyyahu*, trans. W. Braude and I. Kapstein (Philadelphia: The Jewish Publication Society of America, 1981).

Buber, *Midrasch Tehillim*, ed. S. Buber (Vilna: Romm, 1891).

Braude, *The Midrash on Psalms*, trans. W. Braude (YJS 13, 1-2; New Haven: Yale University, 1959), 2 volumes.

Visotzsky, *The Midrash on Proverbs*, trans. B. Visotzsky (YJS 27; New Haven: Yale University, 1992).

Wünsche, "Der Midrasch Sprüche," German by A. Wünsche in *Bibliotheca Rabbinica* (Leipzig: Schulze, 1885) 4.1-77.

Eshkol, *Pirqe Rabbi Eliezer*, Eshkol edition (Jerusalem: Eshkol, 1973).

Higger, *Pirqe R. Eliezer*, ed. M. Higger in *Horeb* 8 (1944) 82-119; 9 (1946) 94-116; and 10 (1948) 185-294.

Friedlander, *Pirke de Rabbi Eliezer*, trans. G. Friedlander (New York: Hermon, 1970; original London, 1916).

Spira, *Yalquṭ Ha-Makhiri on Isaiah*, ed. J. Spira (Berlin, 1894).

Milikowsky, *Seder Olam. A Rabbinic Chronography*, ed. and trans. Ch. Milikowsky (1981 Yale University Ph.D. dissertation).

Wünsche, *Aus Israels Lehrhallen*. German by A. Wünsche (Leipzig: Pfeiffer, 1907-1909; reprint Hildesheim: Olms, 1967), 5 volumes.

Jellinek, *Bet ha-Midrasch,* ed. A. Jellinek (Jerusalem: Wahrmann Books, 1967³), 6 volumes in 2.

Wertheimer, *Batei Midrashot,* ed. S. Wertheimer, second edition A. Wertheimer (Jerusalem: Cook, 1954), volume 1.

Kasher, *Encyclopedia of Biblical Interpretation,* vol. VII, Exodus, ed. M. Kasher (New York: American Biblical Encyclopedia Society, 1967). Vol. VIII, 1970.

VII. *Apocrypha, Pseudepigrapha, Philo, Josephus and the Dead Sea Scrolls.*

Apocrypha: see Rahlfs, *Septuaginta.*

OTP. The Old Testament Pseudepigrapha, ed. J. Charlesworth (Garden City, New York: Doubleday, 1983-1985), 2 volumes.

APOT. The Apocrypha and Pseudepigrapha of the Old Testament, II. Pseudepigrapha, ed. R. Charles (Oxford: Clarendon, 1913).

Harrington, *Les Antiquités Bibliques,* ed. D. Harrington, French by J. Cazeaux (SC 229-230; Paris: du Cerf, 1976), 2 volumes.

LCL, *Philo,* Greek and English translation by F. Colson, G. Whitaker, J. Earp and R. Marcus (Cambridge, Massachusetts: Harvard University, 1971), 10 volumes with 2 supplements.

LCL, *Josephus,* Greek and English translation by H. Thackeray, R. Marcus and A. Wikgren (Cambridge, Massachusetts: Harvard University, 1969), 9 volumes.

Martínez, *The Dead Sea Scrolls Translated,* trans. F. Martínez (Leiden: Brill, 1994).

Fitzmyer, J., *The Dead Sea Scrolls.* Major Publications and Tools for Study (SBLRBS 20; Atlanta; Scholars Press, 1990).

VIII. *Dictionaries and Reference Works.*

BDB, *A Hebrew and English Lexicon of the Old Testament,* by F. Brown, S. Driver and C. Briggs (Oxford: Clarendon, 1962).

Jastrow, *A Dictionary of the Targumim, the Talmud Babli and Yerushalmi, and the Midrashic Literature,* by M. Jastrow (New York: Pardes, 1950), 2 volumes.

Levy, *Neuhebräisches und chaldäisches Wörterbuch über die Talmudim und Midraschim,* by J. Levy (Berlin and Vienna, 1924²), 4 volumes.

Alcalay, *The Complete Hebrew-English Dictionary*, by R. Alcalay (Tel Aviv and Jerusalem: Massadah, 1965).

Krauss, *Griechische und Lateinische Lehnwörter in Talmud, Midrasch und Targum*, by S. Krauss (Berlin: Calvary, 1898-1899).

Krauss, *Talmudische Archäologie*, by S. Krauss (Leipzig: Fock, 1911; reprint Hildesheim: Olms, 1966).

Hyman, *Torah Hakethubah Vehamessurah*. A Reference Book of the Scriptural Passages Quoted in Talmudic, Midrashic and Early Rabbinic Literature, by Aaron Hyman, second edition by Arthur Hyman (Tel Aviv: Dvir, 1979), 3 volumes.

Schürer, *The history of the Jewish people in the age of Jesus Christ (175 B.C. – A.D. 135)*, by E. Schürer, ed. G. Vermes, F. Millar and M. Black (Edinburgh: Clark, 1973-1986), 3 volumes.

Jeremias, *Jerusalem in the Time of Jesus*, by J. Jeremias (London: SCM, 1969).

Strack and Stemberger, *Introduction to the Talmud and Midrash*, by H. Strack and G. Stemberger (Minneapolis: Fortress, 1992). At times I refer to the German, *Einleitung in Talmud und Midrasch* (Munich: Beck, 1982[7]).

Ginzberg, *The Legends of the Jews*, by L. Ginzberg (Philadelphia: The Jewish Publication Society of America, 1968), 6 volumes and index.

JE, *The Jewish Encyclopedia* (New York: Funk and Wagnalls, 1905), 12 volumes.

EncJud, *Encyclopaedia Judaica* (Jerusalem: Keter, 1971), 16 volumes.

LSJ, *A Greek-English Lexicon*, by H. Liddell, R. Scott and H. Jones (Oxford: Clarendon, 1966[9]).

BAGD, *A Greek-English Lexicon of the New Testament and Other Early Christian Literature*, by W. Bauer, W. Arndt, F. Gingrich and F. Danker (Chicago: University of Chicago, 1979[2]).

TDNT, *Theological Dictionary of the New Testament*, ed. G. Kittel and G. Friedrich (Grand Rapids, Michigan: Eerdmans, 1964-1976), 9 volumes and index.

Str-B, *Kommentar zum Neuen Testament aus Talmud und Midrasch*, by (H. Strack and) P. Billerbeck (Munich: Beck, 1924-1961), 6 volumes.

Wettstein, J., *Novum Testamentum Graecum* (Amsterdam: Dommerian, 1752; reprint Graz, 1962).

Nickelsburg, *Jewish Literature Between the Bible and the Mishnah*, by G. Nickelsburg (Philadelphia: Fortress, 1981).

IX. *The Early Church.*

The Ante-Nicene Fathers 1, trans. A. Roberts, J. Donaldson and A. Coxe (Grand Rapids, Michigan: Eerdmans, 1979).

Eusebius Werke, 8: Die Praeparatio Evangelica, I, ed. K. Mras, 2. edition by E. des Places (Berlin: Akademie-Verlag, 1982).

P.G., *Patrologia Graeca*, ed. with a Latin translation by J. Migne (Paris, 1857 – 1866), 167 volumes.

P.L., *Patrologia Latina*, ed. J. Migne (Paris, 1841 – 1864), 221 volumes.

Walker, *A History of the Christian Church*, by W. Walker (New York: Scribner's, 1959).

Index of Modern Authors

About the Author

Roger David Aus, b. 1940, studied English and German at St. Olaf College, and theology at Harvard Divinity School, Luther Theological Seminary, and Yale University, from which he received the Ph.D. degree in New Testament Studies in 1971. He is an ordained clergyman of the Evangelical Lutheran Church in America, currently serving the German-speaking Luthergemeinde in Berlin-Reinickendorf, Germany. The Protestant Church of Berlin-Brandenburg (Berlin West) kindly granted him a short study leave in Jerusalem, Israel, in 1981. His study of New Testament topics always reflects his great interest in, and deep appreciation of, the Jewish roots of the Christian faith.

South Florida Studies in the History of Judaism

South Florida Academic Commentary Series

243039	The Talmud of Babylonia, A Complete Outline, Part I, Tractate Berakhot and the Division of Appointed Times A: From Tractate Berakhot through Tractate Pesahim	Neusner
243040	The Talmud of Babylonia, A Complete Outline, Part I, Tractate Berakhot and the Division of Appointed Times B: From Tractate Yoma through Tractate Hagigah	Neusner
243041	The Talmud of Babylonia, A Complete Outline, Part II, The Division of Women; A: From Tractate Yebamot through Tractate Ketubot	Neusner
243042	The Talmud of Babylonia, A Complete Outline, Part II, The Division of Women; B: From Tractate Nedarim through Tractate Qiddushin	Neusner
243043	The Talmud of Babylonia, An Academic Commentary, Volume XIII, Bavli Tractate Yebamot, A. Chapters One through Eight	Neusner
243044	The Talmud of Babylonia, An Academic Commentary, XIII, Bavli Tractate Yebamot, B. Chapters Nine through Seventeen	Neusner
243045	The Talmud of the Land of Israel, A Complete Outline of the Second, Third and Fourth Divisions, Part II, The Division of Women, A. Yebamot to Nedarim	Neusner
243046	The Talmud of the Land of Israel, A Complete Outline of the Second, Third and Fourth Divisions, Part II, The Division of Women, B. Nazir to Sotah	Neusner
243047	The Talmud of the Land of Israel, A Complete Outline of the Second, Third and Fourth Divisions, Part I, The Division of Appointed Times, C. Pesahim and Sukkah	Neusner
243048	The Talmud of the Land of Israel, A Complete Outline of the Second, Third and Fourth Divisions, Part I, The Division of Appointed Times, A. Berakhot, Shabbat	Neusner
243049	The Talmud of the Land of Israel, A Complete Outline of the Second, Third and Fourth Divisions, Part I, The Division of Appointed Times, B. Erubin, Yoma and Besah	Neusner
243050	The Talmud of the Land of Israel, A Complete Outline of the Second, Third and Fourth Divisions, Part I, The Division of Appointed Times, D. Taanit, Megillah, Rosh Hashannah, Hagigah and Moed Qatan	Neusner
243051	The Talmud of the Land of Israel, A Complete Outline of the Second, Third and Fourth Divisions, Part III, The Division of Damages, A. Baba Qamma, Baba Mesia, Baba Batra, Horayot and Niddah	Neusner
243052	The Talmud of the Land of Israel, A Complete Outline of the Second, Third and Fourth Divisions, Part III, The Division of Damages, B. Sanhedrin, Makkot, Shebuot and Abldah Zarah	Neusner
243053	The Two Talmuds Compared, II. The Division of Women in the Talmud of the Land of Israel and the Talmud of Babylonia, Volume A, Tractates Yebamot and Ketubot	Neusner
243054	The Two Talmuds Compared, II. The Division of Women in the Talmud of the Land of Israel and the Talmud of Babylonia, Volume B, Tractates Nedarim, Nazir and Sotah	Neusner

243055	The Two Talmuds Compared, II. The Division of Women in the Talmud of the Land of Israel and the Talmud of Babylonia, Volume C, Tractates Qiddushin and Gittin	Neusner
243056	The Two Talmuds Compared, III. The Division of Damages in the Talmud of the Land of Israel and the Talmud of Babylonia, Volume A, Tractates Baba Qamma and Baba Mesia	Neusner
243057	The Two Talmuds Compared, III. The Division of Damages in the Talmud of the Land of Israel and the Talmud of Babylonia, Volume B, Tractates Baba Batra and Niddah	Neusner
243058	The Two Talmuds Compared, III. The Division of Damages in the Talmud of the Land of Israel and the Talmud of Babylonia, Volume C, Tractates Sanhedrin and Makkot	Neusner
243059	The Two Talmuds Compared, I. Tractate Berakhot and the Division of Appointed Times in the Talmud of the Land of Israel and the Talmud of Babylonia, Volume B, Tractate Shabbat	Neusner
243060	The Two Talmuds Compared, I. Tractate Berakhot and the Division of Appointed Times in the Talmud of the Land of Israel and the Talmud of Babylonia, Volume A, Tractate Berakhot	Neusner
243061	The Two Talmuds Compared, III. The Division of Damages in the Talmud of the Land of Israel and the Talmud of Babylonia, Volume D, Tractates Shebuot, Abodah Zarah and Horayot	Neusner

South Florida-Rochester-Saint Louis
Studies on Religion and the Social Order

245001	Faith and Context, Volume 1	Ong
245002	Faith and Context, Volume 2	Ong
245003	Judaism and Civil Religion	Breslauer
245004	The Sociology of Andrew M. Greeley	Greeley
245005	Faith and Context, Volume 3	Ong
245006	The Christ of Michelangelo	Dixon
245007	From Hermeneutics to Ethical Consensus Among Cultures	Bori
245008	Mordecai Kaplan's Thought in a Postmodern Age	Breslauer
245009	No Longer Aliens, No Longer Strangers	Eckardt
245010	Between Tradition and Culture	Ellenson
245011	Religion and the Social Order	Neusner
245012	Christianity and the Stranger	Nichols
245013	The Polish Challenge	Czosnyka

South Florida International Studies in
Formative Christianity and Judaism

242501	The Earliest Christian Mission to 'All Nations'	La Grand
242502	Judaic Approaches to the Gospels	Chilton
252403	The "Essence of Christianity"	Forni Rosa
242504	The Wicked Tenants and Gethsemane	Aus